*English Romantic Writers*

# ENGLISH ROMANTIC WRITERS

*by*

## HENRY M. BATTENHOUSE

*Florida Southern College / Lakeland, Florida*

## BARRON'S EDUCATIONAL SERIES, INC.

*Great Neck, New York*

# Table of Contents

*Preface*
*Introduction*

## THE NEW POETRY

| | |
|---|---|
| The Spirit of the Age | 15 |
| James Thomson | 20 |
| Edward Young | 23 |
| William Collins | 25 |
| Thomas Gray | 28 |
| Minor Poets of Romance | 32 |
| Realists and Antiquarians | 36 |
| William Cowper | 41 |
| Robert Burns | 45 |
| William Blake | 50 |

## WILLIAM WORDSWORTH

| | |
|---|---|
| The Poet and His Art | 57 |
| His Youth and Education | 61 |
| The Period of Storm and Stress | 65 |
| The Early Poetry | 70 |
| Years of Literary Productivity | 77 |
| Wordsworth's Power and Influence | 83 |

## SAMUEL TAYLOR COLERIDGE

| | |
|---|---|
| The Intellectual Poet | 91 |
| The Young Coleridge | 94 |
| Poetry of Power and Pain | 105 |
| Criticism of Life and Literature | 112 |
| The Man and Estimates of Him | 118 |

## LORD BYRON

| | |
|---|---|
| The Inimitable Poet | 125 |
| Education and Travel | 128 |
| Fame and Changing Fortune | 133 |
| In Exile from England | 142 |
| Great Literary Productivity | 150 |

## PERCY BYSSHE SHELLEY

| | |
|---|---|
| The Rise of Genius | 165 |
| Formative Years | 171 |
| Period of Transition | 179 |
| Golden Years of Poetry | 184 |

## JOHN KEATS

| | |
|---|---|
| Time of Preparation | 201 |
| First Creative Period | 206 |
| Year of Trial and Victory | 210 |
| The Miraculous Year | 214 |
| Remaining Days | 227 |

## MINOR ROMANTIC WRITERS

| | |
|---|---|
| Sir Walter Scott | 233 |
| Jane Austen | 247 |
| Charles Lamb | 254 |
| William Hazlitt | 267 |
| Thomas De Quincey | 274 |
| The Lesser Romantics | 282 |
| The Literary Reviews | 300 |
| | |
| *Bibliography* | 306 |
| *Index* | 319 |

# PREFACE

It is good to step directly into the stream of literature and to measure for oneself its depth and the strong direction of its current. This is a pleasurable and a required experience for the educated man. But in order to make a good crossing of the stream, or to travel exploratively up any literature's main current to the original and traditional source, the general reader and the college student, alike, are in need of some special help.

It is this help that the author of the present volume offers to give. He wishes to provide the reader with a few technical tools and a chart for his journey through the Romantic period of English literature. Beyond this, he would be pleased to aid him in finding here and there *en route*, in some secluded place and "spot of time," the enchanting moment that will give meaning to his entire study. For it is scarcely conceivable that the literature of the Romantic revival can be read without the occurrence of such a moment. Dates and literary characteristics, and other data, are not to be ignored. They are the devices that open, and close, the door to the mansions of poetry and the halls of prose. But the main event is the festival within —the feast, together, of the reader and the poet and the high entertainment offered by the master of fine prose. To make these good things available is this book's ultimate objective.

For this reason the author has not hesitated, in the treatment of the individual writers, to include frequent interpretative paragraphs wherever these have been thought to be helpful: not as substitutes for independent study, but as a stimulus to it. The reader will find here the suitably arranged historical, biographical and other critical material—including a working bibliography—necessary to a scholarly approach to the English Romantic writers. It is hoped that the concise summaries and estimates of the authors' works, the selected quotations, and the style of the volume may commend it to the use of college students who desire to increase their present acquaintance with this important period of our literature.

To readers of good books, scholars, wayfarers, all who out of pure pleasure may wish, with the poet Keats and his contemporaries, to travel through half-forgotten "realms of gold," through "many goodly states and kingdoms," and "Round many western islands" which these "bards in fealty to Apollo hold" — to them the author dedicates this volume, with his best wishes for a profitable journey.

HENRY M. BATTENHOUSE

# English Romantic Writers

# INTRODUCTION

The background of the Romantic period in English literature is rich and varied. It stretches, like a vast and picturesque valley, into distant places, and through years of time. It reaches across the English Channel into Germany, Italy and France, and extends in history to the Renaissance and from there through the Middle Ages, even to Aeneas and Dido in the story of Virgil. Wherever, on some spot of ground, and in some suitable climate, the imagination is set free and young men have visions and old men dream dreams — have visions and dreams of fairer things in this world and out of it, of signs and wonders in the mind of man and in the society in which he lives — there we have the background, and there is the spirit of Romanticism.

We may say that Romanticism is, in a real sense, a native English plant. Its roots lie deep in English soil. In its literature they extend as far back as Anglo-Saxon times. We cannot resist being moved by the sight of the march of the lances, "singing together," as Beowulf's men move shoreward to come to the help of Hrothgar; or by the sound of the harp of the gleeman as he chants of times long past. The same note of surprise and wonder is struck in the medieval Metrical Romances in which the deeds of Charlemagne, Alexander the

Great, the Trojan warriors, and Roland and Oliver, as well as those of the great King Arthur, are remembered and extolled. Chaucer delights in his use of the borrowed romances of Boccaccio; and the *Cuckoo Song* in England's new springtime tells its own story.

> Sumer is icumen in,
>> Lhude sing, cuccu!
> Groweth sed and bloweth med
>> And springth the wude nu.
>> Sing, cuccu!

In Elizabethan England the Romantic note, touched by the early sonneteers, swells into a chorus in the poetry of Edmund Spenser and William Shakespeare. Romanticism's song has begun in earnest, reaching a pitch of perfection in the Elizabethan lyric and in the poems of the young Milton. Nor is the Romantic note forgotten, or allowed to fade out, in the epic *Paradise Lost*. The idyllic scene of Adam and Eve alone in the Garden of Eden is an example at hand.

> Thus talking, hand in hand alone they passed
> On to their blissful bower . . . The roof
> Of thickest covert was inwoven shade,
> Laurel and myrtle . . . Each beauteous flower,
> Iris all hues, roses, and jessamine
> Reared high their flourished heads.

In the Seventeenth Century the classical strain asserts itself in the poetry of Ben Jonson. But the "Metaphysical" poets and "Cavalier" poets alike revel in the artistry of a romantic theme. George Herbert's poems *The Collar* and *The Pulley* strive toward the highest freedom in which the soul finds its rest in God. Robert Herrick, Cavalier that he was, made of his parish a hermitage for his mind's delight, telling us in *The Argument of His Book,*

**3**

> I write of groves, of twilights, and I sing
> The Court of Mab, and of the Fairy King;
> I write of Hell; I sing (and ever shall)
> Of Heaven, and hope to have it after all.

And, to refer again to Milton, we note how the companion poems *L'Allegro* and *Il Penseroso* reflect in a most vivid manner the daytime and nighttime moods of a young romantic poet.

It was not until after the restoration of the monarchy, in 1660, that Classicism as a prevailing attitude began to assert itself. It came in the wake of a movement to make reason the rule of all action, in law and government, in the advance of science, in social and religious activity, and in the art of writing. The great master of literary thought in that time was John Dryden. In him a giant intellect strove for passionate expression, together with a power to control it. He fed his mind on the ancient classics, imitated them, and unburdened his thoughts in heroic couplets of stately satire and sharp criticism. His death, in 1700, was followed by the Age of Pope.

The Age, called Augustan, continued to 1740. In it Classicism was the literary rule. It meant that writers to be respected must entertain the royal court, please the aristocracy while criticizing it, and write "correctly," solidly, without giving way to any form of fancy, or appeal to the emotions, especially to the emotions of men wishing to be free. As the century progressed the Popean formula of obedience to law—law that fitted the behavior of the cosmos—was sternly applied to literature. The result was two-fold. It brought forth a crop of artificial writers; and it produced a ground swell of protest on the side of those who wished literature again to be creative and imaginative and individualistic, as it had been in the greater days of Queen Elizabeth.

The years between 1740 and 1780, represented in literary

history as the Age of Johnson, were years of transition. In them the main currents of Classicism and Romanticism ran in full force against each other, often intermingling in their over-flow, as in the poetry of Thomas Gray whose melancholy passion and fastidious artistry Dr. Johnson did not approve. There was in Gray's *Elegy Written in a Country Churchyard* a feeling for common humanity, expressed in notes of pathos, that was the opposite of the contented optimism of the English Deists, the learned wit of the French Encyclopedists, and the powder-wigged snobbishness of the coterie of Voltaire. It was humanity speaking once more, at first in the quiet tones of Collins and Cowper, and presently more boldly through the voices of Burns and Blake, and at last with affirmation and authority in the poems of Wordsworth and Coleridge and the sounding minstrelsy of Scott. A new day had dawned. A new poetry was alive in the land of Chaucer, Shakespeare and Spenser.

What happened in literature was also taking place in other fields. The men who wrote down their thoughts in prose or poetry were men of their own time; they assimilated, tested, and gave creative expression to the germinating ideas of the age. These ideas—seed thoughts for the poet's mind—were taking form in multiplying clusters around the political, the social, and the religious life of the English people.

Among the leaders of thought in mid-Eighteenth Century England, three men deserve especial mention. Two of them were professional historians; the third was an outstanding par-liamentarian. They were David Hume, Edward Gibbon, and Edmund Burke. Hume, writing his *Political Discourses* in 1752, and following them with a Tory type of History of Great Britain, begun in 1754—both of them in the mid-Century's atmosphere of Naturalism—was an outstanding example of the cold classical logic against which the Romanticists rebelled. He held that a people's general interests, its domestic economy, its politics and its moral behavior, follow in their normal process the "laws of nature." This meant that, so far as man's freedom and destiny are concerned, these laws are fixed and arbitrary. They are, by definition, subject to no man's will. Man's thinking on these questions, or matters, may be regulative; but it is not determinative. All knowledge, said Hume, is relative; all science is fragmentary. The mental world of man is built up by his own impressions. These impressions are based on an association of ideas. The link between the world of the mind and that of objective phenomena is vague, incidental, casual. To Hume religion, too, is wholly "natural"; not a revelation. And the idea of liberty is one that opposes and instinctively thwarts the authority of government. In short, Hume was an empiricist and a skeptic who reasoned by the process of an analysis of the facts, and followed the hard conclusions of his own logic.

It is noteworthy that the English Romantic writers of the half-century to follow did not entirely escape the influence of such naturalistic thought. Wordsworth and Coleridge, in their youth, were not free of it; and a little more than a glance at the poem *Don Juan* will show that it was a hidden element in Byron's recurring skepticism, when he said:

> Thou shalt believe in Milton, Dryden, Pope;
> Thou shalt not set up Wordsworth, Coleridge, Southey;
> Because the first is crazed beyond all hope,
> The second drunk, the third so quaint and mouthy.

The "crazed" moments for Wordsworth, of course, were those in which he gazed intently on the little violet, or daisy, or celandine; and the strongest wine tasted by Coleridge was that of German transcendental philosophy. Southey, no doubt, at times was talkative. But so also was Byron. Most poets are; and it is, by all means, their talk that we want to hear; whether the words they toss at us be roses or spears, and the tone of their voice be mellow or hard. The influence of Hume's ideas on the poets was indirect; but it was definite and undeniable. Poets are, of all beings, the most impressionable.

Edward Gibbon, too, was an analytical scholar and a skeptic of the classical school. In *The Decline and Fall of the Roman Empire*, he insists that the rise of Christianity *caused* the fall of Rome—not aware that Rome, lying in ruins under barbarian arms, may have created a spiritual and cultural vacuum which the Christian faith found and filled. We must imagine the calm faith with which the poet William Cowper met the accusation of Gibbon the deist, in the affirmative Olney hymn:

> God moves in a mysterious way
> His wonders to perform;
> He plants His footsteps in the sea,
> And rides upon the storm.
>
> Blind unbelief is sure to err,
> And scan His work in vain:
> God is His own interpreter,
> And He will make it plain.

In Edmund Burke the growing Romantic movement found an intuitive voice. His speech *On Conciliation with the Colonies*, delivered in 1774, was spoken for the people—the English people living in the land across the Atlantic, a freedom-loving, hardy people who, like their kinsmen in the home land, had become conscious of their right to the "pursuit of life, liberty and happiness." It was this application of a Romantic principle to political and domestic life that twenty years later was to prompt Coleridge, in his visionary dream of founding a Pantisocrasy on the banks of the Susquehanna, in America, to write:

# INTRODUCTION

O'er the ocean swell
Sublime of hope, I seek the cottage dell
Where virtue calm with careless steps may stray,
And dancing to the moonlight roundelay,
The wizard passions weave an holy spell.

Thus were the dreams of a new and better world transferred across the sea to a land far off, carrying with them the hopes of political freedom, social justice, individual liberty, and the spiritual contentment that the Romanticist could not then find in Eighteenth Century England.

Among those whose influence on our English Romantic writers was most strong, none exceeded J. J. Rousseau. He was himself the symbol of excess. His life, as the *Confessions* indicate, was irregular, erotic, erratic. His novel *Héloïse* advocated a social return to nature, away from the traditional concept of marriage and the family. His *Social Contract,* with its demand that the head of a state be held responsible to the people he leads, contributed to the outset of the French Revolution. His *Emile* was an astonishingly modern tract on general education. In him, and in the ideas he advanced, what was good and bad for Romanticism were strangely intermixed. In his stress on the natural goodness of man, he placed the cause of all evil in society in man's environment. He held civilized society responsible for man's errors in thought and act. Man, he said, is by nature good. A benevolent Deity made him such. He has a soul that is immortal and designed to be free. Such teaching, some of it an obvious distortion of traditional Christian orthodoxy, was found to have in it a great appeal to persons of a Romantic temperament; more particularly to writers of the Sentimental School—to those who liked to find a subject of deep pathos and to treat it sentimentally, enlarging especially on the theme of goodness corrupted, and innocence seduced by evil. The seduction of virtue had been the particularly popular subject of Samuel Richardson's novel *Clarissa Harlowe*, from which Rousseau had drawn his inspiration for the novel *Héloïse*. This work, in turn, had inspired Oliver Goldsmith to write *The Vicar of Wakefield*, a novel of pure and playful sentiment, based on a study of the best instincts of man in a free and open world in which good deeds and humanitarian impulses are recognized and respected.

In *The Vicar of Wakefield*, a refined moral attitude, a pleasing gracious manner, a respect for the behavior of simple people, for domestic virtues, for patriotic feeling, and for religion, constitute a kind of code of English conduct—so aptly is it purged, by Goldsmith's Irish good humor, of Smollett's picaresque coarseness and, at the same time freed from a restricting Puritanic severity. This wholesome strain, uniting good morals with good taste, is traceable, backward, in the essays of Addison and Steele, and continues to be felt in Gray's *Elegy*, and in *The Eve of St. Agnes* of Keats and, afterwards, in the sane humanitarianism of the Victorian novels of Dickens. Good morals and good taste, softened by a tender sentiment, became the expression of a dominant English trait, emerging in the Eighteenth Century and signalizing the rise of the common man, giving recognition to his importance in society, his gifts in the newly developing areas of science and industry, and his readiness to join the company of artists and the fraternity of philosophers.

Thus, was another dream of Romanticism seen to come true. To this end, also, had the mid-Century tea-houses and coffee-houses been established; places where the rising middle class could find entertainment, learn good manners, and develop those sensitivities to moral and religious values in behalf of which the *Tatler* and the *Spectator* had been crusading in the mercantile heart of London. Out of this sensibility to human values, touched with a dream of a better society and with a genuine compassion for suffering humanity, together with a fondness for country life and a return to nature—all amply illustrated in Goldsmith's poem *The Deserted Village*—the later Romantic writers were able to take both material and inspiration for many of their best works.

In looking for the influence of one writer on another, one finds it interesting to trace, in the study of Shakespeare, a common sensitivity to the great poet's art in the criticisms, for example, of Addison, Johnson, Coleridge, Hazlitt and De Quincey. Or one may note, with equal satisfaction, how the delightful and delicate halftones of Steele's essays portray the same sly accent of humor to be found in Lamb's *Essays of Elia*. There will be observed differences, of course; differences that distinguish a Classical from a Romantic type of prose: Steele's elegance, in contrast to Lamb's homeliness; Steele's cool and playful comedy, in contrast to the underlying pathos in Lamb's spontaneous laughter. But the tie that binds them is there; and it essentially Romantic—a tie of human sentiment and genuine sympathy. This underlying kinship—though with contrasting stress—is further demonstrated in a comparison of Goldsmith's *Deserted Village*, published in 1770, with George Crabbe's poem *The Village*, written thirteen years later. In the first poem the picture of village life is idyllic and ideal; in the second, it is somber, grim and real. The one moves us to pleasing tears; the other leaves in us a dull ache. Yet both are Romantic because they represent the free interplay of the poet's emotion and imagination with the selected facts.

We have noted that the Eighteenth Century was one of controversy. In politics it was a battle between the interests of liberty and those of authority; in philosophy it was a contest between reason and intuition; in economics it was the losing struggle of the traditional handicraftsman against the new machine age. But the controversy and the disturbance did not end there. They had wide-reaching social implications. These involved the transition, in England, from a chiefly rural to an urban way of life. They affected the nation's family solidarity, bringing up for solution the problem of child labor, of the city slums, of providing charity for the poor; with the result that the leaders of the people were stirred to give an account of themselves in their attitude toward these gathered masses of humanity, huddled together in mines and factories and city huts, and faced with poverty, misery, and disease. The French Revolution, when it came, had a theoretical origin in philosophical thought. The preceding industrial revolution in England began as practical, technological and economic discovery. The two events most responsible for it were the invention of the spinning jenny by James Hargreaves, in 1764, and the invention of the steam engine by James Watt, in 1765. These after mid-Century events date the beginning of the great change of which both Goldsmith and Crabbe give us their contemporary accounts. Goldsmith thinking fondly of past better days, says:

> A time there was ere England's griefs began
> When every rood of ground maintain'd its man;
> For him light labor spread her wholesome store,
> Just gave what life required, but gave not more:
> His best companions, innocence and health,
> And his best riches, ignorance of wealth.

And Crabbe, letting us see the skeleton of a starved and half-abandoned seaside village, completes the picture of what was happening in these hard times:

**11**

# INTRODUCTION

> Here joyless roam a wild amphibious race,
> With sullen woe displayed in every face,
> Who far from civil arts and social fly
> And scowl at strangers with suspicious eye.

We are to infer from this sketch of the scene before us that the time had come for nation-wide social reform. It was obvious that the germination of Romantic ideas of the sacredness of the individual was beginning to bear fruit. The first harvest came, perhaps unexpectedly, in the form of a movement known as the Wesleyan Revival. The way, in no small part, had been prepared for the movement by another philosopher, George Berkeley, who had been born in Ireland, had come to England early in the Century, had visited America in an attempt to evangelize the Indians, and had, in 1734, become a bishop in the Anglican Church. Bishop Berkeley had taught that men do indeed live by *ideas,* not by material things. The existence of material things, he held, is in our preception of them. Our real world is mental; our real life is spiritual. The ancient poet-philosopher Plato had insisted on this truth. But Berkeley went further with it, arriving at a Christian conception of God, of man, and of the world—a position later found to be notably attractive to Wordsworth and Coleridge. To Berkeley *ideas* were a "divine language" through which God reveals Himself to us. This revelation, as it breaks through to us, is accompanied by the exercise of our imagination and intuition, and by an experience of religious emotion. The ultimate comprehension of truth is mystical.

But the direct predecessor of the Wesleyan movement was the intellectual mystic William Law. Inspired by the teaching of the Seventeenth Century German philosopher Jacob Boehme, he wrote, first, in 1726, *A Practical Treatise on Christian Perfection,* and, three years later, his *Serious Call to a*

*Devout and Holy Life.* These books became the seed bed of a Romantic religious revival. It began with Wesley's preaching at the Bristol coal mines, and spread rapidly throughout England. Its moral influence on the nation was extraordinary. It helped the English people to steady themselves against the excesses that were to overtake France during the Revolution. It counteracted the hard skepticism and false rationalism current throughout much of the Century. It stimulated the impulse to a broader humanitarianism among men everywhere; and it prepared England for a new harvest of great literature. The hymns of Issac Watts, tempering the Puritanism in them with a mystical piety, had already become a part of the English people's life. Now those of Charles Wesley were added: hymns less solemnly moving but charged with a livelier sensibility, gospel hymns and songs, awakening the soul and calling men to the activity of their Christian faith and hope. When, presently, the Anglican evangelical movement prompted William Cowper to write the *Olney Hymns,* it became evident that the rising Romanticism in England was taking into itself a fresh and healing element. By it, after Cowper, William Blake was to revitalize poetry by rejuvenating its inward and secret source and giving it the voice of prophecy; and through it, looking on Nature, Wordsworth was to draw that sustenance of the soul by which he could record his experience of the disturbing joy

> Of elevated thoughts; a sense sublime
> Of something far more deeply interfused,
> Whose dwelling is the light of setting suns,
> And the round ocean and the living air,
> And the blue sky, and in the mind of man.

# The New Poetry

## THE SPIRIT OF THE AGE

### JAMES THOMSON
*1700-1748*

### EDWARD YOUNG
*1683-1765*

### WILLIAM COLLINS
*1721-1759*

### THOMAS GRAY
*1716-1771*

## MINOR POETS OF ROMANCE

## REALISTS AND ANTIQUARIANS

### WILLIAM COWPER
*1731-1800*

### ROBERT BURNS
*1759-1796*

### WILLIAM BLAKE
*1757-1827*

# THE SPIRIT OF THE AGE

## THE CLASSICAL TRADITION

English poetry, early in the eighteenth century, expressed two tendencies. The first, represented in the work of Alexander Pope, was classical and was founded on a theory of natural and universal law. According to it, politics, religion and poetry, alike, rested ultimately on the behavior of the cosmos; and art and science were to be regarded as man's way of measuring his wit by nature's law, and shaping his thought to that perfect mold. Here, in classical poetry, it was held, was a realm in which the mind was perfectly fitted to the cosmos. In it reason ruled supreme, dispelling mystery, satirizing stupidity, rationalizing conduct, indoctrinating social opinion, and setting up— while the mid-century's optimism lasted—a temporary utopia on the Popean formula of "whatever is, is right."

## THE ROMANTIC SPIRIT

But by the side of this neo-classical poetry there was the trend toward romanticism. Those who followed it talked less about the law than about the life of poetry. They entered directly into nature, not primarily to examine or to praise it, but to feel and to express it. The men who wrote this poetry entertained no illusions of a perfect natural world. They saw clearly enough the evil around them; they felt the pain and sorrow of life, and they refused to attribute them to man's plain ignorance. Rather, they perceived man's spirit as somehow different from the natural world in which he lived, and pitied him, and so more often wrote tragically than in the mood of criticism and satire which was so congenial to the school of Pope. For example, as early as 1713, while Pope was entertaining English society with the sleek wit of *The Rape of the Lock*, Edward Young was writing the last lines of a long poem on the end of the world, gravely echoing the cry of a lost soul in these words:

> Father of mercies! Why from silent earth
> Didst thou awake, and curse me into birth?

## THIS MYSTERIOUS WORLD

The difference, actually, was not between Young and Pope. It was not merely individual, but penetrated to a distinction between two views of life: the naturalistic and the supernaturalistic. The poetry of deism, like its philosophy, was grounded in the natural man and in human reason. The new poetry—new only after its comparative neglect in the late seventeenth century—was a protest against a correct but closed and cold world. Men like William Collins and Thomas Gray, following Young, voiced this protest in lines as smooth and controlled as those of Pope; but what they wrote was strongly infused with the sense of conflict, of pathos verging on pain. The reason, of course, was not that the times had changed; for Pope and Young were contemporaries. It was a fundamental antithesis of ideas on poetry and life that separated them.

## REPRESENTATIVE ROMANTICS

The spirit of poetry was, in fact, breaking through natural barriers. With Young it was the "original genius" he so daringly praised in his *Conjectures*. In the poetry of Robert Blair it was the medieval sense of the mysterious, together with a stress on the violent and irregular notes of music, that in a later day came to be known by the name of "Gothic." In the odes of Collins this

self-liberating spirit struggled within the strained lines which
were often reduced to slow motion, giving the impression of
being "clogged and impeded with clusters of consonants." One
easily observes, for example, the controlled brilliance, didactic
measure and rhetorical finesse of these lines of Pope:

> Vice is a monster of so frightful mien,
> As to be hated needs but to be seen;
> Yet seen too oft, familiar with her face,
> We first endure, then pity, then embrace.

But then one notes, by contrast, the tortured thought and turgid
movement of these lines in Collins' *Ode to Fear*:

> Thou to whom the world unknown,
> With all its shadowy shapes, is shown;
> Who see'st, appall'd th' unreal scene,
> While Fancy lifts the veil between;
> > Ah Fear, ah frantic Fear,
> > I see, I see thee near!
> I know thy hurried step, thy haggard eye!
> Like thee I start, like thee disorder'd fly.

Similarly anyone reading the odes of Gray will note at once that
there is in them an element that is at opposite poles, for example, to Dryden at his best. The impassioned but subdued
grandeur of *Alexander's Feast* yields and gives way to a tense,
almost disintegrating flux of feeling as one reaches the end of
the first epode of *The Bard* in which Gray writes of the martyred Welsh poets:

> Dear lost companions of my tuneful art,
> Dear as the light that visits these sad eyes,
> Dear as the ruddy drops that warm my heart,
> Ye died amidst your dying country's cries—
> > No more I weep. They do not sleep.
> On yonder cliffs, a grisly band,
> I see them sit; they linger yet,

Avengers of their native land:
With me in dreadful harmony they join,
And weave with bloody hands the tissue of thy line.

## CHARACTERISTIC TRENDS

Yet these poets, and others including Oliver Goldsmith, were within the classical tradition. We are wont to say, sometimes, that their manner was classical, while the matter of which they wrote was romantic. This, if said with restriction, is true. And it is also true that the growing romantic attitude of poets like Thomas Chatterton, William Cowper, Robert Burns and William Blake did in time change both the subject matter and the metrical structure of the late eighteenth century poetry. The change, when it came, was radical, and it was wrought from within and by a powerful and fundamentally reconstructive ideology. This ideology, or core of integrated concepts we now call romantic, had in it distinctive elements. One of them was medievalism, variously interpreted as antiquarianism, as a return to chivalry, as Aristotelian ethics, as pre-Renaissance Christianity. Another element was a return to a love, and a fear, of nature. Still another was a stress on individual artistic tastes and human rights and responsibilities. Perhaps the most significant part of the romantic tradition was its emphasis on original genius, on genuine emotion, and on the reality and integrity of the human spirit. Poets, more than at any other time since the Renaissance, found it possible to believe themselves overshadowed by a supernatural presence, a creative informing Spirit.

## NATURE AND SPIRIT

But the more earthy or naturalistic tradition of the age survived also. It expressed itself in the discipline of the passions, or in their release, according to either the classical or the romantic trend. Nature therefore became a theme for poetry, and writers generally dealt with it, according to their individual attitudes, on three levels: (1) on the lower level of physical or vegetative existence; or (2) on the higher level of human reason, of moral values, of universal law; or (3) on the transcendental plane of a transformed nature, where ultimate realities were considered to be spiritual, and the supernatural was brought into a mystical juxtaposition with the natural.

## THE AGE IN SUMMARY

History was viewed similarly, either as physical warfare, or as a battle of wits, or as a record of providence. So also was religion. Followers of Rousseau gave sanction to animal impulses and passions; adherents to Deism rationalized in favor of a cosmic religion; evangelical piety, strong enough to produce an eighteenth century religious movement, aspired to the supernatural, but laid an Adam's curse on human nature; and neo-Platonism, very popular with the poets, moved on an ascending and descending scale to bring the natural and supernatural together in graduations under the sovereignty and unity of being, and, beyond being, of the great *ONE*. Finally Catholicism, mindful of its own tradition, and distinguishing between the two orders of the spiritual or eternal, and the physical or temporal, asserted the authority of faith and of the church over human conduct, social institutions, and the course of human history. In all fields of interest, including that of politics, the new poetry was known by these signs and trends. Attitudes toward history, nature, the problem of evil, human reason and destiny, and the existence and providence of God, ran like undercurrents through the eighteenth century, touching and feeding the poet's minds. In this way their art, though intensely individual, was kept alive and sincere.

# JAMES THOMSON

## NATURE AND MAN

It will be convenient to give our attention to the *Seasons*, published in 1730, as marking the rise of the new poetry. It is not the date that matters in noting this event; it is what we find in the poem, or poems. There are, as we should expect, four of them, one for each of the seasons of the year. Looking briefly at the poem *Winter*, written before 1726, the earliest and the best, we note how it describes the approach of winter: the cold rain, the bitter wind, the gray sky, the falling snow. The poet's mind, we observe, is not on the wonders of the cosmos, but on the weather. Capricorn and Aquarius are not now heavenly rotating planets. They are signs of heavy weather, the freezing foggy air, the general dejection in nature. Winter brings misery and human want. It stirs the poet's humanitarian spirit, his social sympathy. Human misfortune rather than the orderly behavior of nature impresses itself on us as we read:

> As thus the snows arise, and foul and fierce
> All Winter drives along the darkened air,
> In his own loose-revolving fields the swain
> Disastered stands. The thoughts of home
> Rush on his nerves, and call their vigor forth
> In many a vain attempt. How sinks his soul,
> What black despair, what horror fills his heart,
> When, for the dusky spot which fancy feigned
> His tufted cottage rising through the snow,
> He meets the roughness of the middle waste,
> Far from the track and blest abode of man,
> While round him night resistless closes fast,
> And every tempest, howling o'er his head,
> Renders the savage wilderness more wild!

In the poems *Winter, Summer, Spring,* and *Autumn* we see the signs of that reverence for Nature of which Wordsworth was later to be the great exponent. That the author of *The*

*Seasons* found it difficult to free himself from the neo-classical diction of his time, and so to let the earlier Miltonic tradition break through, is noticeable in the opening lines of *Winter:*

> Vapors, and clouds, and storms. Be these my theme;
> These that exalt the soul to solemn thought
> And heavenly musing. Welcome kindred glooms!
> Congenial horrors hail!

But the ground had been broken, and there was a good harvest to come.

## THE PASTORAL TRADITION

The four poems which comprise the *Seasons* belong properly in the pastoral tradition. They are not poetry of a new order, but simply reminiscent of Milton and Spenser. But the *Seasons* differ, for example, from Pope's *Windsor Forest* which also describes nature, but does so by presenting us with a "colorful catalogue of birds and fishes," or, as Wordsworth later said, with "new images of external nature." Thomson, in contrast, compels the scenes from nature to speak to him. He extracts a mood from them, or more correctly, varying moods. We note his free use of fanciful poetical device: birds become creatures of "the tuneful race"; fish, of "the finny tribe." We observe that the lines of the poems run almost into couplets, though unrhymed. Besides this, there is an imitation of Milton's grandeur. But the sentiment is genuine, at least to Thomson; and the emotion called forth in us by the best passages is deep and strong. For lines to move us to admiration of him we need to select only three from his *Hymn* on the seasons in which he directs us to a study of nature in order that we may know its divine Creator:

> Ye forests, bend, ye harvests, wave to Him;
> Breathe your still song into the reaper's heart
> As home he goes beneath the joyous moon.

## A SPENSERIAN POET

Thomson was born in 1700, in Scotland. He was by nature indolent, friendly, good humored and self-assured, capable of laughing at his own laziness, and fond of the wild beauty of his native Cheviot hills. He was trained in theology, but his heart was entirely in poetry. *The Castle of Indolence,* his last important work, entirely suited his temper. The Spenserian influence—its idyllicism, its allegory, its fancy, its language and metre—was his by right of a natural heritage. The poem, evidently, was written out of sheer pleasure. The theme induced the mood in him and he added the measures, so it would seem, out of simple delight. The stanzas, each with its closing hexameter, sometimes stand out as vignettes of a painted landscape, sometimes simply as specimens of versification executed with charming finesse. The appeal to the ear in some of them is more enchanting even than to the eye, as these spoken lines illustrate:

> Each sound, too, here to languishment inclined,
> Lulled the weak bosom, and induced ease.
> Aerial music in the warbling wind,
> At distance rising oft, by small degrees,
> Nearer and nearer came, till o'er the trees
> It hung, and breathed such soul—dissolving airs
> As did, alas! with soft perdition please,
> Entangled deep in its enchanting snares,
> The listening heart forgot all duties and all cares.

# MARK AKENSIDE

## THE SUBLIME IMAGINATION

Thomson died in 1784. He had during his last ten years lived at Richmond, a dozen miles out of London, and only two miles on the other side of the Thames from Twickenham where he had enjoyed the friendship of Pope. Earlier in the century there had lived in Edinburgh, and after that in London, a man by the name of Mark Akenside (1721-1770) who had later become a physician, and who in 1774 had written a poem he called *The Pleasures of the Imagination*. The poem is memorable as a sign post of the romantic movement. Its impetuous energy and mounting imagination suggest Milton whom the poet imitated well enough to write some blank verse of rare musical quality. The poet concerns himself with that innate gift of the moral and esthetic sense whereby the common man, however unlettered he may be, can perceive greatness and place himself in harmony with the universe. Speaking of such persons of genuine natural sensibility, Akenside says:

> To these the Sire Omnipotent unfolds
> The world's harmonious volume, there to read
> The Transcript of Himself.

# EDWARD YOUNG

## MELANCHOLY MEDITATION

But it was to Edward Young (1683-1765), gifted man and an intimate friend of Addison, that the new romantic poetry owed its first decisive impulse. His father had been dean at Salisbury Cathedral, and he himself became a clergyman at the age of forty-four. Before then he had written well but without distinction, producing elegies, odes, satires, tragedies and essays. In 1742 he began writing the *Night Thoughts* to which he gave the long elucidating title: *The Complaint, or Night Thoughts on Life, Death, and Immortality*. In 1759, then in his seventy-sixth year, he published his much valued *Conjectures on Origi-*

*nal Composition.* Around these two works his reputation clings and lives, an ever fresh and green laurel to his name.

## MAN'S SPIRITUAL HUNGER

The *Night Thoughts* are more than mere romantic meditations. Someone has referred to them as the *In Memoriam* of the eighteenth century. They have, we observe, a threefold background: personal, literary, and philosophical. Young, at fifty, had married an earl's daughter, a gifted Christian lady. Her death, eight years afterwards, came like a last sad eclipse of day to him. By then, too, the tradition of melancholy, an old romantic tendency, but renewed in Milton's *Il Penseroso,* was gaining ground. But deeper down in the mind of Young were the stirring thoughts of a man dissatisfied with the current eighteenth century conception of the world. He found the age's deistic optimism, resting contentedly in the lap of natural law, lulled to rest by the soothing voice of reason, inadequate to man's deeper spiritual needs. The soul's aspiration and divine revelation were truths which the physical cosmos of itself could not explain. The acceptance of a higher order of existence, of which the physical world was an undeniable though imperfect manifestation, was, he said, necessary to man's intuitive reasoning. As man thinks *originally*—i.e., when his thinking involves the emotions and is ethical—he must conclude that

> All, all on earth is Shadow, all beyond
> Is Substance: the reverse is folly's Creed.

## THE POET'S STYLE

Here, one says on reading further into the *Night Thoughts,* is poetry suited to blank verse. Dr. Johnson, who for good reasons of his own preferred rime, admits this fact, and adds: "This is one of the few poems in which blank verse could not be changed for rhyme but with disadvantage." Within this "ennobling sphere" the poet finds room for his lofty rhetoric and verbal music, as when he exclaims:

> Death wounds to cure: we fall; we rise; we reign!
> Spring from our fetters; fasten in the skies;
> Where blooming Eden withers in our sight:
> Death gives us more than was in Eden lost.

Yet, almost by contrast, he shows an alternating fondness for the short quotable sentence, as for example, "Death loves a shining mark, a single blow," preferring it to the "wide-wheeling period"—following here Pope's rather than Milton's example.

# WILLIAM COLLINS

## POETRY AND MUSIC

Listening to a poem of William Collins is a singular experience. It is like hearing in some quiet corner of an English garden the music of a water fountain. The *Ode to Evening* is not any mere description in verse: it is something you touch, cool and smooth to the fingers, like a silver flute, from which music and the sensation of beauty pass almost imperceptibly into the mind. It is unrhymed and exquisitely phrased, classical in its restraint, yet romantic in its "enjoyment of nature in solitude and in the twilight hour," a specimen of eighteenth century poetry at its best, and worthy of being compared to an *adagio* of Mozart or a Sheraton chair. The last three stanzas of the *Ode* form one movement; one hears the instrument of the poet's verse, touching the chords of the seasons: the lavishing spring, the sporting summer, the sallow autumn, and the winter "yelling through the troublous air"; but over, above, and through them all, one is aware of the sustained prolongation of the poem's theme to its peaceful end as, one by one, Fancy, Friendship, Science, and "rose-lipped" Health yield to Evening's "gentlest influence," and hymn its "favorite name."

## SENSITIVITY TO BEAUTY

The Greek and Latin influence lay heavily on Collins. It made an Oxford gentleman of him, elegant in his taste and manners, and a scholar skilled in reasoning and rhetoric. The spirit of what was classical seemed actually to rise before him, as if from some page of ancient mythology, to accompany him in his habitual mood of restraint, to offer him "beauty disguised as learning," and to threaten him, as Dr. Johnson said, with a diction that was "often unskilfully laboured," as if caught fast in the intricate network of his verses. The writing of such poetry as that by a lesser poet might have easily resolved itself into empty echoes of the classical masters. But Collins was saved from sometimes singing in falsetto by his extreme sensitiveness. Everything touched him, almost with painful reality: the mysterious beauty of nature; the loveliness of song; the tragedy of human existence. Something of the consuming imagination of Keats burned in him: like Keats, he suffered, though less self-sustained and self-taught; like him, he traveled far into the solitary "realms of gold"; and again like Keats, he died young.

## TALENT AND TRAGEDY

The career of Collins was tragic. He was born in 1721, in Sussex, in the quiet town of Chichester, and under the shadow of its old cathedral. At the age of twelve he was studying in Winchester; at seventeen, fascinated by the Orient, he began writing the *Persian Eclogues*. Soon thereafter he entered Oxford, matriculating at Magdalen College, not liking its discipline, its pedantry, but graduating with the bachelor's degree. At twenty-three, while relatives directed him toward the army, and friends toward the church, he set out on a literary life in London. There he made many friends and large plans; but indolence waylaid him and, until he fell heir to an uncle's legacy, he was homeless and poor. At the time when the inheritance might have brought him comfort, illness came to him; and, after that, complete collapse and insanity. He died at thirty-eight in 1759.

## GRECIAN ART

Most of Collins' work was done between the years 1742 and 1752. Of the ten or twelve poems by which he is known, the Odes *To Fear, To Simplicity, On the Poetical Character, The Passions,* and *To Evening,* are very nearly perfect pieces. All of them are sculpturesque, all excess imagery and emotion being cut away to let the truth come through. What we hear when we listen to their lines is what we also see: subdued horizons merging into twilight; views of wind and rain dissolving into abstract ideas; palpable yet transcendent forms, "viewless forms of air," charged with superterrestrial energy, with spell, with something no longer individual but typical; in short, poetry in which "the music is an emanation of the mood and the form is that of the thought itself."

## MEMORIAL ODE

Such a poem is the now famous *Ode Written in 1746,* a stainless Greek-like epitaph, worthy to be compared to Keats' *Ode on a Grecian Urn,* which it antedates by seventy-three years. It is happily so short that it can be quoted in full:

> How sleep the brave who sink to rest,
> By all their country's wishes blest!

When Spring, with dewy fingers cold,
Returns to deck their hallow's mould,
She there shall dress a sweeter sod
Than Fancy's feet have ever trod.

By fairy hands their knell is rung;
By forms unseen their dirge is sung;
There Honor comes, a pilgrim grey,
To bless the turf that wraps their clay;

And Freedom shall awhile repair,
To dwell a weeping hermit there!

It was in the small quantity of excellent verse of William
Collins that the creative imagination of the new movement
was now seen to be intensely at work. His ode was written
before 1750. It is a little masterpiece of clear diction charged
with overtones of mystery and gentle melancholy. Reading the
*Ode to Evening*, the *Ode to Fear*, and the *Ode to Simplicity*,
we find it hard to accept the complaint of Dr. Johnson that
Collins' diction was too "often harsh and unskilfully labored."
The Romantic spirit is alive in them. And, as we follow the
ode entitled *The Passions*, dedicated to music, weaving in inter-
lacing movements its spell of fear and hope, of pity and
revenge, and are moved by the Muse's art, "filled with fury,
rapt, inspired," we know that we are in Romantic territory.
At that moment we do not ask for a formal definition of
Romanticism. We recognize it by its forceful and pleasurable
hold on us.

# THOMAS GRAY

## CRITICAL VERDICTS

Men, in his time and ours, have differed in their estimates
of the work of Thomas Gray. He was, it is true, a neo-classical
poet. Should he also be listed as romantic? He was scholarly,

deeply read in the ancient writers, a keen critic, a man of marked talent. Did he as certainly possess genuine creative powers? Or is it necessary to trace a differentiating line between artistic talent and original genius in arriving at a critical conclusion about him? Again, was Gray the delicately shy and socially sensitive person we like to imagine, or was he, as Samuel Johnson called him, a "dull fellow?" We must expect the truth about Gray and his poetry to lie in both directions. Perhaps we should say that the poet himself has been rather overrated, while his place in the history of poetry has been underestimated. Gray was not actually half classical and half romantic, as it is sometimes said. His poetry is not so much a bridge between the two historic periods as the extension of a literary draw bridge from classicism with no foundation on the romantic side. *The Fatal Sisters,* for example, is genuinely romantic in tone and tendency, but it is an excursion into Norse mythology rather than an immigration. The Valkyries, the beautiful but terrible choosers of the slain, are real, and we get a shocking glimpse into the grisly fields of Odin as we read:

> Horror covers all the heath,
> Clouds of carnage blot the sun.
> Sisters, weave the web of death!
> Sisters, cease; the work is done.

## THE ELEGIAC MOOD

But the Gray we know best is not associated with such poetry. It is the *Ode on Eton College,* and the *Elegy Written in a Country Churchyard,* that identify him and endear him to us. In them the pastoral and the academic attitudes mingle in pleasurable and careful notes in which the idyllic mood is aptly timed to the poet's intellectual life. The resultant elegiac temper is particularly congenial to Gray. It furnishes him the emotional pattern for the pure and controlled measures that are so patiently interwoven with the familiar and deep-dyed threads of the poet's thoughts. The effect is that of looking intently at a rare piece of tapestry, an antique piece, in which

> Now fades the glimmering landscape on the sight,
> And all the air a solemn stillness holds,
> Save where the beetle wheels his droning flight,
> And drowsy tinklings lull the distant folds.

Poetry like this is rich in associations, full of memories and precious fragments of experience. The reader of vigorous mind will find in it no hint to bold adventure, no breaking through to new vistas. The poet stands in the center of an old world in which ambition has begun to lag, inspiration to fail, and

> The boast of heraldry, the pomp of power,
> And all that beauty, all that wealth e'er gave,
> Awaits alike th' inevitable hour.
> The paths of glory lead but to the grave.

## SCHOLAR AND POET

The same pensive mood pervades the *Ode on Eton College*. Three facts lie behind the poem that help to explain it: the death of Richard West, a close friend; the reconciling influence of Horace Walpole; and Gray's erudite and academic mind. We see in the *Ode* an interesting example of the manner in which the scholar-artist's thoughts revolve with classical precision between two poles: that of pure knowledge, symbolized in the Eton towers,

> Where grateful Science still adores
> Her Henry's holy Shade;

and that of an understanding of this imperfect world which destroys man's paradise, his innocence, and causes the poet to say:

Where ignorance is bliss,
'Tis folly to be wise.

## LIVING WITH LITERATURE

Gray and his poetry are inseparable from Cambridge which continued to be his *alma mater* through the years between 1734 when, at the age of eighteen, he matriculated there, and 1771, the year of his death. Nothing else comparable to living in that academic atmosphere happened to the poet. There were a few events that contributed something to his career: the Grand Tour which Walpole and he set out to make of the Continent; a late journey to Scotland; and a belated professorship in modern history. There were besides, his summer excursions, long miles on foot, to Stoke Poges to visit his mother, and trips to the London Museum. To these we should add his daily companionship with classical literature, "with the Italian writers and Old Norse mythology, with botany and architecture and painting and music." From them, and from within himself, he fashioned the pattern of his poetry, with its constituent elements of a moderated Puritanism, rural sentiment, controlled music and cadence, a mastery of the quatrain, and the coining of unforgettable examples of pure English diction which escaped the listening but untuned ear of Dr. Johnson.

In these eighteenth century writings a poet had effectively done two things. He had brought the pride of the earth's mighty into focus with the common lot of man, insisting that

"the paths of glory lead but to the grave."

And he had found open access to a new and native source of literary interest by his exploration in the areas of Norse and Celtic legend. After reading *The Fatal Sisters* and *The Bard*, later poets might freely mine for ore in scenic Wales, or revel in Germanic mythology among the Valkyries, the grisly "choosers of the slain." That no great number of the later Romantic writers did so is another story. James Macpherson and young Thomas Chatterton did indeed dig up the "literary remains" of a Gaelic tradition, as the *Poems of Ossian* and the *Rowley Poems* indicate. But it is the archaic and cloudy atmosphere of the romances, rather than the literary excellence of their writing, that attracts us to them today.

## MINOR POETS OF ROMANCE

### MAJOR AND MINOR POETS

We cannot easily put literary tags on major writers and call them either classical or romantic. Both tendencies are present in them, though not usually to an equal degree. The great impulse, and its masterly control, are joint factors in all major works of literary activity. But this is less true of the minor writers. For in them the varying tendencies of the age are not completely assimilated, and are for this reason the more easily recognized. When we listen to a minor poet composing his song in the early morning or the late evening of some period in literary history, it is not difficult to identify him by his single note of classical or romantic strain. Such poets, representing the second half of the eighteenth century, are the Wartons, Thomas and his two sons, Thomas the younger, and Joseph, William Shenstone, Christopher Smart, and, more significantly, James Macpherson, Thomas Chatterton, James Beattie, and George Crabbe. Their poetry has the peculiar merit of indicating that the stream of romanticism did not suddenly spring into existence out of the dry sand in an age of classicism, but owed its origin to influences easily recognizable, for example, in Milton, Shakespeare and Spenser, and, before them, in Malory and Chaucer.

# THE WARTONS

## CULTURE AND COUNTRYSIDE

The Wartons were a family of poetasters, following literary trends, sounding out new and old notes, experimenting, imitating the masters; not notably energetic men, but, fond of country life; antiquarians, mildly interested in the church, in Oxford, in the pleasures of solitude. Together, they lived from 1688, the year of the Revolution, to 1800, long enough, as father and sons, to influence Coleridge and Wordsworth. The relationship is, in fact, direct through the person of William Lisle Bowles whom Joseph Warton taught and who inspired the two famous romantic poets. At some time before 1748 Thomas Warton wrote the ode *Retirement,* in praise of the solitary life, rounding out the first stanza of the poem with these three lines:

> Of nature's various charms I sing;
> Ambition, Pride, and Pomp, adieu!
> For what has Joy to do with you?

## POETRY AND LEISURE

The younger Thomas, before he was twenty, was caught fast in the same net of indolence and wrote *The Pleasures of Melancholy.* The poem, elegiac and sentimental, exactly fitted the sophisticated decadence of the time, as a typical man of Oxford would represent it. An appearance of lethargy, hiding from sight an expert classical learning, a moderate passion for the middle ages, a deep-felt contentment with life in a library, a few boon companions, an unmolested unurbanized quiet life —these were what best satisfied the younger Warton who, in 1785, published an excellent edition of some poems of Milton and was appointed poet laureate of England.

## TRADITION AND REVOLT

His brother Joseph differed from him only in his possession of a more vigorous spirit. Joseph became a teacher of boys at Winchester, a friend of William Collins, and a loyal though independent member of Dr. Johnson's literary club. Otherwise he was a true son of the Warton clan, an antiquarian, a lover of solitude, of simplicity, and of natural freedom. His poem, *The Enthusiast*, written when he was only eighteen, contained two very significant lines:

> What are the lays of artful Addison,
> Coldly correct, to Shakespeare's warblings wild?

expressing his revolt against the school of Pope by indicating that he gave original genius a place above imitative skill. It appears certain enough that Young Joseph Warton had been reading Milton and remembered the line referring to "sweetest Shakespeare, Fancy's child."

# WILLIAM SHENSTONE

## THE IDYLLIC MOOD

William Shenstone's poem, *The Schoolmistress*, was written in a graceful imitation of Edmund Spenser. It is a gentlemanly poem, a "charming admixture of laughter and tenderness." It is evident that the poet was in love with everything Spenserian, with the flowers and the soil of his garden, with the ideal of a life regulated by "good taste, moderation, and decorum." He did not desire nature "methodized" according to the formula of Pope; nor, on the contrary, did he fall to the low level of preferring savagery to culture. In *The Schoolmistress* he simply wished to sing the praise of rustic virtue and of obscure merit, to honor in the poem the name of Sarah Lloyd, his early childhood teacher, who loved and chastised her pupils, and dreamed of their future, and taught them well. It is not a great poem; but Goldsmith and Burns liked and imitated it, and that is praise enough.

# CHRISTOPHER SMART

## RELIGIOUS POETRY

Christopher Smart is to some students of literature only a name. To others he is perhaps only a man who was harmlessly mad about religion and who wrote his celestial ravings in half coherent verse. This is a mistaken criticism of him. Smart was a seer and a mystic whom readers who know and praise the poet William Blake can best understand. The time in which Smart lived was not tuned to such a song as his *Song to David*. But it came, and in the year 1763, from a man who had been "through the gates," who had spent two years in an asylum because of his periodic insanity. Naturally the poem would be thought to be infected by madness, and so neglected. Persons not understanding it might treat it with contempt, or with humor. A few, in our later time, have rightly evaluated it. In 1887 Robert Browning, writing in his *Parleyings with Certain People of Importance in Their Day,* placed this humble poet between Milton and Keats:

> Smart, solely of such songmen, pierced the screen
> 'Twixt thing and word, lit language straight from soul.

Religion was the poet's delight. He worshipped, not nature, but God in whom he believed all creation existed and in praise of whom all nature exulted. Poetry was to him such an exultation, a perpetual prayer from the soul of every created thing: of man, beast, bird and blade of grass; a chorus of praise, worthy of the psaltery of David whom the poet lets us see in these lines that suggest both Browning and Blake:

> Blest was the tenderness he felt,
> When to his graceful harp he knelt,
> And did for audience call;
> When Satan with his hands he quell'd
> And in serene suspense he held
> The frantic throes of Saul.

# REALISTS AND ANTIQUARIANS

## JAMES MACPHERSON

### THE OSSIANIC POEMS

A more direct literary effort, and a more sensational one, is associated with the name of James Macpherson. His poems of Ossian alleged to be translations of that third-century Gaelic poet of Scotland, were, in reality, the work of Macpherson's own vigorous imagination, or largely so. That the young poet possessed genius is clear. He was not yet twenty-five when, in 1760, he began work on the Gaelic fragments he had before him—if he had any; and the "translations" he produced created a great stir, at home and abroad, that lasted an entire century. Here was the story of the brave Fingal, told by Ossian his son, in the noble and rhythmical language of the Bible, against a background of shadow-casting mountains and clouds, and depicted in scenes that were at once romantic, exotic, antique and wild.

### AUTHENTICITY AND INFLUENCE

The Macpherson story caught the fancy of an entire Europe. The German poet Goethe, then in his period of "Storm and Stress," wrote: "Homer has been displaced in my heart by the divine Ossian." Thomas Gray was excitedly curious about the Ossianic poems, but confessed himself "plagued" by the question of their antiquity and by what he called the "demon of poetry" in them. Dr. Johnson declared them fraudulent, told Macpherson so, said they were foggy stuff, and declared that anyone might produce their like "if he would but abandon his mind to it." The judgment of Johnson on Macpherson's sources was very near to the truth. But the great doctor could not in his own time evaluate the sonorous prose by means of which the "poems" so directly affected the romantic movement as later to cause Matthew Arnold to say, with true insight, that the best Ossianic passages could well be imagined to have presented themselves to the eighteenth century as "an apparition of newness and power." Excepting only Bishop Percy's collection of old ballads, *Fingal,* more than any other contemporary piece of writing, carried the spirit of the mysterious and the medieval directly into romantic literature. A good Ossianic specimen is presented to us in *Carthon: A Poem,* from the *Collected Fragments.* In it father and son, unknown to one another, meet in battle. Carthon, the son, sees the elderly hero approaching; he rejoices in the dreadful joy of the old man's face; he thinks it may be his father. He says:

> Shall I lift that spear that never strikes, but
> once, a foe? Or shall I, with words of peace,
> preserve the warrior's life? Stately are his steps
> of age! Lovely the remnant of his years! Perhaps
> it is the husband of Moina; the father of Carborne
> Carthon. Often have I heard that he dwelt at the
> echoing stream of Lora.

# THOMAS CHATTERTON

## THE ROWLEY POEMS

Of Thomas Chatterton and his exceptional and early display of genius, much is written in deserved praise, and much in bare speculation. It is hard to look dispassionately on the youth's struggle against adversity and neglect, the critical abuse and the disillusionment he suffered, and to form a calm judgment of him. His tragic death at eighteen, and by his own hand, colors our judgment of his poetry. He was a poet, unmistakably, perhaps too purely and entirely for any long career. He knew no nurturing home life; he had no helpful friends; he received no formal disciplining education. His father died before the child was born. Bristol was not an attractive town, not any part of it except where the cathedral stood, the old Gothic church of St. Mary Redcliffe, outwardly solemn and gloomy, "Bristolia's dingy piles of brick," as Chatterton called it. But to the boy's fancy it was an alluring and sacred place within whose dust-covered, dim-lighted rooms he found what somehow the age looked for, and almost missed—a haven for its new restless and romantic spirit. There, fingering through the dust, opening old chests, he found parchments he could read, but not necessarily understand. But he could use them, hints in them, words and phrases out of which he could construct the ideas for his own original poetry. To these verses, so written, he attached the name of Rowley, after an imaginary fifteenth century priest. The bold adventure succeeded beyond young Chatterton's dreams: the poems were read and accepted as authentic—"such was the ignorance of Middle English, not to say of Anglo-Saxon, even among educated persons of the time."

## TRAGEDY AND GENIUS

Specimens of the "Rowley poems" began soon to be submitted for publication. This was in 1767 when Chatterton, now only fifteen years of age, was forcing himself to read law. In reality, his imagination was filled with antiquities and the excitement of composition. Then, apparently, someone suspected that the Rowley poems were Chatterton's own brilliant fabrications, and not translations; and Horace Walpole's interest, that might have helped the young poet in his personal distress, hardened into indifference. Chatterton went to London, into the very path of tragedy. Ignored and heart-broken and hungry, he took poison. His poems, an offering to "the passion of the past," survived to puzzle the unscholarly, to be denounced by pedants, but to delight men of genius after him, especially men like Coleridge, Keats, Shelley, and Rossetti, and to be remembered in the annals of poetry through Wordsworth's delineating tribute to Chatterton,

> the marvellous Boy,
> The sleepless Soul that perished in his pride.

# JAMES BEATTIE

## SOLITUDE WITH NATURE

James Beattie was born in 1735, and died in 1803. He was a Scottish farmer's son who studied philosophy and divinity, became a schoolmaster in a mountain town, lived in solitude with the classics, studied music, published minor verse, loved wild nature. At the age of thirty he was teaching moral philosophy in Aberdeen, intimately befriending the poet Gray, and writing both poetry and prose. In 1770, the year of Wordsworth's birth, he published his *Essay on Truth*, attacking the skepticism of David Hume. It brought him popularity, admission to London literary society, an interview with King George III, a pension, and, not the least of all, Dr. Johnson's friendship. Between 1766 and 1771, he was writing Book I of *The Minstrel* to which he gave the subtitle *The Progress of Genius.* Book II appeared in 1774. The poems were written in the Spenserian stanza, as Beattie said, to please his ear and for their "Gothic structure." Their theme was primitive nature, man's teacher through the mild discipline of solitude — a Wordsworthian theme, developed by a minor poet of true sensibility and exemplified in these words about Edwin, the village philosopher, whose life is depicted in stanzas XV to XXII:

> In truth he was a strange and wayward sight,
> Fond of each gentle and each dreadful scene.
> In darkness and in storm he found delight,
> Nor less than when on ocean-wave serene
> The southern sun diffused his dazzling sheen.
> Each sad vicissitude amused his soul;
> And if a sigh would sometimes intervene,
> And down his cheek a tear of pity roll,
> A sigh, a tear so sweet, he wish'd not to control.

# GEORGE CRABBE

## NATURE AND REALISM

The place of George Crabbe was definitely with the romantics. His aim was to please his reader with his art, but to do it through an appeal to the rougher and more realistic sensations. His own experience gave him this opportunity. He was born into poverty; his father was not a tolerant man; and life for him in the village of Aldeburgh, on the Suffolk seacoast, was rather harsh and grim. But the chief source of his realism was not in Aldeburgh, but in him. He wrote of what he saw; and his eyes were on life's stern and tragic facts which, for the composition of his poetry, he selected with careful detail.

# GOLDSMITH AND CRABBE

## TWO "VILLAGE" POETS

Oliver Goldsmith, too, in *The Deserted Village,* had written of the countryside and of rural life, and he had himself known poverty and grief. But he had, besides his gift to observe and to pity man's hard lot, the greater power to perceive and portray man's trust in a benevolent Nature and, beyond this, to cast on the entire earthly scene something of "that unfading light that never was on land or sea." It cannot be said that Crabbe misjudged the plain fact of human misery, but only that he recorded in red letters what must be written on the debit side of life's ledger. Accordingly, *The Village,* his most notable poem, became a social document, a protest against the soft sentimentality that fed, like a parasite, on the pastoral tradition in literature and on its idyllic feeling for nature. George Crabbe, scorning sentimentality, had himself no such idyllic feeling. A modern critic has called him "intellectually short-sighted, and emotionally restricted." But he was an honest realist, even if not a great one, and his acidly moralizing humor was in the best English vein. He was exact enough to satisfy Burke, sufficiently practical to please Johnson; and his bold rusticity won for him the regard of Wordsworth and Byron. Scott found in *The Village* something healthily realistic; Lamb, something deliciously bitter and quaint; Tennyson, something ruggedly English. George Eliot was moved by its authentic note of tragedy, and Thomas Hardy felt its acid touch of irony. All of these writers admitted its influence— as did Edgar Lee Masters, whose *Spoon River Anthology* resembles *The Village* closely enough, as is evident in these words of an old man:

> A lonely wretched man, in pain I go;
> None need my help and none relieve my woe;
> Then let my bones beneath the turf be laid,
> And men forget the wretch they would not aid.

# WILLIAM COWPER

**SENSITIVENESS AND SERENITY**

If poetry were to be defined in terms of sustained reasoning, William Cowper could not be called an important writer of it. But in the list of those in whom a certain childlike quality of innocence is associated with a mature and vivid perception of objects in their primary power to heal and inform the human spirit, he is among the first of our English poets. His sensitiveness and serenity are alike astonishing. If he were not in a peculiar way the poet that he is, his versification might strike us as dull; and we do not indeed have to read far to find pedestrian passages in such of his longer poems as *Table Talk, Expostulation,* and *Retirement* that test the patience of the uninitiated reader. Cowper did not go to writing as to a formal exercise in neo-classical art, or romantic fancy. The composition of poetry was a necessity to him: an act of inward quiet breathing, a respite from a haunting fear, a means of grace to a soul beclouded with the continual foreboding of insanity.

## EMOTION TURNED TO ART

Words do not fall at random, like leaves from trees, on a page of Cowper's poetry. Instead they are peculiarly selected and placed together in a colorful pattern of strong emotion. In the poem *Upon the Receipt of My Mother's Picture,* the poet's experience is so faithfully traced in the familiar forms of thoughts and things round about him as to induce in the reader a state of mild excitement and leave him in possession of an enduring truth. The poem is typical of Cowper at his best: an ardent delicacy, fond memory, domesticity, pity for nature's creatures, childlikeness, religious feeling, submissiveness, frail philosophizing, and a particular delight in the art of innocent fancy as a shield against dark thoughts—these are the qualities that endear him to the reader. Here, it is seen, is poetry which only a mature and leisurely person could write; and it is written for those who are as civilized and take as much delight in rustic life as does a Georgian gentleman. What we note, simply and finally, is that the poet succeeds in

communicating to us the crystallized product of the emotion
he felt on the receipt of his mother's picture—and that the
poem ends with an awakening from his dream:

> And now, farewell. Time unrevoked has run
> His wonted course, yet what I wished is done:
> By contemplation's help, not sought in vain,
> I seem t' have lived my childhood o'er again,
> To have renewed the joys that once were mine,
> Without the sin of violating thine;
> And, while the wings of Fancy still are free,
> And I can view this mimic show of thee,
> Time has but half succeeded in his theft—
> Thyself removed, thy power to soothe me left.

## THE LONGER POEM

But Cowper's fame rests on a broader foundation than these
brief and tender lines suggest. Besides the group of eight longer
poems, including the influential *Retirement,* all of them written
in the couplets of the school of Pope whose "mere mechanic
art" he disliked, there are the six books of the poem *The
Task,* which owe something of their origin to the "lovely and
vivacious Lady Austen" whom Cowper came to know in the
little town of Olney, and who presented the poet one day
with the challenge: "A subject? You can write upon any—write
upon this sofa!" The suggestion stirred up jealousy in the good
Mrs. Unwin who had long cared for Cowper at Huntingdon
and Olney, and it cost Lady Austen and the poet the intimate
friendship that was maturing between them. But it produced
a poem, probably his best. Cowper himself tells us that he
acted on the moment's incentive, "and, having much leisure,
brought forth at length, instead of the trifle which I at first
intended, a serious affair—a volume!"

## TAPESTRY IN VERSE

The six idylls of the poem, *The Sofa, The Time-Piece, The Garden, The Winter Evening, The Winter Morning Walk, The Winter Walk at Noon,* are English throughout. They are written from life. Scenes near Olney, the river Ouse, the inviting pastures, a thatched house, trees, deep snow, furnish the delightful tapestry for sheltered meditations such as these: "God made the country, and man made the town"; "Slaves cannot breathe in England; if their lungs receive our air, that moment they are free." In Book III, *The Garden,* Cowper lets us see deep into his life and becomes autobiographical. His lapses into insanity, the lonely misery he knew, the religion which fed and yet allayed his fears, understanding friends, and the silent woods, are described in the poignant lines, beginning:

> I was a sticken deer that left the herd
> Long since; with many an arrow deep infixed
> My panting side was charged, when I withdrew
> To seek a tranquil death in distant shades.
> There was I found by One who had Himself
> Been hurt by th' archers. In His side He bore,
> And in His hands and feet, the cruel scars.
> With gentle force soliciting the darts,
> He drew them forth, and healed, and bade me live.

## MELANCHOLY RESIGNATION

The last days were clouded for Cowper. The creative passion had never been strong in him, nor the will to live; and in consequence, after the death of Mrs. Unwin, he sank into a melancholy loneliness. He died, in peaceful resignation, in 1800. His two famous hymns, "O for a closer walk with God," and "There is a fountain filled with blood," are his sufficient

Christian monument. A modern writer has noted, for our attention, that the dates of Cowper's birth and death are exactly a century later than those of John Dryden.

# ROBERT BURNS

## THE MAN AND HIS CHARACTER

On first acqaintance there seems to be nothing at all mysterious or enigmatic about Robert Burns. He stands boldly exposed, hiding nothing from us, not either his tender and sincere heart, nor his irony. But it is difficult, at one glance, to bring together the widely various traits in him and to make one picture of them. It is not in any sense a question of making a patterned moral man of him: poets, like other men, know good and evil; and Burns was wholehearted and headlong in whatever he did. What is apt to disturb the casual reader who perceives the tenderness of a song like *Highland Mary,* and then finds that it was written by the author of a poem familiarly addressed to the devil, is something more than an antithesis of literary traits in the poet. It is, more profoundly, the sign of a generic weakness in our human nature, openly exposed in the poet as in some character in the Bible, or in a play of Sophocles. We are moved to pity by the life of Burns as he himself was moved to pity and fear by nature's beauty and life's essential tragedy. To understand the poet it is necessary to dispel the popular opinion that the name of Burns is nothing more than the symbol of a romantic love reduced to frustration against a background of austere nature and relentless fate.

## A LIFE OF TRAGEDY

Thomas Carlyle, in his *Essay on Burns,* looks on the poet through transcendental eyeglasses. He sees the poet exalted, but the man abased. Like Byron, we are told, Burns "has a poet's soul, and strives toward the Infinite and the Eternal; and soon feels that all this is but mounting to the house-top to reach the stars." To reach with his poetry, and to fail with his life— that, Carlyle intimates, was the tragedy of Burns; and Carlyle quotes, as his conclusion, the words of Milton: "He who would write heroic poems must make his whole life a heroic poem." Obviously, Burns lacked the strength to do this thing: his was not Shakespeare's or Dante's gift "to sing the heroic poet". The gift of Burns was indeed the gift of song: the song of love; the song of good company; the song of the plow. These represent his genius. But existence was by no mean's simply a joy to him. It was hard labor, sorrow over lost love, at life's fading joy, his own declining health, the death of friends. Of the days of his youth Burns himself said: "This kind of life, the cheerless gloom of a hermit and the unceasing toil of a galley-slave, brought me to my sixteenth year." Later, when he thought of the hard days and of his unfulfilled longings, he likened them to the "blind gropings of Homer's Cyclops round the walls of his cave." What, mostly, kept Burns alive as he neared the age of twenty was his good-humored Scottish capacity to take life's punishment.

**FORMATIVE INFLUENCES**

By then, however, three influences had begun to act on him. They were the reading of literature, an intense love of nature, and the impulse to patriotism. Literature had begun to exist for him when, through the patient teaching of an old servant of the house, he had come to know many of Scotland's legends and to recite its ballads. To this small literary store he added by good reading, and from it there issued his own poetry, first in oral rhymes, and after that in the more careful composition of writing. Such were his background and growth to the year 1781, when Burns, then in his twenty-third year, left the farm, went to live in an Ayrshire town, became a flax-dresser, fell in and out of love, learned to drink and thought himself a mature man and a boon companion. Three years later, in 1784, after his father's death, he returned to the farm; and, in the midst of grim hardship, he met and fell in love with Jean Armour.

## POETRY AND FAME

Out of the pleasure and pain, chiefly of the next two years, came his first volume of poetry, a small edition printed in the nearby town of Kilmarnock, in 1786. It contained forty-four poems and it marked the literary crisis of his life. In the next year appeared the larger Edinburgh edition. Fame, it appears, had come just in time to keep Burns from sailing for Jamaica in the hope of striking a better fortune. Instead, he went to Edinburgh to be honored as the "heaven-taught ploughboy," and to be subjected to the scrutiny of a literary society. The young peasant poet, as Carlyle says, stood up well enough under the "dazzling blaze of favor." But the experience hindered rather than helped Burns, and added little to his future poetry. The wealth and gaiety he saw displayed there only served to exaggerate his social misfortune. Had he been a Scot as strong of will as he was emotionally sensitive, this contrast of others' wealth with his own poverty might not have embittered his spirit. As it was, his very humanitarianism caused this bitterness to grow, especially after his return from Edinburgh to the hard life of the farm and of an exciseman in the town of Dumfries. There, in the round of menial duty, he fell into further brooding and sentimental excesses. To top his unwisdom, as his own countrymen judged it, he hailed the progress of the French Revolution. His marriage to Jean

Armour, at this time, was an acknowledged compensation for her loyalty and love.

## SORROW AND SONG

The German poet Heine once said: "Out of these my great sufferings write I the little songs" (*Aus diesen meinen grossen Schmertzen mache ich die kleinen Lieder*). It was so of Burns. Like his sense of humor, his power to produce poems and songs did not fail him even in these later hard years, as we note in such lyrics of intermingled pleasure and pathos as *John Anderson My Jo, A Red, Red Rose,* and *Highland Mary.* In the first of these, once a ribald song, but now as humorous as it is tender, we can almost read the story of the poet's life:

> John Anderson, my jo, John,
> We clamb the hill thegither;
> And monie a cantie day, John,
> We've had wi' ane anither:
> Now we maun totter down, John,
> And hand in hand we'll go,
> And sleep thegither at the foot,
> John Anderson, my jo.

## THE PLEASURES OF POETRY

The first thing one notices about Burns is that he is a solidly earthy poet. After that, no one can fail to observe that he possesses the supreme gift of music, of uniting tender personal feeling with tuneful words. Nor does he lack imaginative force, manly vigor, and human understanding. As an apt master of song he is easily comparable to Chaucer in warmth of emotion, in carefree gaiety and in good-humored, gloom-dispelling laughter. The power to imitate nature, to draw from the earth its sweet breath of love, to associate some deep experience in us with a familiar spot of ground, some tune of far-off times, or some healed but not forgotten sorrow—this gift is the unfading glory of Burns. To readers of cosmopolitan tastes, the poems *Tam o'Shanter* and *The Jolly Beggers,* with their picturesque description of the rude aspects of Scottish life, their broad uproarious comedy, their satire on superstition, hypocrisy and cant, will best represent the poet they know: the exultant Burns; the social critic; the boon companion of caustic tongue and provincial pride; the artist who takes a swing at life and, by his brilliance, comes through victoriously. But poet lovers, generally, will relinquish these specialized pleasures to the coterie of the more deeply initiated and settle for a song, composed in familiar English, that begins and ends, for example, on such an ingratiating note as this:

> Flow gently, sweet Afton, among thy green braes,
> Flow gently, I'll sing thee a song in thy praise;
> My Mary's asleep by the murmuring stream,
> Flow gently, sweet Afton, disturb not her dream.

In the lyrics of Burns, Romanticism came to earth, literally, tenderly, and with a touch of satire. Burns loved Scotland, his country, and liked to write ballads about it. He loved the most gentle and beautiful of Scotland's daughters and knew how to express this love in verses of lyric tenderness and passionate fervor. With all this, he was a man's man with strong emotions toward honor, fair play, domestic tranquillity, and the solid rugged virtues of the common people. The poem's *My Luve is like a Red, Red Rose, A Man's a Man for A' That,* and *The Cotter's Saturday Night* — the last of these prefaced by a stanza from Gray's *Elegy*—sum up what the later Romantic poets, from Wordsworth to Lord Byron, were to find rich and enduring in Burns: his homely depiction of rural life in a setting of natural repose and dignity; and his sharp, native satirical instinct, set in close proximity to his sincere praise of innocent, romantic love. In Burns, we may say, Romanticism looked out upon the world with frank and open eyes, and so became fully conscious of itself as a source of power in the poetry of the age to come. Wordsworth sensed this power when, in 1803, after visiting the grave of Burns, he wrote:

> I mourned with thousands, but as one
> More deeply grieved, for He was gone
> Whose light I hailed when first it shone,
>     And showed my youth
> How Verse may build a princely throne
> On humble truth.

# WILLIAM BLAKE

## HIS MYSTICISM

The name of William Blake has become a passport to the realm of the imagination. In his upward and downward movement of thought he stands in marked antithesis to Burns whose fancy generally follows a horizontal course close to the earth's surface. Burns extracts feeling from the natural and social situation in the world of which man is a part. Blake, too, senses the aliveness of nature, laying his hand on its dilating pulse. But he knows it for what he believes it to be: the outer physical form of an inner motion of the spirit. Nature and the soul, alike, are realities to this mystical poet. They are not identical, but they are *One*. Only to Blake, as he says, commenting on the prophetic poem *The Marriage of Heaven and Hell,* "that call'd Body is a portion of Soul discern'd by the five senses, the chief inlets of the soul in this age." Therefore to understand this poet it is necessary to approach him through his belief that two orders coexist in the world, the natural and the spiritual, and that the natural is the spiritual made real to our senses. This belief is at the core of the poet's mysticism.

## PASSION FOR SOCIAL REFORM

But there is a practical and social side to Blake's poetry. He is as revolutionary as he is metaphysical—a fact that puzzles those to whom his poems are mainly visionary. His interest in the ancients, in Biblical history, in the Renaissance, in the French Revolution and in the economic and social thought of his contemporary England, establish him among the most vigorous of modern reformers. Among the so-called prophetic books of the poet there is one entitled *Milton*, written close to the year 1808. It contains lines now set to music, and the words in them strike as sharp spears at the existing evils of the time, when he says,

> Bring me my bow of burning gold!
> Bring me my arrows of desire!
> Bring me my spear! O Clouds, unfold!
> Bring me my chariot of fire!
>
> I will not cease from mental fight,
> Nor shall my sword sleep in my hand,
> Till we have built Jerusalem
> In England's green and pleasant land.

## SOURCES OF INSPIRATION

While Blake's calling was poetry, and his passion was social reform, he was by occupation a seller of prints and by profession an engraver. He was born in London in 1757, a dry-goods merchant's son, and privately and informally educated. He learned what he came to know mainly by absorption and domestic example, and was soon talking theology, having visions, walking "in the company of angels," making ingenious drawings of what he saw, and composing the imitative but visionary lyrics that were published in 1783 under the title of *Poetical Sketches*. Of the rules of grammar and spelling he had at first little knowledge, and of the art of composition he learned only what was convenient from the academic books. Nor, apparently, did he have any need of them; for his clear imagination seems to have been his teacher, inducing him to learn directly from life how to portray life. His sources of inspiration, as far as they can be traced, were principally these: (1) the Bible; (2) the mystical and theological teachings of Immanuel Swedenborg; (3) the poetry of Shakespeare and Milton; and (4) the noble monuments and interior arches of Westminster Abbey where, for several years before he was twenty, he almost literally lived. From religion, poetry, and architecture, therefore, he derived those forms of beauty which, whether as engravings in copper, or drawings in color, or lines of lyric verse, were to shape themselves into the delicate symbolism of his almost escaping and always elevating thoughts.

## POET AND ENGRAVER

Blake opened his printer's and engraver's shop in 1789; and in that year he published the *Songs of Innocence*. The poems were romantic, tender, symbolical and humanitarian. The engravings that accompanied them were masterly in design; the tinting, by the poet's own hand, was a blending of color with sense and sound. When the volume was completed, it was a compositional unity, a thing of beauty, of genius. Yet, though the book was priced at four shillings, the sales were few—such, then as now, was the over-the-counter value of poetry. But Blake was unambitious and happily occupied, working intensely, keeping long hours, and trusting time for the outcome. To Blake poetry was simply translated vision: the artist was the seer. Language might sometimes fail him; but the poet's intuition kept the course of vision clear, even when the line or verse of poetry, like a sea-going ship, faded into the distant horizon beyond sight. At such times he was content to think of what had been revealed to him as intelligible chiefly to himself. This is the Blake of the later *Prophetic Books* in which, as someone has recently said, we hear the poet uttering his thoughts with "the effect of a majestic soliloquy."

## SONGS OF EXPERIENCE

The six years between 1788 and 1794 were among Blake's happiest. During them, aided by his faithful wife, he composed, illustrated and printed the two famous books of poetry, *Songs of Innocence* and *Songs of Experience*. There is in both of them the same blithe but scrutinizing note of joy, but with the difference their titles suggest. The first is well typified by the poem *The Lamb;* the second by the poem *The Tiger.* God made the lamb, the poet says, as He made the little child; for did not the Christ Child become the sacrificial Lamb of God? This is the poet's song of innocence. Then speaking out of experience, and knowing the affirmative answer, he asks boldly:

> Tiger, Tiger, burning bright
> In the forests of the night, . . .
> When the stars threw down their spears
> And watered heaven with their tears,
> Did He smile His work to see?
> Did He who made the lamb make thee?

## VOICE OF PROPHECY

Except for a few years in Sussex, Blake lived his entire life in London. Outwardly the years were uneventful. The age, still rationalistic, considering itself correct and mannerly, thought him queer and half mad when, in the midst of its noise and commerce, he professed to hear the voice of judgment against outraged humanity, and wrote:

> A robin redbreast in a cage
> Puts all Heaven in a rage . . .
> A dog starved at his master's gate
> Predicts the ruin of the state.

There passed for Blake ten years of comparative waiting until the creative spirit again moved him, this time sublimely and resolutely. Following, as he believed, the inner light of divine imagination, he set out to produce such masterpieces as his one hundred drawings on the Book of Job and such prophetic literary works as *Milton* and *Jerusalem,* the latter celebrating, through gloom and terror, the victory of man over sin and death and his return to Eternity. In a manner typical of this work, and as an answer to the disputation of the Deists of his and other times, ancient and modern, he bequeathed this parting word in praise of the Christian martyr:

> Titus! Constantine! Charlemaine!
> O Voltaire! Rousseau! Gibbon! Vain
> Your Grecian mocks and Roman sword
> Against this image of his Lord!

> The bitter groan of a martyr's woe
> Is an arrow from the Almighty bow.

In Blake's poetry, we see a departure from almost everything that was neo-classical. In the place of formal pedantry, here was verse of a blithe spirit and of a delightful ease of expression. The didactic couplet gave way to the free line and open stanza. Here was poetry, not for the aristocratic ear, the critical eye, but for the human mind and heart. It was tenderly and thoroughly humanitarian. Yet it was also richly symbolical and mystical. Everywhere in the *Songs of Innocence* the childlike words and rhymes give off overtones of a deeper meaning, as in the poem *The Lamb,* which begins with the line "Little Lamb, who made thee?" and ends, saying,

Little Lamb, I'll tell thee,
Little Lamb, I'll tell thee:
He is callèd by thy name,
For He calls Himself a Lamb,
He is meek, and He is mild;
He became a little child.
I a child, and thou a lamb,
We are callèd by His name.
Little Lamb, God bless thee!
Little Lamb, God bless thee!

In the *Songs of Experience* the verbal felicity is the same. But the mystery is deepened, as, for example, in the poem *The Tiger* in which the sensation of terror unites with that of beauty, and in *The Clod and the Pebble* in which the striking opposites of the "self" and "another" are brought together under the reconciling concept of love. Here at last, in Blake, the Romantic spirit reaches its highest expression in the symbolism of religious faith. Beauty and truth are united in the embrace of language in a manner that suggests Coleridge's supernaturalistic poetry and Hazlitt's idea of divine inspiration.

# William Wordsworth
### 1770-1850

## THE POET AND HIS ART

## HIS YOUTH AND EDUCATION
### 1783-1791

## THE PERIOD OF STORM AND STRESS
### 1791-1796

## THE EARLY POETRY
### 1796-1805

## YEARS OF LITERARY PRODUCTIVITY
### 1805-1845

## WORDSWORTH'S POWER
## AND INFLUENCE

# THE POET AND HIS ART

## THE POET'S SELF-REVELATION

Two strong and determining tendencies meet in the poet Wordsworth. We may, at this beginning, call them the moral and the confessional. Both of them are rooted in his instinctive desire to lay bare his soul to the world. It is the same instinct that he finds in nature: in the flower opening its petals to the sun; in the earth inviting the rain; in the heavens spreading their starry mantle above the night.

## NATURE AND THE SOUL

It is this act of self-revelation in the poet that makes him at once so simple and so profound. He does not write as one intent on unearthing something hidden in nature; instead, he quietly and joyously tells his reader of what he has found, of what lies unexpectedly uncovered before him. Nature and his own soul are alike an open book to him. It is as a poet-seer that he appears before us; and as such he must be recognized and studied. His words have the august character and authenticity of prophetic utterances. In contrast to much of our mundane talk, they belong to the category of the inspired. For this reason even those dull passages that are sometimes found in his poetry have a more than ordinary worth; for in them, as in a handful of common earth, some essential meaning is implicit; some value touching the poet's life lies waiting, like a seed in good soil, for its germinating time to come. It is this attitude of objectivity toward emotions which in men generally are too deep for words, or are simply passed by as trivial and ordinary, that makes Wordsworth the poet he is—a poet of the soul who makes his communion with nature, as Professor Oliver Elton aptly says, a "eucharistic experience" of the divine in natural form.

## WORDSWORTH'S NOBLE LYRICISM

When in his august reverence for life Wordsworth writes in his own typical metaphysical style, the effect upon the reader is overpowering and positive. Beginning with some pastoral setting in which the vagrant fancy, or heated temper, of our daily life is gradually subdued, the typical poem of Wordsworth moves in measures of accelerating intensity, like some giant figure, across the earthly scene, casting a magic shadow on the landscape, scarcely observed by the passer-by, but greeted with joy by the receptive reader who shares the life of some little creature of nature at the poet's feet. Such, for example, is the poem *To the Cuckoo* in which by slow degrees all the valley is awakened while the cuckoo sings and the poet listens to the song's echo, and later records the meaning of what he has heard in these concluding lines:

> O blessed Bird! the earth we pace
> Again appears to be
> An unsubstantial, faery place,
> That is fit home for thee!

## HIS RANK AS POET

It is fitting that a study of the nineteenth century in English literature should begin with Wordsworth. He comes first in time and rank. The depth and the durability of his best work have earned him a place next to Shakespeare and Milton. He is an original poet whose thoughts, beginning within himself, find

their ultimate expression in stately poems of objective reality—
the dual yet integrated reality of the natural world and the
divine spirit. This close integration is immediately perceived
by almost anyone who casually opens the volume of the poet
and reads:

> The eye—it cannot choose but see;
> We cannot bid the ear be still;
> Our bodies feel, where'er they be,
> Against or with our will.
> Nor less I deem that there are Powers
> Which of themselves our minds impress;
> That we can feed this mind of ours
> In a wise passiveness.

## HIS STATELY SIMPLICITY

Looking more closely at the poetry of Wordsworth, we are
impressed by the fact that he ignores nothing that is common to
man. He is guided, but never lured, by a poet's fancy. He feels
no urge to side-step the plain truth, no inclination toward art
for art's sake, no fear of appearing dull to his readers. The
reminiscences of Wordsworth may at times seem tedious to
those who are unprepared to read them; but the monotony of
the poems is never merely something artificial. It is as natural,
and often as moving, as the spacious monotony of the tranquil
ocean. His style is free from literary dexterity, from over-subtle
or abstruse inference, from the harshly shocking word, the
superlative epithet. His poetry is stately, simple and serious.
It is evidently written to instruct and to give pleasure.

## A NEW POETRY

But Wordsworth did not simply write poetry; he started a
movement in it, a "school" known—at first derisively—by the
name of the Lake Poets. The new poetry began as a protest

against the rationalism of the eighteenth century: against its skeptical attitude toward revealed religion; against its distrust of human nature, of the common man, of political liberty; and against its stress on external rules of literary composition.

## THE POET'S CREED

The literary aristocracy of the past century had done important things for the cultural life of the people. It had exalted reason. It had established English good sense. It had enforced popular social discipline. It had cultivated an exact style of writing. But the century had forgotten its greater and richer heritage: the gift to English literature of its earlier great poets, men of original genius like Chaucer, Shakespeare, and Milton. It had actually all but ignored them. This neo-classical age which had so greatly influenced Alexander Pope, and had in turn been greatly influenced by him, had turned away both from the chivalry and romance of the Middle Age, and from the thirst for knowledge that had marked the Renaissance, and had itself become emotionally barren. Trying to escape from the dark marshes of an extreme romanticism, it had wandered into the dry desert of an extreme classicism.

## A FREE PEOPLE'S POETRY

Wordsworth held that the English spirit was no longer creative because it was no longer free. Literature, he believed, needed to become fresh and strong again. It needed for this reason to be the expression of a sturdy and free people; a people whose source of strength lay in communion with nature rather than in conformity to social convention; who found their kinship with living beings as real as their belief in cosmic law; and who looked on poetry as an expression of life rather than as an exercise in literary art. It was with this conviction nurtured, first in an early solitude with nature, then in the revolutionary atmosphere of France, and after that in a return to nature, his first love, that Wordsworth began his work as a poet.

## HIS YOUTH AND EDUCATION

### WORDSWORTH'S CHILDHOOD

The Romantic period, lasting from 1798 to 1832, falls directly into the middle of Wordsworth's life. He was born in 1770 in Cockermouth, a little town on the river Derwent, in the Lake District in northwestern England. His father was a lawyer, a sturdy character, and fond of the natural beauty of the Cumberland region. His mother died when William was only eight; his father five years later. The orphaned children, including two brothers and a sister, Dorothy, were separated, and William was sent to a preparatory school at Hawkshead, a village set in the heart of the Lake District.

### AT HAWKSHEAD

Here the boy, sensitive and lonely, drank in the wild beauty of the scenery around him. The hills, the clouds, the water, the bird life and the flowers—on these he fed his young imagination, filling it with what he later called the joy of "holy forms" of beauty. In his first published poem, *An Evening Walk*, written when he was eighteen, and when the Hawkshead days were still a present sensation and hardly yet a memory, he tells of seeing two pairs of majestic swans, and singling out the leader among them, says:

> The eye that marks the gliding creature sees
> How graceful pride can be, and how majestic, ease.

It is not the lines of the verse that strike us here. They plainly remind us that he wrote in heroic couplets in his Cambridge days. It is the young Wordsworth's awakened mind, his sense of the latent beauty in the forms of nature, that arrest us. It is of this sensitivity to form in the poem that Dorothy Wordsworth was aware when, at a later time, she wrote to a friend, saying: "I hope you will here discover many beauties which could only have been created by the imagination of a poet."

## FORMATIVE INFLUENCES

Of the Hawkshead years, between 1783 and 1787, Wordsworth has himself given us a good account in the poem called *The Prelude*, which he began in 1799 and completed in 1805. The poem is retrospective and philosophical, and interprets for us the youthful sensations and intuitions underlying the conscious art of the mature poet. In a passage in the first book of the poem, typical of Wordsworth's early consciousness of the "soul of nature", there is a description of the boy as the later man sees him. He is unloosing his boat from an old willow within a rocky cove, and pushing out into the lake, stealthily and in a mood of "troubled pleasure", surrounded by mountain echoes, the little waves "glittering idly in the moon," fixing his eye on the summit of a craggy ridge, rowing lustily, as he says, and "heaving through the water like a swan," until suddenly from behind the ridge

> A huge peak, black and huge,
> As if with voluntary power instinct,
> Upreared its head. I struck and struck again,
> And growing still in stature the grim shape
> Towered up between me and the stars, and still,
> For so it seemed, with purpose of its own
> And measured motion like a living thing,
> Strode after me. With trembling oars I turned,
> And through the silent water stole my way
> Back to the covert of the willow tree;
> There in her mooring-place I left my bark,—

And through the meadow homeward went, in grave
And serious mood; but after I had seen
That spectacle, for many days, my brain
Worked with a dim and undetermined sense
Of unknown modes of being; o'er my thoughts
There hung a darkness, call it solitude
Or blank desertion. No familiar shapes
Remained, no pleasant images of trees,
Of sea or sky, no colors of green fields;
But huge and mighty forms that do not live
Like living men, moved slowly through the mind
By day, and were a trouble to my dreams.

## MEMORIES OF LUCY

Those were the Hawkshead days. He entered Cambridge in 1787, at the age of seventeen. But he took the Lake Country with him in his memory of visions, especially those of Lucy, or the maiden he later called by that name, who dwelt beside the springs of Dove. The Lucy-poems, written in 1799 and 1800, are too real and poignant not to be autobiographical. In them Wordsworth recorded, with profound and delicate feeling, the truth which lay at the basis of his conception of poetry and of life, namely, that man and nature are united in a divine and eternal mystery of being—a mystery to which a faith in God alone is the key. Who Lucy was is not known. But it is clear that she symbolized three things: (1) the ecstasy of his youthful affections, (2) the omnipresent tutelary soul of the mountainous Lake District, (3) the deep intuitive sense of divine reality within which all nature moved, as objects move by means of thoughts within the mind in calm repose.

## THE POWER OF INTUITION

These intuitions, early and formatively at work in his mind, are the essential Wordsworth. To trace them, as we can, for example, in Section Five of the famous Lucy-group, is to see how from the beginning the power of mystical vision was present in the poet. Writing of Lucy who has lived unknown and now is dead, he records in these lines his remembered feelings of those days:

> A slumber did my spirit seal;
> I had no human fears:
> She seemed a thing that could not feel
> The touch of earthly years.
> No motion has she now, no force;
> She neither hears nor sees;
> Rolled round in earth's diurnal course,
> With rocks, and stones, and trees.

## AT CAMBRIDGE

But between Wordsworth's departure from Hawkshead and the time when he wrote these lines, while touring in the Hartz Forest in Germany, there was an intervening period of ten years. First, within that period, came the four years at Cambridge where, in 1791, he received the A. B. degree, but without citation of especial honors. He writes, in the *Prelude,* of his Cambridge experiences: of the loyal students who were faithful to their books; of the "half-and-half idlers", and the "honest dunces"; of richly nurtured friendships; of "unprofitable talk at morning hours"; of his laughter with Chaucer; of his moving with Spenser "through his clouded heaven with the moon's beauty and the moon's soft pace"; of Milton, once also a Cambridge student, but now an "awful soul," yet a comrade among poets, to whose memory one day he himself, aspiring to be a poet, and in the very room which Milton once occupied, poured out libations and drank wine "till pride and gratitude grew dizzy" in his brain as he sped off to reach the chapel door before it closed. It was here at Cambridge, the seat of learning, the ruling place of the mighty living among the world's dead, that Wordsworth became fully aware of that especial gift entrusted to him, the gift of the poet's imagination.

> Imagination—here the Power so called
> Through sad incompetence of human speech,
> That awful Power rose from the mind's abyss
> Like an unfathered vapor that enwraps,
> At once, some lonely traveller. I was lost;
> Halted without an effort to break through;
> But to my conscious soul I now can say—
> "I recognize thy glory."

## THE SUMMER VACATION

But of more importance, and never to be forgotten, was that almost holy time, during the Cambridge summer vacation, of which he writes in the fourth book of the *Prelude,* when, after a night spent in social gayety and dancing, he walked homeward alone, and into the "roseate magnificence" of the morning. Behind him he heard the laughter of the sea; before him rose the sun. The hills stood there crimson-tinctured. The dew glistened with gold. The birds poured forth song. It was a grave yet joyous hour. In the later quiet retrospect of it the poet says:

> Ah, need I say, dear Friend! that to the brim
> My heart was full; I made no vows, but vows
> Were made for me; bond unknown to me
> Was given, that I should be, else sinning greatly,
> A dedicated spirit.

# PERIOD OF STORM AND STRESS

## IN FRANCE

In the late autumn of 1791 Wordsworth went to France. There, in the midst of the Revolution, he caught the time's excitement: (1) he felt the influence of the teaching of Rousseau who attributed the evil in the world, not to man's sin, but to organized society; (2) he began, with other revolutionaries, to look on kings as the major cause of political evil; (3) he joined the progressive party of the republican Girondists; (4) he fell romantically and tragically in love with Annette Vallon whose sympathies, fundamentally, were with the Royalist cause. The years between 1791 and 1795, consequently, were for him years of both exalting and agonizing experience. During them his highest hopes were momentarily realized and then gradually turned to bitter disappointment; and it was only through the timely help of his sister Dorothy, and his friend Coleridge, that the world was for him again set upright and in order and that, by 1797, he was able to resume his vow to be a poet.

## THE VOW AGAINST TYRANNY

We can well imagine that going to France was for Wordsworth an experience for which he was quite unprepared by the quiet time at Hawkshead and the scarcely more eventful days at Cambridge. The Revolution set his imagination on fire. Rousseau was right: so Wordsworth now began to think. Man was essentially noble; he must therefore be free. Monarchy, the breeder of tyranny, must be stamped out. There was something in the temper of the French nation that pleased Wordsworth. He liked the patriotic passion joined with the type of gallantry he found represented in the person of a Captain Michel de Beaupuy who became his friend and with whom, as he says, he often conversed on "dearest themes—man and his noble nature," on heroes and philosophers, and on man's injustice to man. Wordsworth tells us in the Ninth Book of the *Prelude* how the Captain and he chanced

One day to meet a hunger-bitten girl,
Who crept along fitting her languid gait
Unto a heifer's motion, by a cord
Tied to her arm, and picking thus from the lane
Its sustenance, while the girl with pallid hands
Was busy knitting in a heartless mood
Of solitude; and at the sight my friend
In agitation said, " 'tis against *that*
That we are fighting."

## ROMANCE AND TRAGEDY

Thus, intellectually stirred, and moved to social sympathy, Wordsworth met and fell in love with Annette Vallon. The revolutionary time did not make for temperate thinking, and the impasse to which their love led them was marked by unanticipated tragedy and suffering. In December, 1792, a child was born to Annette, a daughter, Anne Caroline. Wordsworth, financially distressed but eager to be married to Annette, hurried to England. Within sixty days, in February, 1793, England declared herself at war with France. Wordsworth was shocked and dismayed. To enter French territory now would mean his arrest. But we have evidence that he dared to go, and it is possible that he saw Annette for a few days in Paris in October, 1793. After that the way to France was barred and remained closed by the war that lasted through the end of the century. Nine years later, in 1802, Wordsworth, accompanied by his sister Dorothy, met Annette and the child again in Calais, France. To us who review the story the meeting was eventful chiefly because out of it came the poet's masterly sonnet beginning with the line "It is a beauteous evening, calm and free," and ending with the touching notes of tribute to the daughter Caroline:

Dear child! Dear girl! that walkest with me here,
If thou appear untouched by solemn thought,

**67**

> Thy nature is not therefore less divine:
> Thou liest in Abraham's bosom all the year;
> And worship'st at the temple's inner shrine,
> God being with thee when we know it not.

## HOPE AND DESPAIR

Besides the tragedy of this separation, Wordsworth now faced with horror the violent course which the Revolution was taking in France. He could not understand how so reasoning a people as the French could quench its thirst for freedom with the blood of the Reign of Terror. Yet, as late as 1793, he affirmed his belief in the cause of France. Referring afterward, in the *Prelude,* to that crucial time, he said that till then, though there were few hopeful signs to those "who looked for the shoots and blossoms of a second spring," yet

> In me, confidence was unimpaired;
> The Senate's language, and the public acts
> And measures of the government, though both
> Weak, and of heartless omen, had not power
> To daunt me; in the people was my trust.

But suddenly the tide turned. England, surprised and frightened, declared war, and Wordsworth's humanitarian hope turned to despair. Added to his personal sorrow, this loss of his faith in a free mankind was a great blow. In his dispairing mood he felt himself deceived by his emotions; and it was but natural that he should later place the blame for his error on his overtime adherence to the teachings of the School of Sensibility.

## THE REVOLUTIONARY CRISIS

The change which overtook the poet was abrupt and radical. Fortunately it was also of short duration. He tells us, again in the *Prelude,* how for a time he gave himself up to a destroying rationalism. The story is vividly told in Book XI, in lines 1-356. It was a shocking, bewildering, dulling experience for the poet. His finer senses seemed to atrophy within him, to dry up the springs of his faith. He lets us guess at the Dantean descent of his spirit as he begins with the famous lines,

> Bliss was it in that dawn to be alive
> But to be young was very Heaven!

That was, as he says, his high attitude, before 1795, when suddenly, with England at war with France, he found himself bewildered, deceived by his affections, and, as he writes, his "sentiments soured and corrupted, upwards to the source." After that, he continues to record, wild theories were afloat in his brain, theories which congealed, at last, into a resolve to make "reason's naked self" his lord. He summoned his best skill to "anatomize the frame of social life," but found himself betrayed, misguided, confounded,

> Dragging all precepts, judgments, maxims, creeds,
> Like Culprits to the bar; now believing,
> Now disbelieving; endlessly perplexed;
> Till, demanding formal *proof*,
> And seeking it in everything, I lost
> All feeling of conviction, and, in fine,
> Sick, wearied out with contrarieties,
> Yielded up moral questions in despair.

## INFLUENCE OF GODWIN AND HARTLEY

William Godwin, once a dissenting minister, but at this time an enemy of all institutions of religion and politics, now attracted Wordsworth. Godwin had, in 1793, written his best known book, his *Enquiry Concerning Political Justice,* denouncing the need of laws and states, and exalting reason as the sole guide to harmonious living. David Hartley, a physician and psychologist, had, in 1749, published a treatise against the view that the moral sense is innate in man. Morality, he had held, was to be attributed to the habitual association of ideas in the mind, and was therefore a strictly rational exercise in the selection of the highest good. Godwin taught that man's highest end was his developed reason; Hartley maintained that man's mind was a society of atoms. Together, their influence on Wordsworth was important and varied: Godwin's was powerful, but brief; Hartley's was modified, but more lasting.

# THE EARLY POETRY

## THE MATURING YEARS

Wordsworth, now in his twenty-fifth year, was being accustomed to endurance. His genius was maturing. It was at this time also that his sister Dorothy greatly helped him, and that he met Coleridge. By the end of the year 1795 he was settled with Dorothy at Racedown, in the south of England. There, in quiet Dorchester, living on a timely legacy of nine hundred pounds, near to Coleridge, Wordsworth thought his way through to new conclusions. Fundamentally, these conclusions were two: (1) to free himself from the rationalism of Godwin; and (2) to dedicate his future years to poetry.

## THE INFLUENCE OF COLERIDGE

The period of the poet's recovery extended through three years, to 1797. By the summer of that year William and Dorothy Wordsworth had moved to Alfoxden, on the Bristol Channel, not far from Nether Stowey, the home of Coleridge. In the exchange of influence between the two men, Coleridge's was at this time the greater. Later, recalling this time of his association with Wordsworth, he wrote of the "invaluable blessing" it afforded him to be near one to whom he could look up with equal reverence "as a poet, a philosopher, or a man." Coleridge had himself, before then, been intellectually awakened, had studied the philosophers critically, Godwin among them, and, besides them, scientists like Hunter and Hartley, and had given up their mechanistic view of the universe for a Christian-Platonic philosophy. He had come to accept this philosophy, partly through the influence of the German Immanuel Kant, but chiefly through his close study of the English metaphysical and Platonist poets of the Seventeenth century. With their help he had come to make a clear distinction between the faculties known as the *understanding* and the *reason.* This was Coleridge's conclusion: the *understanding*, submitting to the senses and therefore to the external world, recorded things as they appeared to be; the *reason,* looking within, built the world of reality from its own conception of essential being and from its intuitive authentic knowledge of God.

## THE POET'S RECOVERY

Wordsworth, now willingly instructed by Coleridge, drank in what was to be to him a full regenerative draught of new learning. Of the help, besides all this, that he received from his sister in this crises he writes repeatedly and reverently. Her words of admonition were like a brook that ran along a lonely road. It was through her wise and sustaining guidance that the poet in him came to life. Next to her, he tells us, it was Nature's instructing voice that led him back

> To those sweet counsels between head and heart
> Whence grew genuine knowledge fraught with peace.

The growth of the poet's mind, which was the theme of the *Prelude,* was now complete. The early Hawkshead days in the

# WILLIAM WORDSWORTH

Lake Country, the formative years at Cambridge, the Revolution in France and the greater spiritual revolution within the man himself; after that the healthful companionship of his sister and his friend Coleridge; and last of all the healing power of Nature; all these influences had accomplished their end. His natural gifts had been made pure and sublime in him through a rebirth in sorrow and suffering. Wordsworth was now prepared to measure and evaluate through his restored imagination and taste what, in Book XIII, lines 1-10 of the *Prelude,* he speaks of as the hidden depth of power behind all poetry, as he says:

> From Nature doth *emotion* come, and moods
> Of *calmness* equally are Nature's gift:
> This is her glory; these two attributes
> Are sister horns that constitute her strength.
> Hence Genius, born to thrive by interchange
> Of peace and excitation, finds in her
> His best and purest friend; from her receives
> That energy by which he seeks the truth,
> From her that happy stillness of the mind
> Which fits him to receive it when unsought.

## THE "LYRICAL BALLADS"

Late in the year 1797 Wordsworth and Coleridge were much together. Coleridge was writing the *Ancient Mariner,* and Wordsworth contributed valuable suggestions toward its composition. In 1798, the two poets together published the *Lyrical Ballads,* the second edition of which appeared in 1800 with the epoch-making *Preface.* There had been an agreement between them, Coleridge tells us in his *Biographia Literaria,* that he should depict "the effects of a supernatural influence on human character," while it was to be Wordsworth's task to "give the charm of novelty to things of every day." Their work, together, was to set forth two complementary aspects of man's nature: Wordsworth's stress on the outward and upward motion of the divine spirit which is in man, and which he shares with all creation; and Coleridge's attempt, by the incantation of his verse, to suggest and symbolize the power of this divine spirit to invade, to disturb, and to regenerate the nature of man and the world.

## THE FLOWERING OF GENIUS

The winter of 1798-9 was spent by the Wordsworths and Coleridge in Germany where the Lucy-poems were written. In 1799 William and Dorothy settled permanently in the Lake District, moving into the Dove Cottage at Grasmere. In 1800, in the revised *Preface* to the second edition of the *Lyrical Ballads*, Wordsworth announced his poet's creed of "utmost simplicity of subject and diction." Besides setting forth the principles that ruled the poetry he was composing, he undertook to outline what he thought poetry itself to be, and, granting the validity of his definition, how it should be written. The *Preface* turned out to be a masterpiece in literary criticism. In it Wordsworth declared that poetry, to be worthy of its vocation, should be sincere, simple and unaffected in style and diction; that its language should, as much as possible, be that of the common man; and that it should, above all else, be instinct with emotion gathered from a close communion with Nature. The poet himself, in composing a poem, Wordsworth said, passes in successive stages from a strong sensation of the object, through moments of intense emotion centering on it, to a state of its "recollection in tranquillity" in which the poem gradually takes form. His statement that "poetry is the spontaneous overflow of powerful feelings," is one with which no other Romantic poet, or critic of poetry, would disagree.

# WILLIAM WORDSWORTH

## TINTERN ABBEY

In 1801, Wordsworth traveled in Scotland. In 1802 he married Mary Hutchinson, Dorothy's close friend. After that, established within himself, and in his household, he gave himself resolutely to poetry. No poet, we may say, was ever more justified in his calling. The remarkable *Tintern Abbey* had already been written in 1798. In it Nature, art, and the poet's mystical faith join in a united endeavor to give us a clear concept of Wordsworth's genius. The poem is a masterpiece of impassioned thinking. In it the poet's thought moves in articulate stages through the sensations of childhood, the kindled emotions of youth, and the meaningful intuitions of the mature man, and comes to rest on the exalted plane of metaphysical reason. The river's "inland murmur" and the poet's "serene and blessed mood" disturb the reader, as they do the poet, with the joy of elevated thoughts and with

> a sense sublime
> Of something far more deeply interfused,
> Whose dwelling is the light of setting suns,
> And the round ocean and the living air,
> And the blue sky, and in the mind of man,
> A motion and a spirit, that impels
> All thinking things, all objects of all thought,
> And rolls through all things.

## FIRST GREAT POETRY

The pastoral poem *Michael* was one of the first pieces to be written after Wordsworth's return to Grasmere. It was composed in blank verse descriptive of life in the Lake District—a grave and noble poem of chaste diction and an elevated but melancholy mood. Michael, its principal character, has the quiet grandeur of a man who stands up under sorrow with

dignity and without bitterness. He understands that pain is
Nature's severe but kindly teacher, and that grief itself need
not destroy the soul's peace. The famous Pastoral does not
attain the high level of Milton's "dramatic artistry of tragic
passion," so evident, for example, in *Samson Agonistes*. But
Wordsworth's tranquilizing touch is more closely felt, and his
hand is assuring and steady. We are held as by a spell as he
draws the picture before us—of Michael the father, Isabel the
mother and Luke the son, living in idyllic peace until, through
misfortune and poverty, Luke is forced to leave the land and
his father's house. And when months have passed and word
comes to Michael that his son has fallen into evil ways in the
dissolute city, and ignominy and shame fall on the old man's
head, we are moved to pity as we see him crushed. He walks
about the farm but cannot work. The sheep-fold in the hollow
dell goes to decay and ruin.

> And to that hollow dell from time to time
> Did he repair, to build the Fold of which
> His flock had need. 'Tis not forgotten yet
> The pity which was then in every heart
> For the old Man—and 'tis believed by all
> That many and many a day he thither went,
> And never lifted up a single stone.

## SONGS AND SONNETS

There followed now, shortly after 1800, a brilliant display
of Wordsworth's gift of writing short spontaneous verse. Poem
after poem appeared, dedicated to simple objects and creatures
of nature, such as the sparrow, the cuckoo, the daisy and the
butterfly; and, presently, such little personal lyrics, as the one
beginning with "My Heart Leaps Up," began to be almost as
numerous as the flowers at the door of Dove Cottage where

they were composed. Besides these there were sonnets, literary
gems, a starry cluster of them, mostly belonging to the year
1802, on diverse subjects: one, for example, on Buonaparte;
another beginning, "Earth has not anything to show more fair;"
another written at Calais in tender dedication to his daughter
Caroline; and, purest of them all in its serene and austere
beauty, that on Milton containing the lines,

> Thy soul was like a Star, and dwelt apart:
> Thou hadst a voice whose sound was like the sea,
> Pure as the naked heavens, majestic, free.

Whatever might be said of Wordsworth's occasional artistic
uncertainty, or the rise and fall of inspiration in his narrative
poems and ballads, it was evident that in the sonnet he had
achieved the mastery of a form especially suited to his desire
to express, in simple dignity and disciplined language, the
thoughts contained in the several hundred existing stanzas of
this type. We have good examples of the masterly ease and
variety of Wordsworth's use of this fourteen-line poem in the
four sonnets called *Personal Talk*, belonging to the year 1806,
and including these lines,

> Wings have we,—and as far as we can go
> We may find pleasure: . . . and books, we know,
> Are a substantial world, both pure and good:
> Round these, with tendrils strong as flesh and blood,
> Our pastime and our happiness will grow.
> There find I personal themes, a plenteous store,
> Matter wherein right voluble I am,
> To which I listen with a ready ear;
> Two shall be named, pre-eminently dear,—
> The gentle Lady married to the Moor;
> And heavenly Una with her milk-white Lamb.

# YEARS OF LITERARY PRODUCTIVITY

## THE POET'S LONG CAREER

The years of Wordsworth's life immediately after 1802—or after 1805 when he completed the *Prelude* and wrote the dedicatory *Ode to Duty*—belong to the golden realm of English literature. His career as a poet, now well begun, moved on to a natural fulness and completion, like a stream, coursing its way through a deep quiet channel to the sea. Between the *Preface* in which Wordsworth defined the direction his poetry was to take, and his death in 1850, lay exactly fifty years. Some critics see in this long period chiefly a continuous decline of the poet's creative powers. It may seem regrettable that he became so early in his life a political conservative. Wordsworth, on occasion, himself felt and expressed this regret. But world events, and the spirit of solitude in the poet, made such a course natural and perhaps inevitable. However, his poetical gifts were not dead in him, even at the age of seventy when he wrote a sonnet beginning, "A Poet!—He had put his heart to school," in which both his philosophical judgment and his sensitiveness to natural beauty are sufficiently evident. If there is a less spontaneous rapture in the older Wordsworth, we are pleased to find in him a compensating deep serenity, and to take to ourselves a more solid comfort from the nobility of thought and mastery of diction that never fail him. Late, as early, in his life he offered this unerring counsel to every hopeful poet:

> Thy art be Nature; the live current quaff,
> And let the groveller sip his stagnant pool,
> In fear that else, when critics grave and cool
> Have killed him, scorn should write his epitaph.

# WILLIAM WORDSWORTH

## WORDSWORTH'S PERSONALITY

In physical appearance Wordsworth was not, even in his earlier years an attractive person. He was by nature grave and austere, severe in outward manner, uncouth in habit and dress, not gallant, without any trace of Chaucerian humor or Johnsonian wit, and a little too self-consciously "dedicated" to poetry. Henry Crabb Robinson, who knew the Wordsworths intimately, observed that the poet was self-absorbed and without social grace; but that "moral purity and dignity and elevation of sentiment are characteristic of his mind and muse." It was Wordsworth's preoccupation with moral rather than political issues that made him the conservative man that he later became. As always, spontaneity remained the essence of his best poetry. It was simply that he could not hide that newborn sense of duty which, through the shock of experience, tempered in him the earlier passion for freedom. But the desire to be free, to live out his life, to pursue his art, never forsook him. This desire he cherished, as he did his religious faith, to the end.

## SELF-DEDICATION

The *Ode to Duty* was composed in 1805; in sorrow, after his brother's death; in remorse, no doubt too, at the thought of Annette; in weariness that cried out:

> Me this unchartered freedom tires;
> I feel the weight of chance-desires;—

and in joyous resolution. It marked a new beginning in his career, as had *Tintern Abbey,* in 1798. It was an act of rededication for him; and it was from a sense of being in accord with the divine law of his own nature that he could look on duty as if it were a heaven-born creature, happy in its earthly state, and wearing "the Godhead's most benignant grace," and could say:

> Nor know we anything so fair
> As is the smile upon thy face:
> Flowers laugh before thee on their beds
> And fragrance in thy footing treads;
> Thou dost preserve the stars from wrong;
> And the most ancient heavens, through
> Thee, are fresh and strong.

Later, on a befitting occasion, he wrote: "Many and many a time have I been twitted by my wife and sister for having forgotten this dedication of myself to the stern lawgiver." The *Ode* is a flawless poem of Platonic-Christian thinking and Horatian style, worthy to be placed beside Gray's *Ode to Adversity*, its model; even though, in a less sympathetic moment, one may regard Wordsworth's work, beside Gray's, as a little too "pulpy with philosophical preaching."

## MEMORIALS OF SCOTLAND

In the year 1803 Wordsworth toured Scotland where he met Sir Walter Scott, visited the grave of Robert Burns, and composed, as a memorial of the tour, fourteen excellent poems. The most perfect of these songs is *The Solitary Reaper*. The diction in it blends faultlessly with the scene and the mood, and one readily perceives in the Highland maiden's singing the poet's own delight in the power to transform pain into melodious song. One listens with him, transported, as he concludes the poem:

> Whate'er the theme, the Maiden sang
> As if her song could have no ending;

> I saw her singing at her work,
> And o'er the sickle bending;—
> I listened, motionless and still;
> And as I mounted up the hill,
> The music in my heart I bore,
> Long after it was heard no more.

In 1804 Wordsworth composed, among others, the poems, *She Was a Phantom of Delight,* and *I Wandered Lonely as a Cloud.* In them his intuitive and descriptive powers are so evenly united as to give the effect of sheer joy, so typical are they of Wordsworth, of his gift of looking on nature minutely, and of remembering with rich pleasure what he has seen. The closing lines of the latter are memorable also as indicating the poet's habit of composing his verses in a mood of passive and pensive retrospect. He has wandered "lonely as a cloud," over hill and valley, and has suddenly been surprised by the sight of the "golden daffodils" dancing in the wind at the water's edge; and he now concludes the poem:

> For oft, when on my couch I lie
> In vacant or in pensive mood,
> They flash upon that inward eye
> Which is the bliss of solitude;
> And then my heart with pleasure fills,
> And dances with the daffodils.

## PHILOSOPHICAL POETRY

But it is in the *Ode on Immortality,* written between 1803 and 1806, that the elements of experience, reason, and imagination are seen to be fused together in Wordsworth's mind and that we find philosophy happily united to poetry. The now familiar intuitive process; the poet's joyous reminiscence; his love of Nature; evidence of his sound, deep reading, particularly in Plato; a noticeable influence of Christian thought; a chaste simplicity and restraint of diction — these traits, and more, all of them typical of the poet, characterize the poem. They prove Wordsworth to be more than simply a nature poet. The *Ode* is mystical-philosophical. There is in it a motion "transfiguring for us the world of sense" and transcending all practiced artistry. Wordsworth himself tells us that the poem owes its origin to an observation of two simple facts: (1) the genius of the child to create from within himself the world in which he lives; (2) the later, fond turning of the adult mind from this circumstantial world, so created yet now so changed, to the blessedness of its original, its purer and more authentic form. The thought of death is a grim foreboding and a life-long burden to the adult mind; it is something not native to the soul of man, and subsequently acquired; but the poet through his gift of recollection, of probing backward into the forgotten child in him, is able to dispel it from his own and from the reader's mind, as the light of day dispels the outstretched night. The *Ode* deserves our attention as a pattern of Wordsworth's best style. At first quietly reminiscent, moving in cheerful yet solemn measures, true to the temper and tradition of the heroic line; then rising and descending in cadences to suit the poet's momentary gladness and his settled philosophic mind, it carries its thought "alive into the heart by passion," as in these lines:

> O joy! that in our embers
> Is something that doth live,
> That Nature yet remembers
> What was so fugitive!

And it comes to its close at last, in serene splendor in the evening of the day, when

> The clouds that gather round the setting sun
> Do take a sober coloring from an eye
> That hath kept watch o'er man's mortality;
> Another race hath been, and other palms are won.

## LITERARY PRODUCTIVITY

Other memorable poems followed, after 1807; many of them: odes, sonnets, in a rich second series, nature lyrics, songs and, besides these, the *Excursion,* begun in 1802 and published in 1814. During these years, and till his death in 1850, Wordsworth wrote continually, and traveled. From Rydal Mount, near Grasmere, which became the Wordsworth home after 1813, he made at least three tours to the Continent, one to Ireland, two to Scotland, and one to Italy. Two of his children died in 1812. Between 1813 and 1843 he held the office of county distributor of stamps at a salary of four hundred pounds a year. The University of Oxford gave him an honorary degree in 1839.

## HONOR AND FAME

In 1843 Wordsworth succeeded Robert Southey to the office of poet laureate. Fame came to him slowly but surely. Coleridge's estimate of him, in 1817, in the *Biographia Literaria,* had proved to be substantial and enduring. After analyzing and correcting Wordsworth's theory of poetical diction, and listing the few defects and major virtues of his poetry, Coleridge summed up his criticism in these words: "In imaginative power Wordsworth stands nearest of all modern writers to Shakespeare and Milton." Such words of eulogy were enough to console Wordsworth, who well knew himself to be a poet, and whose thirst for fame was by now well disciplined. He died at the age of eighty, and was buried, at his request, in the little churchyard at Grasmere.

# WORDSWORTH'S POWER AND INFLUENCE

## THE TREND OF CRITICISM

Estimates of Wordsworth vary. Some of them are based primarily on the man and his character; others on his art and his own theory of it. Occasionally—forgetting that Coleridge has plowed the ground thoroughly—someone digs up the old stories about *The Idiot Boy,* and other such poems, in disparagement of the poet. Increasingly, however, critics are probing beneath the defects of his minor poetry, his insistent stress on moral values, and his simple love of nature, and are seeing, beyond these and the chaste austerity of his style, a fundamental philosophy.

## THE POET'S BACKGROUND

Coleridge saw in Wordsworth a philosophical poet, a poet of ideas, and not simply an amateur naturalist with an astonishingly lyrical voice, or a devout rustic bard recording primitive sensations. This much about him now seems clear: that— *first,* from his earliest association with Nature, his strong religious feelings, and his Cambridge reading of the poets, *second,* from his experience in France and the suffering it brought, *third,* from his brief resort to Godwin and to Hartley, and his abrupt abandonment of them, and, *fourth,* from his knowledge of the teachings of Plato and of Christianity—he derived the profound thoughts about man, nature and God which are the foundation of his best poetry. A good example of the sublimated essence of these thoughts is given us in these lines, once more from the first book of the *Prelude:*

> Wisdom and Spirit of the universe!
> Thou Soul that art the eternity of thought,
> That givest to forms and images a breath

And everlasting motion, not in vain
By day or star-light thus from my first dawn
Of childhood didst thou intertwine for me
The passions that build up our human soul;
Not with the mean and vulgar works of man,
But with the high objects, with enduring things—
With life and nature—purifying thus
The elements of feeling and of thought,
And sanctifying, by such discipline,
Both pain and fear, until we recognize
A grandeur in the beatings of the heart.

## HIS PHILOSOPHY

A close study of Wordsworth's poetry lets us see the orderly pattern into which these thoughts fall. In their broad outline, they follow this course. Between Nature and man, and between man and God, the poet perceives an existing unbreakable bond of union. Through his communion with Nature, man discovers this bond's essential being or character; and he recognizes it as the essence or *form* of all reality, including the moral instinct of man, as we see it exemplified, more particularly and outwardly, in his little unremembered acts of duty and kindness. By these gentle acts, as by a tie of divine kinship, man is brought into a blissful relationship with the universe, with his fellow men, and with God. This relationship, to Wordsworth, was vital and social because it was deeply natural. But it was also mystical. There were moments in the poet's experience, "spots of time," he called them, in which a deeper sense of the oneness of all creation, held together by the infinite Spirit, flashed upon his inward eye; moments of still contemplation when objects of reason became transparent, like invisible glass, and he saw, not the parts but the whole, not the many but the *One*. These moments of insight and bliss, Wordsworth held, belonged by divine right to the poet; and he associated them with the poet's higher reason, or imagination, before which

> The unfettered clouds and region of the Heavens,
> Tumult and peace, the darkness and the light—
> Were all like workings of one mind, the features
> Of the same face, blossoms upon one tree;
> Characters of the great Apocalypse,
> The types and symbols of Eternity.

## STAGES OF EXPERIENCE

Nature and the human spirit, "the soul of man," are fully integrated in Wordsworth's pattern of thought. His poetry merges them into a higher divine synthesis. Of the three aspects of human existence—the life of the senses, the growth of reason and self-knowledge, and the larger consciousness of being at home in the universe—the poet holds that each is in its own way of special importance. Together, they represent the soul's progress or history, from childhood, through adolescence, to maturity. In each stage of this development, something is contributed, something essential to individual happiness, to social progress, and to the larger world outlook. Human values and poetry, alike, are found to be rooted in fundamental simplicity. Trustworthy sensations; wholesome natural feelings; and a worshipful sense of familiarity with the Eternal Spirit: from these, says Wordsworth, spring good deeds and immortal poems.

## THE POET'S INTUITION

But a poem, like a life in its discovery of itself, must move toward its cause or source, as well as issue from it. Intuition, or imagination, which is "the godlike way of knowing truth," is the poet's way to this source. It is also his way of revealing the world to us. To Wordsworth it is essentially the way of religion, chosen by such of his teachers as Plato, Jacob Boehme, Spinoza,

Immanuel Kant, Bishop Berkeley, and Coleridge. In the expanse between physical nature, including human nature, and the larger divine intuition of the poet, there is spread before man the broad and level area of logical reason and common sense; and in it he may find opportunity for both the exercise of his scientific mind and the writing of meaningful prose.

## WHAT POETRY IS

Of Wordsworth's theory of poetry, as set forth in the *Preface* to the second edition of the "Lyrical Ballads," the only further word to be added is that the poet bases his ideas and his art on humble and rustic life because "in that condition the essential passions of the heart find a better soil." The poet, Wordsworth concludes, is a man speaking to men. He is a man endowed with uncommon sensibility, who finds an elevated pleasure in his own thoughts, and is able to hold the memory of a strong passion in a joyous suspended state of contemplation. Poetry, so conceived and written, Wordsworth defines as the "breath and finer spirit of all knowledge;" to him poetry is truth carried impassioned and alive into the heart of man. That as a poet he sufficiently accomplished what in theory he proposed to do is attested by Coleridge. There were, we concede, differences of opinion between the two poets, both on what poetry is and how it is to be written; but on the question of what especially distinguishes a poet they were in complete agreement. Coleridge, speaking for both poets, says that it is finally "the poetic genius itself, which sustains and modifies the images, thoughts, and emotions of the poet's own mind." And when Coleridge adds that "the poet, described in ideal perfection, brings the whole soul of man into activity, with the subordination of its faculties to each other according to their relative worth and dignity," he is in full accord with Wordsworth's statement that "poetry is the first and last of all knowl-edge—it is as immortal as the heart of man."

## WORDSWORTH'S HEALING POWER

Much may be said of Wordsworth's poetry as a "means of grace," a power to heal men's souls. His was a capacious mind in which thoughts moved like objects, not in isolated parts, but as complete wholes, in an orderly system, like planets in their orbits, unimpaired by chance or passing circumstance. The world in which he lived and which he invited his reader to share with him was one of divine law, unchanging but benevo-lent and comforting. And he held that nature, though some-times recalcitrant, as man sometimes is, shared with man this deep instinct of obedience to the divine law by which all crea-tion is moved to a humble but stately subservience to the Almighty Will. The quiet grandeur of this view is most simply expressed in the little groups of poems written by Wordsworth under the adopted title of *Lucy*. In them the freshness of earthly things, the quickening of natural affection in the poet, love of country, soil and fireside, nature in its playful moods, its severer "motions of the storm," and its role as nourishing and disciplin-ing mother, are all summed up in the life-story of a little girl who grew to maidenhood and died, leaving to the poet

> This heath, this calm and quiet scene;
> The memory of what has been,
> And never more will be.

## HIS ELEVATED STYLE

While not all who read Wordsworth may confess themselves ennobled or consoled by him, there is no question about the effect of his stately style, nor about his apt invention and original use of poetical forms. The ballad, the sonnet, the pastoral and the ode are but a few of the types of poetry that he either brings to perfection or modifies and reinvigorates beyond their conventional patterns. Besides his liberty with these forms, he works in new directions with other poems, long and short, extending their limits, pressing poetry as far as it can go toward prose, insisting on the language of the common man, and dealing with realism and pathos in as factual a manner as good taste will allow; sometimes indeed, and without apology, overstepping the posted margin of decreed poetical usage and so letting us know where the areas of poetry and prose meet and divide. In all these bold experiments—in such poems as *Michael, Ruth,* and *Lucy Gray*—he drives literary convention before him in stories of passion or sorrow, in natural situations that fairly throb with innate feeling and vary in pace as the chosen meter decrees. In the poem *Lucy Gray,* for example, the reader is left with Lucy's distraught parents near the narrow bridge to which they have traced their lost child. Breathless with apprehension they detect the child's footsteps and follow

> from the snowy bank
> Those footmarks, one by one,
> Into the middle of the plank;
> And further there were none!

But the poet does not leave the reader standing there contemplating the scene of the child's hard fate. He concludes the poem:

> Yet some maintain that to this day
> She is a living child;
> That you may see sweet Lucy Gray
> Upon the lonesome wild.
>
> O'er rough and smooth she trips along.
> And never looks behind;
> And sings a solitary song
> That whistles in the wind.

## THE BEST OF WORDSWORTH

We can see that Wordsworth is at his best writing a "lyrical ballad" such as this about Lucy. He finds it exactly suited to the swift telling of the legend he finds ready in the region round about him. In such a poem we find the essential Wordsworth. Then, moving by degrees to a more elevated plain, we come to the poet's sustained narratives that approach the epic grandeur of Milton's *Samson Agonistes;* poems in which the hero's suffering is justified by the nobility of spirit in which this suffering is endured. Such poems are *Michael,* and *The Brothers,* and especially *Laodamia,* the most Grecian of his works of which Wordsworth very interestingly says: "It cost me more trouble than almost anything of equal length I have ever written." The result is that lofty union of discourse and story that he often achieves, crowning the summit of his Parnassian fame with oracular words like these:

> "Be taught, O faithful Consort, to control
> Rebellious passion: for the Gods approve
> The depth, and not the tumult, of the soul.

# Samuel Taylor Coleridge
### 1772-1834


## THE INTELLECTUAL POET


## THE YOUNG COLERIDGE
### 1782-1795


## POETRY OF PAIN AND POWER
### 1795-1816


## CRITICISM OF LIFE AND LITERATURE
### 1808-1830


## THE MAN AND ESTIMATES OF HIM

# THE INTELLECTUAL POET

In Coleridge, born in 1772, two years after Wordsworth, the Romantic movement found its most profound interpreter. He gave the movement both sinew and spirit, a hard core of reality combined with "an atmosphere of mystery, wonder, and pathos." It is significant to note that Wordsworth who knew Coleridge best called him a "most *wonderful* man." For his mind was indeed the symbol of wonder and awe. In him, and in his best poetry, the strange and the marvelous attached themselves to everyday things, simple events, and to the common nature of man. To him the ordinary and daily observation of Nature was more real than romantic. It dealt with the facts as they were, many of them relentless and hard. Something else was needed to give them life and tenderness and meaning. This something else, greater than the hard facts, was the poet's vision and faith. The power of intellectual vision, or higher reason, by which he was able to see everywhere the mysterious interpenetration of the supernatural and the natural, of spirit and matter, of good and evil was Coleridge's special gift. He owed much of it to his study of philosophy; but more of it to his visionary temperament, his extraordinary creative imagination, and his profoundly religious nature.

## WORDSWORTH AND COLERIDGE

A traditional tie binds the study of Coleridge to that of Wordsworth. Their writings, in general, are very unlike; so also are their personalities. But, in the words of someone who once applied them to Plato, both possessed minds that were "large in design, and magnificent in surmise." One underground stream fed their thoughts to which they gave diverse expression as the genius of each determined. Both were Romantic poets in search of transcendental values: Wordsworth, by infusing them with tender passion; Coleridge, by linking them with psychological experience. Wordsworth sought to keep realism from becoming hard; Coleridge, to keep romance from becoming sensational and soft.

## REPRESENTATIVE POEMS

The poems *Tintern Abbey* and *The Ancient Mariner* are unlike in outward construction; they arouse different feelings in us; yet we sense in them the common aim of exalting the human spirit in a setting of natural grandeur; and there is in both the poet's fidelity to the truth that lies beyond external appearance. Wordsworth's debt to Coleridge is summed up in his reference to him in the *Prelude* as that "capacious Soul, placed on earth to love and understand." And the manner in which Coleridge acknowledged the unbreakable bond between the two poets is shown in these lines composed by him on the night after he had listened to Wordsworth's reading of selections from the *Prelude:*

> Friend of the wise! and teacher of the Good!
> Into my heart have I received that lay
> More than historic, that prophetic lay
> Wherein . . .
> Of the foundations and the building up
> Of the human spirit thou hast dared to tell
> What may be told to the understanding mind
> Revealable; and what within the mind
> By vital breathings secret as the soul
> Of vernal growth, oft quickens in the heart
> Thoughts all too deep for words!

## POET AND PHILOSOPHER

Coleridge, we now understand, was an intellectual poet. Ideas, we rightly infer, were more authentic to him than bodily sensations. In his now famous *Biographia Literaria* we read that he regarded the poet's imagination as "a living repetition, in the finite mind, of the eternal act of creation in the infinite *I AM*." That definition would be willingly accepted by Wordsworth. It gives us also the key to a study of Coleridge. We see from it that he was a metaphysical poet; not a brain-poet only; nor only a dream-poet; but a worker in fire, an inspired alchemist, toiling at the re-creation of the world, restless through the six days of his labors, till he might see the plan of his life-work completed in some vision of a celestial Sabbath.

## A BURDENED MAN

But such a blissful outcome was, in fact, denied him. For Coleridge was a curst as well as a blest man. His great thoughts often worked upward while he himself wandered in the dark, without the solace of a happy marriage, beset with ill health, a victim of melancholy moods, of opium, of indolence, driven to find refuge in abstruse speculation, tormented by his Chistian conscience and by the unfulfilment of his grandiose dreams —a man whose art poets envied, whose learning astonished scholars, whose criticism of literature was unexcelled, whose "great, renovated scheme of metaphysics, ethics, and aesthetics," as Professor Elton has said, "remained in splinters, which flew far and pierced deep"—yet a man of the tenderest nature, at times childlike in his innocence, and then altogether irresistible in his appeal to our sympathy, as when, in the poem *The Pains of Sleep,* he says, almost inaudibly,

> To be beloved is all I need,
> And whom I love, I love indeed.

# THE YOUNG COLERIDGE

## SCHOOL DAYS

Coleridge was born at Ottery St. Mary, in Devonshire, October 21, 1772. He was the son of an Anglican clergyman. When he was ten years old he entered Christ's Hospital, a London school for poor boys. Charles Lamb who was also a school-boy there tells us in one of his *Essays of Elia,* written thirty-five years later, how the two youths lived at the charity school together. Coleridge was more fortunate than Lamb, we may infer from the latter's vivid comparison in the *Essay.* While the unlucky Lamb was called out of bed, "and waked for the purpose, in the coldest winter nights, to receive the discipline of a leathern thong," Coleridge had the protection of a patron— though, thanks to one of his kind schoolmasters, Matthew Field, Lamb was happy in his studies. There is a well known passage in the *Essay* from which we get a vivid momentary picture of the Coleridge that was to be. Looking back across the span of the years, Lamb says:

> "Come back into memory, like as thou wert in the
> dayspring of thy fancies, with hope like a fiery
> column before thee — the dark pillar not yet turned —
> Samuel Taylor Coleridge — Logician, Metaphysician,
> Bard! — How have I seen the casual passer through
> the Cloisters stand still, entranced with admiration
> (while he weighed the disproportion between the
> *speech* and the *garb* of the young Mirandula), to
> hear thee unfold, in thy deep and sweet intonations,
> the mysteries of Jamblichus, or Plotinus (for even
> in those years thou waxedst not pale at such
> philosophic draughts), or reciting Homer in his
> Greek, or Pindar — while the walls of the old Grey
> Friars re-echoed to the accents of the *inspired
> charity-boy!*"

## YOUTH AND DREAMS

Coleridge entered Cambridge in 1791, at nineteen. Outwardly, the events of his three years there were few. He was a student, but restless; not actually happy except in his eager and very wide reading; and he left the university twice, and finally without graduating. In 1793, harassed by debt, and heart-sick over a disastrous love affair, he went suddenly away, to London, assumed the name Silas Tomkyn Comberbacke, and enlisted in the King's Light Dragoons. But Coleridge was no calvaryman, or a very ludicrous one, and he was soon glad to have his brothers buy his discharge. He returned to Cambridge; but only for a year. In 1794, while on a visit to Oxford, he met Robert Southey, and, to judge from the ensuing events, unfortunately. The two young men presently fell into an idealistic scheme of establishing a Pantisocratic society, in which, as Coleridge wrote,

> No more my visionary soul shall dwell
> On joys that were; no more endure to weigh
> The shame and anguish of the evil day.
> Wisely forgetful! O'er the ocean swell
> Sublime of hope, I seek the cottaged dell
> Where virtue calm with careless step may stray,
> And dancing to the moonlight roundelay,
> The wizard passions weave an holy spell.

Cambridge's formal education was forgotten. The Pantisocracy which was to be set up in Pennsylvania, on the banks of the Susquehanna, failed. So also did Coleridge's marriage to Sara Fricker, hastily entered into as a part of the colonization plan. Only there was this difference, that the marriage was a lasting failure, whereas the Pantisocracy simply collapsed, and so could be forgotten. It was good luck for Coleridge that, in 1795, he met and learned to know Wordsworth; for with that friendship began Coleridge's literary career.

**95**

# SAMUEL COLERIDGE

## MATERIALISTIC INFLUENCE

But, between the years 1791 and 1795, other events were taking place in the life of Coleridge, inward events contributing to the growth of his mind. These may be listed according to their four sources. First among them were those leading to radicalism. Coleridge's father had been a vicar in the Church of England. But Coleridge himself, in his Cambridge days, had gradually dissented from the doctrine of the established church, and drifted toward Unitarianism. In his reading he had yielded to the influence of Hobbes and Hartley who held to the materialistic view that all knowledge is gained through a sense impression and a subsequent association of ideas, and that the mind cannot build its world from within. Coleridge, later, was able to refute this theory, but not until he had had time to look more deeply into the philosophy of such ancients as Saint Augustine and Plato. Now, however, his radicalism took the form of an admiration rather than a criticism of this mechanistic and rationalistic position, prompting him at one time to say: "I am a complete necessitarian, and believe in the corporeality of thought." Coleridge at this time was still in his early twenties. Meanwhile the spirit of political reform was a fermenting passion in him; but he forced himself to base the reason for it on his confessed adherence to the anarchistic teachings of Godwin who sympathized with the French Revolution. With every humanitarian impulse in him, he felt obliged to turn to pacifism and to denounce England's war against France.

## THE SCHOOL OF SENSIBILITY

A second noticeable trend in the young Coleridge's thought was toward the current poetry of sensibility. It was in the sonnets of the Reverend William Lisle Bowles that he found, according to a later remark, "that poetry which proceeds from

the intellectual Helicon, that which is *dignified,* and apper-
taining to *human* feelings, and entering into the soul." This
experience of dignified humane feeling, so strongly represented
for example in writers like Goldsmith, was to be a major con-
necting link between the eighteenth and nineteenth centuries
in English Literature. Coleridge gives expression to it in an
early version of a sonnet, written at some time close to 1796,
in which he offers us a moment's glimpse into the pleasure and
pain of these his formative years.

> My heart has thank'd thee, *BOWLES!* for those soft strains,
> That, on the still air, floating tremblingly,
> Wak'd in me Fancy, Love, and Sympathy!
> For hence, not callous to a Brother's pains
> Thro' Youth's gay prime and thornless paths I went;
>> And, when the *darker* day of life began,
>> And I did roam, a thought-bewilder'd man,
> Thy kindred Lays an healing solace lent.

## GREEK THOUGHT

But Coleridge's talents did not allow him any time to rest
in the lap of sensibility. His critical mind, bent on a search for
knowledge, was fascinated by the mystery of those things which
lie beyond the grasp of man's unaided reason. Reading more
deeply, beyond Godwin and Hartley, he found his way into
Greek philosophy. Plotinus and the 17th century Cambridge
Platonists, particularly, appealed to him; for here were thinkers
who were at the same time mystics and men of faith, and who
were able to show that the reasoning mind was by its own
nature conscious of itself, of truth, and of God.

## THE CHRISTIAN TRADITION

Finally, there were the Christian poets, chiefly Milton; and
there was the Bible. He steeped his thought in them, reading

them with theological insight. In his *Religious Musings,* written at Christmas in 1794, he was, even though only twenty-two, clearly the scholar, the theologian and the poet. The French Revolution was pictured by him in the language of the book of Revelation:

> The Lamb of God hath opened the fifth seal:
> And upward rush on swiftest wing of fire
> The innumerable multitude of wrongs
> By man on man inflicted.

That by 1798 Coleridge had definitely freed himself from Godwinian materialism and returned to his earlier religious faith—with an acknowledgment of having been misled—is noted by him in a letter to his brother George, in which he says:

> "Of guilt I say nothing, but I believe most
> steadfastly in original sin; that from our mother's
> wombs our understandings are darkened; and even
> where our understandings are in the light, that
> our organization is depraved and our volitions
> imperfect; and we sometimes see the good without
> wishing to attain it, and oftener *wish* it without
> the energy that wills and performs. And for this
> inherent depravity I believe that the *Spirit* of the
> Gospel is the sole cure."

But before this time, as we note further in the *Religious Musings,* the young poet had already found his way back to orthodoxy as expressed in these words ending in a passage of noble dedication:

> Lovely was the death
> Of Him whose life was Love! Holy with power
> He on the thought-benighted Sceptic beamed
> Manifest Godhead, . . .
> And first by Fear uncharmed the drowsed Soul.
> Till of its nobler nature it 'gan feel
> Dim recollections; and thence scared to Hope . . .
> From Hope and firmer Faith to perfect Love.

## MATURING YEARS

Meanwhile, leading to his maturity as a poet, other tendencies were shaping the way for Coleridge. Among them was his ardent humanitarianism which led him to write, in a poem entitled *To A Young Ass.*

> Innocent foal! thou poor despis'd forlorn!
> I hail thee *Brother*—spite of the fool's scorn!
> And fain would take thee with me, in the dell
> Of peace and mild equality to dwell
> Where toil shall call the charmer health his bride,
> And laughter tickle plenty's ribless side!

—touching overtones of the entry into Jerusalem, recorded in *Matthew* 21, and referring to the Pantisocracy, which failed. In 1795 he wrote *The Eolian Harp,* beginning with "My Pensive Sara!" and referring to Mrs. Coleridge, to whom he was not at the time a very provident husband. But it was a poem exhibiting the true mark of his genius. Two great gifts seemed to rise in him at once: the power to describe nature; and the faculty of comprehending life's meaning. At one moment, we are conscious, while repeating his own magic words, of

> Such a soft floating witchery of sound
> As twilight Elfins make, when they at eve
> Voyage on gentle gales from fairy-land.

But in another, we are carried far out beyond sound and sight to

> the one Life within us and abroad,
> Which meets all motion and becomes its soul,
> A light in sound, a sound-like power in light,
> Rhythm in all thought, and joyance everywhere—
> Methinks, it should have been impossible
> Not to love all things in a world so filled;
> Where the breeze warbles, and the mute still air
> Is music slumbering on her instrument.

# SAMUEL COLERIDGE

## THE PROPHETIC POET

In 1796 Coleridge started a newspaper, *The Watchman,*
which ran from March 1 to May 13, and failed. Against this
journalistic failure stands his memorable *Ode On The Departing Year,* written in December, 1796, after the death of
Catherine the Great, Empress of Russia. To Coleridge her
public crimes and private vices were particularly abhorrent, an
offense against womanhood. He felt himself compelled to say:
"I rejoice, as at the disenshrining of a demon—as at the extinc-
tion of the evil principle impersonated." In stanza 8 of the *Ode*
he adds this visionary warning to England, then at war with
France:

> Abondoned of heaven; mad avarice thy guide,
> At cowardly distance, yet kindling with pride—
> Mid thy herds and thy corn-fields secure thou hast stood,
> And joined the wild yelling of famine and blood!
> The nations curse thee! They with eager wondering
>> Shall hear Destruction, like a vulture scream!
>> Strange-eyed Destruction! who with many a dream
> Of central fires through nether seas up-thundering
>> Soothes her fierce solitude; yet as she lies
>> By livid fount, or red volcanic stream,
>> If ever to her lidless dragon-eyes,
>> O Albion! thy predestined ruin rise,
> The fiend-hag on her perilous couch doth leap,
> Muttering distempered triumph in her charmed sleep.

## COLERIDGE AND HAZLITT

Of unusual interest to the student of literature, in evaluating
this early period of Coleridge's literary career, is William
Hazlitt's account of how he himself once walked ten miles to
hear Coleridge preach. It was in the year 1798 and Coleridge
was by then a famous person. Hazlitt describes, in the essay
*My First Acquaintance With Poets,* first, Coleridge's homely

personal appearance, wearing "a short black coat like a shooting jacket;" then, his brilliant, incessant talk on his arrival at the parish, from which "he did not cease while he stayed, nor has he since, that I know of;" and, finally, his sermon:

> The preacher then launched into his subject, like an eagle dallying with the wind. The sermon was upon peace and war; upon church and state—not their alliance, but their separation—on the spirit of the world and the spirit of Christianity, not as the same, but as opposed to one another. He talked of those who had "inscribed the cross of Christ on banners dripping with human gore."

It was the young Hazlitt who felt so moved. But he was, even then, a good critic. His judgment that in Coleridge "Poetry and Philosophy had met together," that "Truth and Genius had embraced, under the eye and with the sanction of Religion," is exact and final. To complete the criticism Hazlitt added this picture of Coleridge's person at the age of twenty-eight or thirty:

> His forehead was broad and high, light as if built of ivory, with large projecting eyebrows . . . His mouth was voluptuous, open, eloquent; his chin good-humored and round . . . His nose was small . . . Coleridge in his person was rather above the common size, inclining to the corpulent . . . His hair was then black and glossy as the raven's.

## THE LYRICAL BALLADS

The intimate friendship between Coleridge and Wordsworth began in 1797. They lived near together at Nether Stowey and Alfoxden in the south of England. Wordsworth had passed through some severe trials and had come out of them to self-mastery. By now the genius of both men was apparent. Together they planned and published—with the companionship of Dorothy Wordsworth—the *Lyrical Ballads*. It was an epoch-making book. The critics of the time did not think so; but the volume is now regarded as the inaugural event of the Romantic movement. It appeared in three editions: the first in 1798, the second in 1800, and the third in 1802. Coleridge's chief contribution to it was *The Ancient Mariner*. The ballad is a remarkable literary composition. It has everything that poems of its kind should have: a vivid story, dramatic action, verbal music, a scenic setting, a unifying element of feeling, moral tone, and mystery. Besides these traits, the "narrative speed, minute actuality, and medieval glamour" of the poem are nothing short of amazing.

## POETRY AND SYMBOLISM

The most familiar term to be applied to the *Ancient Mariner* is the term supernatural. The poem lifts the reader out of himself into the world of spiritual values in which earthly things, events in nature, are but the shadows of thoughts. The mariner, telling his story as an act of penance, is not simply a "natural" man, breathed on by the spirit in Nature, as, for example, is Wordsworth's hero in *Michael*. He is a voice within man: the voice of the immortal spirit, crying out in the wilderness of the world. The ship at sea under the burning sun, and the albatross, are symbols, signs in nature of invisible realities beyond nature, and active in the mind as proofs of divine love and forgiveness and man's sense of sin. The poem in its entirety suggests a concerto movement in seven parts, in patterns of repetitive rhyme; it owes its deserved popularity to an achievement that is at once artistic and philosophical; and it may be regarded as the poet's confession of faith, comparable to that to which John Keats was later, in the *Ode on a Grecian Urn*, to give this expression:

> "Beauty is truth, truth beauty,"—that is all
> Ye know on earth, and all ye need to know.

It is difficult to find in all ballad literature such magical grace, displayed against a background of intense realism, and moving so freely within a controlling framework of religious thought, as is found, for example, in this typical stanza:

> Oh sleep! it is a gentle thing,
> Beloved from pole to pole!
> To Mary Queen the praise be given!
> She sent the gentle sleep from Heaven,
> That slid into my soul.

## THE POEM'S REALISM

Yet we are not to look on the *Ancient Mariner* as a supernaturalistic poem only, as though it were simply an excursion into the realm of the poet's metaphysical fancy. There is in it too much realism for such a view. Everything, or almost everything in it is, first of all, taken from real life: the old Navigator himself, as Coleridge called him, his ship and the ocean and all its creatures, for instance, are so minutely detailed from actual experience that the poem seemed to Robert Southey, a contemporary poet, to be but "a Dutch attempt at sublimity." It is clear that Coleridge kept "a watchful eye on truth" as he proceeded with the poem. This all-embracing truth, given the form of the poem's theme or central idea, may conveniently be expressed in such words as these: Life is ONE, both terrifying and beautiful; we must accept it so, imaginatively love it and live it. The Mariner himself sums it all up, including the peace that comes to him:

> O happy living things! no tongue
> Their beauty might declare:
> A spring of love gushed from my heart,
> And I blessed them unaware:
> Sure my kind saint took pity on me,
> And I blessed them unaware.

> The self-same moment I could pray;
> And from my neck so free
> The Albatross fell off, and sank
> Like lead into the sea.

Here, in *The Ancient Mariner*, we see the unfolding of his romantic genius: his fanciful journeyings in lands afar; his bold psychological experimentation in the realms of good and evil; the sublimity of his philosophical thought by which, in a revolutionary age, as Thomas Carlyle expressed it, he "saved his crown of spiritual manhood"; and, finally, his mastery of a form of poetical diction in which accent, imagery and rhythm are joined together to make of his style—as Nietzsche would say—a dance.

Coleridge's descriptions, illustrated in *The Ancient Mariner*, are memorable. When in the First Part of the poem the ship is driven by a storm toward the South Pole, encountering vast regions of ice, we not only see but hear the writhing of the ice against the ship in the lines:

> The ice was here, the ice was there,
> The ice was all around:
> It cracked and growled, and roared and howled,
> Like noises in a swound.

And then, in the Second Part, after the mariner has shot the albatross, the "pious bird of good omen," and the ship, driven into the Pacific, is suddenly becalmed, we feel and see the silent ocean under the "hot and copper sky," as the poet continues:

> Down dropt the breeze, the sails dropt down,
> 'Twas sad as sad could be;
> And we did speak only to break
> The silence of the sea.

# POETRY OF POWER AND PAIN

## THE GOLDEN PERIOD

The years between 1797 and 1802 were Coleridge's happiest. In them the creative mood was stronger than the dejective. Pain and melancholy, it seems, were almost from the first his lot, and to them he owed the opium habit which now began slowly to fasten itself on him. The dream-fragment *Kubla Khan* was written at this time. De Quincey would probably have assigned the poem to the early pleasures of opium. In contrast to the pleasure of opium, its pain was less shadowy and of longer duration. It was to torment Coleridge intermittently during the following fifteen years until, almost hopeless, he was to place himself in the skillful hands of Dr. James Gillman, his personal friend and physician. In *Kubla Khan* the especial gift of the poet to summon visions of the phantom-world and to give them corporeality in striking images and haunting music, is wondrously demonstrated. The strange proximity of terror to beauty that is so true to life—the eerie fascination of the light that dazzles on the brink of destruction—is unforgettably depicted in the "incense-bearing tree" and the "sunny spots of greenery" that border the chasm from which, "with ceaseless turmoil seething," a fountain spewing forth rocks like hail flings up a river that, after a brief "meandering with a mazy motion," sinks "in tumult to a lifeless ocean." The phantom-picture assumes reality when to the accompaniment of contrasting voices—that of the bright fountain and the dark cave—the poet lets us see the dome of pleasure as

> a miracle of rare device,
> A sunny pleasure-dome with caves of ice!

## THE MATERIAL OF THE POEM

But, like *The Ancient Mariner,* the poem *Kubla Khan* is not simply the product of an artist's hallucination. It is full of images from real life, of historical place names and of Coleridge's wide remembered reading—for example, from Samuel Purchas' *Pilgrimage,* referring to Kubla Khan the thirteenth century Mongol emperor and his Oriental pleasure palace, and from Milton's *Paradise Lost.* As Coleridge himself said, the images in the dream-poem "rose up before him as *Things*"; and it is their vivid reality to the imagination that carries us away with the poet as he concludes the fragment:

> A damsel with a dulcimer
> In a vision once I saw:
> It was an Abyssinian maid,
> And on her dulcimer she played,
> Singing of Mount Abora.
> Could I revive within me
> Her symphony and song.
> To such a deep delight 'twould win me,
> That with music loud and long,
> I would build that dome in air,
> That sunny dome! those caves of ice!
> And all who heard should see them there,
> And all should cry, Beware! Beware!
> His flashing eyes, his floating hair!
> Weave a circle round him thrice,
> And close your eyes with holy dread,
> For he on honey-dew hath fed,
> And drunk the milk of Paradise.

## GERMAN PHILOSOPHY

The important poem *Christabel* was written during this same period, and in two parts: the first, in 1797 or 1798, at Nether Stowey; the second, in 1800, at Keswick. During the interval between them Coleridge went with William and Dorothy Wordsworth to Germany. There, supported by the generous Wedgwood family of pottery fame, he studied German literature and philosophy. He found the land of Goethe and Schiller in the ferment of a Romantic revival. The movement in that country was organized and thorough-going, with the critic Friedrich Schlegel as its distinguished leader. It had a precise program, a well-formed foundation in metaphysics, a set theory of art; and its aim, as Professor H. A. Beers has said, was "to interpret all human activities from a central principle, to apply its highest abstractions to literature, government, religion, the fine arts, and society." This disposition toward a synthesis of literature and philosophy exactly suited Coleridge. He read far and wide into the systems of the philosophies of Kant, Fichte, Schelling, and Hegel. In the *Biographia Literaria*, fifteen years later, he remembered, in the midst of his speculative studies—which then were more original than any found elsewhere in English literature — to pay his respect to Kant, "that illustrious sage of Koenigsberg," who by his clear and compact reasoning, Coleridge added, "took possession of me as with the giant's hand."

## MYSTICISM AND RELIGION

At this time also Coleridge was acquainting himself with the mystical teachings of Jacob Boehme, the early seventeenth century peasant philosopher who, while engaged in making shoes in Gorlitz, Germany, was found to have speculated with amazing results on the unity of the divine *One* who transcended the contrasting *Many*. Coleridge had before this time, as he tells us, already immersed his thought in Plato and Plotinus. The result was the overthrow in him of the authority of Hume and Hartley. He preferred, after that period of deeper insight, to follow such thinkers among his own countrymen as the poet Milton and the theologian William Law. The religious influence of Law on Coleridge was hardly less than it had previously been on John Wesley and Samuel Johnson. It was, in fact, revolutionary.

## ILL HEALTH

Coleridge returned from Germany, in 1799, ready to take up the task in behalf of poetry, literary criticism and philosophy. The year 1800 marked a point of transition in his career. By that time he had moved to Keswick, in Cumberland, again to be near the Wordsworths. Here, as we have said, he wrote the second part of *Christabel.* Although now married, he found himself in love with Sarah Hutchinson, sister to Mary who was engaged to Wordsworth. Coleridge's home life, it was known, was not happy; his impaired health was adding to his wretchedness; and by now, also, he found that opium had its own bitter pains. It evokes little wonder in us, therefore, to have Coleridge say that at the time he undertook to write the second part of *Christabel* his poetic powers began to be "in a state of suspended animation." The fact is evident in a comparison of the two parts of the poem. The second continues the theme of the first; but the vision of evil, its bewildering effect upon the sensitive innocent soul, and the subtilized portrayal of the poet's own suffering are less magically presented in it. The reference to the bard Bracy's dream-picture of the fluttering dove fastened in the coils of the green snake tells us all too plainly how much the poet has suffered. That he still has the power to describe what he feels is observable in the almost autobiographical lines:

> For in my sleep I saw that dove,
> That gentle bird . . . I saw the same

Fluttering, and uttering fearful moan,
Among the green herbs in the forest alone.
Which when I saw and when I heard,
I wondered what might ail the bird;
For nothing near it could I see,
Save the grass and green herbs underneath the old tree.
I stooped, methought, the dove to take,
When lo! I saw a bright green snake
Coiled round its wings and neck,
Green as the herbs on which it couched,
Close by the dove's its head it crouched;
And with the dove it heaves and stirs,
Swelling its neck as she swelled hers!
I woke; it was the midnight hour,
The clock was echoing in the tower;
But though my slumber was gone by,
This dream it would not pass away—
It seems to live upon my eye!

## DESPONDENCY

In these years of his wretchedness, between 1802 and 1810, Coleridge turned more than ever toward philosophy, as much for consolation as for intellectual inquiry. Bowed down to earth by affliction, by the decline, as he said, of his "shaping spirit of Imagination," he sought in "abstruse research" to find a companion to take the place of his deserting muse. He was not forsaking poetry; poetry, or the power to write it, was forsaking him. Already sufficiently grieved, he tormented himself further by a self-accusation of neglectful indolence. Still, in truth, he was an active man, even if tortured into activity. A chief source of pain which was also a source of inspiration to him was his hopeless love for Sarah Hutchinson. Being separated — by the fact that he was married — from the one woman he loved was depressing and tragic. But it served, together with other dire circumstances, at certain times to make a "mad lutinist" of him, driving him to poetry in order to charm or dispel the viper thoughts that coiled about his mind. At other times it moved him to tenderness, as in the dream-poem *Love,* in which all sorrow was forgotten and she whom he loved dearly was won to listening to his plaintive lute while he played a soft and doleful air, until

> She listened with a flitting blush,
> With downcast eyes, and modest grace;
> And she forgave me, that I gazed
> Too fondly on her face!
> She wept with pity and delight,
> She blushed with love, and virgin-shame;
> And like the murmer of a dream,
> I heard her breathe my name.

## POETRY AND PAIN

In *The Pains of Sleep,* written in 1803 in a low spirit, as he contemplated the evil of opium, Coleridge laid bare the terror of his "fantastic passions," his sense of guilt and the remorse he endured even while, unlike the habitual evil-doer, he longed for peace and desired only to be blest, adding at the poem's end these lines—now twice quoted—that are worth an entire chapter on the poet's essential character:

> To be beloved is all I need,
> And whom I love, I love indeed.

## THE CONSCIOUS CHANGE

But it was the *Ode to Dejection* that marked for Coleridge the end of one period and the beginning of another. He now felt his poetical resources exhausted within him. Like Sir Patrick Spense in the old ballad, he beheld himself facing a journey from which he had no hope of returning: he "saw the new Moon with the old Moon in her arms"—the sign, for him, of impending stormy weather. The *Ode* is a masterpiece in execution. It was written in 1802; first dedicated to Wordsworth; sent to Sarah Hutchinson for her approval; and revised in 1817. The strong contrast between Wordsworth's state of mind and his own heightens the temper of the poem. It brings back to Coleridge's own thought the earlier happy and enlarging days of their companionship together in the vicinity of Bristol; and with them that still earlier seed-time of his life, when his thoughts grew at their own will in the tropical atmosphere of the *Arabian Nights*. Thinking of those days now so at war with the years that were making a thorny wasteland of the poet's career, he strikes an account of the losses, holds them up against the gains, and concludes:

> We receive but what we give,
> And in our life alone does Nature live:
> Ours is her wedding garment, ours her shroud!
>    And would we aught behold, of higher worth,
> Than that inanimate cold world allowed
> To the poor loveless over-anxious crowd,
>    Ah! from the soul itself must issue forth
> A light, a glory, a fair luminous cloud
>    Enveloping the earth—
> And from the soul itself must there be sent
>    A sweet and potent voice, of its own birth,
> Of all sweet sounds the life and element!

The poet is thus drawn back, as an anchor to his heavy thoughts, to the teachings of the Platonists to whom all nature and the world order were regarded as the outward expressions of the eternal Spirit. In so doing he reaffirms what he has already said in the *Ode to France*, that Freedom, the heavenly goddess, must forgive him for having ever thought that liberty could

> Mix with Kings in the low lust of sway,
> Yell in the hunt, and share the murderous prey.

**111**

### WORK WITHOUT HOPE

The years from 1802 to 1816, as we have said, were the most wretched for Coleridge. But it is necessary, at this juncture in our study, to distinguish between the personal fortunes of the man and the work he did. He was dejected and broken in health; he went to the Mediterranean, to Italy and to Malta, hoping to appease the demon of melancholy; he moved to Grasmere, in 1808, to live with William and Dorothy Wordsworth; and he continued to cling desparately to his love for Sarah Hutchinson, until at length the Wordsworths intervened. After that, stricken and hurt, in 1811, he entered a short and depressing period of estrangement from them. Besides all this, in the same year, Thomas Wedgewood recalled one half of his annuity to Coleridge. Only a few men in England apparently now believed in him: one among them was Charles Lamb; another was Henry Crabb Robinson. How Coleridge felt, near the end of this prolonged period of spiritual degradation, he himself most succinctly put into words in his invocation to a play he wrote in 1812, and saw staged the next year at Drury Lane under the title of *Remorse:*

> Hark! the cadence dies away
> On the quiet moonlight sea:
> The boatmen rest their oars and say,
> Miserere Domine!

## CRITICISM OF LIFE AND LITERATURE

### THE SHAKESPEARE LECTURES

But it was not how Coleridge felt, but what he did, that made even these years of his dejection memorable. It was during them, principally in 1808, that he delivered his lectures on Shakespeare and Milton. Only notes from these lectures survive; but in them the thoughts of Coleridge burn like iridescent stars. Though always a Romantic critic who freely uses his creative imagination, he penetrates beyond the flower to the stem and root of a piece of writing. His method of unearthing a fact, of bringing it to light, instead of covering it over with comments to dazzle the reader's eye, is shown by this note taken from a lecture on Shakespeare having to do with the fact that there are exact laws governing the art of poetry:

"Imagine not that I am about to oppose genius to rules. The spirit of poetry, like all other living powers, must of necessity circumscribe itself by rules, were it only to unite power with beauty. It must embody in order to reveal itself; but a living body is of necessity an organized one. . . This is no discovery of criticism; it is a necessity of the human mind."

## POETRY'S GOVERNING PRINCIPLE

But this order to which poetry subscribes is not imposed upon it. It is not something external to poetry, but the product of the poet's shaping mind, his purer reason, in contrast to a man's limited search toward understanding. The poet writes according to a *law* which is above all *theory*. Rising above the plane of relativity and expediency by which a man's individual knowledge is limited, he moves in the realm of the governing *principle* by which all things live and move and have their being. In this vein of literary criticism Coleridge continues to say:

"One character belongs to all true poets, that they write from a principle within, not originating in anything without; and that the true poet's work in its form, its shapings, and its modifications, is distinguished from all other works that assume to belong to the class of poetry, as a natural from an artificial flower, or as the mimic garden from an enamelled meadow."

# SAMUEL COLERIDGE

## COLERIDGE'S CRITICAL METHOD

Such criticism presupposes a comprehensive reading of the text. It inquires as much into how good poetry comes to be written as into the literary structure of an individual stanza of masterly verse. In chapter XV of the *Biographia Literaria* Coleridge lets us see how he approaches the study of such a poem, for instance, as Shakespeare's *Venus and Adonis.* He proceeds by noting (1) "the perfect sweetness of the versification," (2) "the choice of subjects very remote from the private interests and circumstances of the writer himself," (3) "the images modified by a predominant passion," and (4) "the depth and energy of the poet's thought." At the climax of his criticism he indicates the general principle that governs him as a literary critic. "No man was ever yet a great poet," he says, "without being at the same time a profound philosopher. For poetry is the blossom and the fragrancy of all human knowledge, human thoughts, human passions, emotions, language." After pointing out that in Shakespeare's poems "the creative power and intellectual energy wrestle as in a war embrace," he concludes that in the Shakespearean drama the creative-romantic and the intellectual-classical forces are reconciled after fighting "each with its shield before the breast of the other."

"Or like two rapid streams, that, at their first meeting within narrow and rocky banks, mutually strive to repel each other and intermix reluctantly and in tumult; but soon, finding a wider channel and more yielding shores, blend and dilate and flow on in one current and with one voice."

## HIS EXTRAORDINARY MIND

The *Biographia Literaria* belongs to the most select body of English critical prose. It consists of twenty-four chapters held together like beads, by a slender thread of autobiography in which Coleridge's early education and his close association with Wordsworth are given especial attention. Its intrinsic worth is in its extraordinary erudition and originality. It is not an easy book to read. Coleridge's thought in it, to quote Sir Arthur Symons, "has to be pursued across stones, ditches, and morasses, with intermittent lingering and disappointment; it turns back, loses itself, fetches wide circuits, and comes to no visible end. But you must follow it step by step; and if you are ceaselessly attentive, you will be ceaselessly rewarded." The reward will consist in knowing a great man's thoughts, the mind of one who was, at once and in large measure, poet, critic, scholar, philosopher, theologian, preacher, lecturer, editor, conversationalist, humanitarian and, by Aristotelian standards, a political agrarian.

## AIM OF THE BIOGRAPHIA LITERARIA

Like Wordsworth in *The Prelude,* Coleridge desired in this work to trace the growth of his own mind. Only Wordsworth's stress was on the mind of the poet while Coleridge's was on the mind of the critic. More particularly, Coleridge wanted, in the language of criticism and philosophy, to tell the story of how his mind was set free from the materialism of Hartley and Hobbes and found refuge in the teachings of Plato, Shakespeare, Milton and Immanuel Kant. He now wished to restate, with its implications for literature, what he had formerly said in his second essay of *The Friend* in which he had summed up the distinction between the Reason and its lesser instrument, the Understanding. Before indicating that the Understanding is limited, relative and "possessed in very different degrees by different persons," he speaks of Reason as the absolute and ultimate principle by which the mind of man rises to the liberty and sovereignty of its own nature; and then says, eloquently:

"Reason! best and holiest gift of God and bond of union with the giver;—the high title by which the majesty of man claims precedence above all other living creatures;—mysterious faculty, the mother of conscience, of language, of tears, and of smiles;—calm and incorruptible legislator of the soul, without whom all its other powers would 'meet in oppugnancy';—sole principle of permanence amid endless change,—in a world of discordant appetites and imagined self-interests the only common measure. . . Thou alone, more than even the sunshine, more than the common air, art given to all men, and to every man alike".

## JUDGMENT AND TASTE

Without attempting to dig up the entire deposit of this rich treasury, it may be said that a major aim of Coleridge's criticism, after its famous distinction between the Reason and the Understanding, is the consequent distinction between the Imagination and the Fancy, and the wise use of this distinction in examining the works of ancient classic literature and of Shakespeare, Milton and Wordsworth. The Reason, Coleridge has said, is more than a function of the mind. It is a special and original faculty, a supersensuous gift to man not possessed by the animal creation. Its highest exercise is the act of the creative imagination. A genuine work of literature is therefore a true interpretation of life. And good criticism is the application of the Reason and the Imagination to the study of such a piece of literature, or any other work of art. This means that a good critic instinctively recognizes the merits of a literary production; the higher reason within him is his guide; to follow it is to have good taste. But this faculty of the Reason, being a supersensuous gift, rests on a metaphysical foundation. It is related to life in its entirety and to a consideration of ultimate human values; and to these values a piece of literature, in order to be an enduring work of art, or noble work of man, must ultimately conform. It is this union of esthetic and philosophical considerations, or principles, that gives a systematic character to Coleridge's criticism, making of it a discipline applicable to religion and politics as well as to literature and art. In a word, Coleridge is a universal critic of combined judgment and taste.

## THE IDEAL POET

What Coleridge was in search of was a voice of *authority*. He found it summarily, and finally, in Plato, the poet-philosopher of the primary and ultimate Ideal. It was the Ideal from which all that is imagined to be real emanates and to which all explanations of reality must return. It is the sublime whole of which all elements, however discordant, are a part; and it is the reconciliation of these discordant parts into an ever renewed and balanced synthesis. For Coleridge's estimate of "the poet described in *ideal* perfection" we may turn again to the classical passage found at the close of Chapter XIV of the *Biographia Literaria*:

"The poet, described in *Ideal* perfection, brings the whole soul of man into activity, with the subordination of its faculties to each other, according to their relative worth and dignity. He diffuses a tone and spirit of unity, that blends, and *fuses*, each into each, by the synthetic and magical power to which we have exclusively appropriated the name of imagination. This power, first put in action by the will and understanding . . . reveals itself in the balance of reconciliation of opposite or discordant qualities: of sameness, with difference; of the general, with the concrete; the idea, with the image; the individual with the representative; the sense of novelty and freshness, with the old and familiar objects; a more than usual state of emotion, with more than usual order; judgement ever awake and steady self-possession, with enthusiasm and feeling profound or vehement; and while it blends and harmonizes the natural and the artificial, still subordinates art to nature; the manner to the matter; and our admiration of the poet to our sympathy with the poetry. . . . Finally, GOOD SENSE is the BODY of poetic genius, FANCY its DRAPERY, MOTION its LIFE, and IMAGINATION the SOUL that is everywhere, and in each; and forms all into one graceful and intelligent whole."

# THE MAN AND ESTIMATES OF HIM

## THE LATER YEARS

In 1816, after living here and there with friends, Coleridge at last made his home with Dr. Gillman, at Highgate, just outside London. There, recovering as well as he could from the opium habit, he worked, lecturing on Shakespeare, in 1818, with much success, and preparing his notes and other earlier writings, old and new, for publication. He dreamed away much time, as he acknowledged regretfully, speculating on the system of philosophy he was attempting to formulate. For this he incurred and endured the attacks of the literary editors, losing some followers, but keeping his old friends. Among them was Emerson who came to visit him from America. English churchmen came under the influence of his theology, and all who heard him in those last years yielded to the spell of his brilliant conversation. "He would talk," Lamb wrote, "from morn to dewy eve, nor cease till far midnight, yet who ever would interrupt him,—who would obstruct that continuous flow of converse, fetched from Helicon or Zion." By the year 1825 he had become the center of London's literary life. At this time he wrote the poem *Youth and Age* which, besides giving proof that the magic art of versification was still his, indicated the heavy loss he felt with the declining years:

> Verse, a breeze mid blossoms straying,
> Where Hope clung feeding, like a bee—
> Both were mine! Life went a-maying
>   With Nature, Hope and Poesy,
>     When I was young!
> Flowers are lovely; Love is flower-like;
> Friendship is a sheltering tree;
> O! the joys, that came down shower-like,
> Of Friendship, Love, and Liberty,
> Ere I was old!

## FAREWELL TO POETRY

Two years after writing *Youth and Age* Coleridge expressed in even more poignant verse, in *Work Without Hope*, the state of things as they concerned him. His muse, he felt, had finally forsaken him; and Nature, once so close to his heart, mocked and chided him: even "slugs leave their lair," while the poet, "the sole unbusy thing," sits useless and silent. He knows but cannot do: that is the tragedy for him, as he concludes the poem:

> Yet well I ken the banks where amaranths blow,
> Have traced the fount whence streams of nectar flow.
> Bloom, O ye amaranths! bloom for whom ye may,
> For me ye bloom not! Glide, rich streams, away!
> With lips unbrightened, wreathless brow, I stroll:
> And would you learn the spells that drowse my soul?
> Work without hope draws nectar in a sieve,
> And hope without an object cannot live.

## AIDS TO REFLECTION

That Coleridge was indeed growing old, old before his time, was evident. But he bore the change with dignity, making use of his talents for the time that remained in writing such important works of prose as the *Aids to Reflection* and the *Constitution of the Church and State*. Both works were basically theological. The first, consisting of timely "Aphorisms," was intended to be a guide to those who sought to understand the truths that form the foundation of the Christian faith. The second, following a political as well as religious course of inquiry, set out to define the functions of the church and the state and prepared the way for the Oxford Movement whose influence was soon to be felt throughout England. Nothing was said in them that contradicted the scientific or logical understanding. But Coleridge would not content himself with the evidences of religion based solely on an observation of nature. His inquiring mind needed to penetrate to the fountain of the Reason where it involved the *will* in an act of self-subjection to the light that flowed from this universal source, quickening the spirit within man, until this higher reasoning faculty—which Coleridge regarded as identical with "the spirit of the regenerated man"—qualified him to discourse and to judge of those transcendent truths which surround and give meaning to human existence. This faculty of higher reasoning is the "seeing light," the "enlightening eye" of the soul, as the soul itself is the lamp of the body and of all Nature. Coleridge calls it Reflection. It is the light reflected in the mind of the deeply religious man, a reflection of the thought or mind of God. Here is what Coleridge says of it in *Aphorism IX* of *Aids to Reflection:*

"Life is the one universal soul which, by virtue of the enlivening *breath*, and the informing *word*, all organized bodies have in common, each *after its kind*. This, therefore, all animals possess, and man as an animal. But, in addition to this, God transfused into man a higher gift, and one specially inbreathed:—even a living—that is, self-subsisting—soul, a soul having its life in itself. 'And man became a living soul'. He did not merely *possess* it, he *became* it. It was his proper *being*, his truest *self*, *the* man *in* the man. None then, not one of human kind, so poor and destitute, but there is provided for him, even in his present state, *a house not built with hands*. Aye, . . . a house gloriously furnished. Nothing is wanted but the eye, which is the light of this house, the light which is the eye of this soul. This *seeing* light, this *enlightening* eye, is Reflection."

## ULTIMATE VALUES

This "house not built with hands" was indeed that in which Coleridge now mostly lived. By means of his reflective imagination he was able to bring into the orbit of his thinking the great dream-concepts of both literature and philosophy and, as Hazlitt indicated, to accomplish their union in religion. He had himself said that he desired all his work of criticism to stress the "reciprocal relations of poetry and philosophy to each other; and of both to religion." But religion was more than a studious discipline to Coleridge. It was a source of self-intuition, an impelling instinct in him by which he discerned man's true nature and destiny. This higher gift of spiritual apperception given to him is well illustrated in the following epitaphic statement:

"They and they only can acquire the philosophic imagination, the sacred power of self-intuition, who within themselves can interpret and understand the symbol, that the wings of the air-sylph are forming within the skin of the caterpillar; those only, who feel in their spirits the same instinct which impels the chrysalis of the horned fly to leave room in its involucrum for the antennae yet to come. They know and feel, that the *potential* works *in* them, even as the *actual* works on them."

## CONVERSATIONS

A study of Coleridge remains incomplete without a reference to his miscellaneous writings summed up by his nephew

Henry Nelson Coleridge and published, a year after the poet's death, under the title of *Table Talk*. These discourses, together with his letters to such of his friends as Thomas Poole, Robert Southey and Charles Lamb, reveal him in a more intimate manner as a man among men and throw a colorful light on his multiple gifts and natural shortcomings. His extemporaneous remarks on Plato and Aristotle, on Tennyson and Keats, on negro emancipation, property tax, and the criterion of genius, are flashes of inner revelation and profound truth. There is, for the moment, little left to say on subjects like these when Coleridge has spoken:

"Every man is born an Aristotelian, or a Platonist. I do not think it possible that any one born an Aristotelian can become a Platonist; and I am sure no born Platonist can ever change into an Aristotelian. They are two classes of men, beside which it is next to impossible to conceive a third. The one considers reason a quality, or attribute; the other considers it a power. I believe Aristotle could never get to understand what Plato meant by an *idea*". . .

"A poet ought not to pick nature's pocket; let him borrow, and so borrow as to repay by the very act of borrowing. Examine nature accurately, but write from recollection; and trust more to your imagination than to your memory."

## VALEDICTORY

On July 13, 1834, twelve days before his death, Coleridge wrote to his godchild:

" . . . I now, on the eve of departure, declare to you, and earnestly pray that you may hereafter live and act on the conviction, that health is a great blessing; competence, obtained by honest industry, is a great blessing; and a great blessing it is, to have kind, faithful, and loving friends and relatives; but that the greatest of all blessings, as it is the most ennobling of all privileges, is to be indeed a Christian."

## THE VERDICT

Estimates of Coleridge vary according to the critics' viewpoint and deeper insight into the man and the poet. Thomas Carlyle in his *Life of Sterling*, at times not quite knowing whether to praise or blame him, pictured Coleridge sitting

"on the brow of Highgate Hill in those years, looking down on London and its smoke tumult like a sage escaped from the inanity of life's battle, attracting towards him the thoughts of innumerable brave souls still engaged there . . . A sublime man; who, alone in those dark days, had saved his crown of spiritual manhood; escaping from the black materialisms, and revolutionary deluges, with 'God, Fredom, Immortality' still his: a king of men."

The poet Shelley, viewing the genius of Coleridge as overshadowed by his infirmity, wrote:

> You will see Coleridge; he who sits obscure
> In the exceeding lustre and the pure
> Intense iridiation of a mind
> Which, with its own internal lightning blind,
> Flags wearily through darkness and despair—
> A cloud-encircled meteor of the air,
> A hooded eagle among blinking owls.

## CONSUMMATE PRAISE

But Wordsworth and Lamb saw another side of him. Moved less than Shelley by considerations of abstract truth and beauty, and more like Coleridge himself by a preoccupation with the arduous upward struggle of mankind, Wordsworth spoke of Coleridge as "the most *wonderful* man" he had ever known; and Lamb mourned his death in these now classical words:

"His great and dear spirit haunts me. I cannot think a thought, I cannot make a criticism on men and books, without an ineffectual turning and reference to him. He was the proof and touchstone of all my cogitations."

# Lord Byron
### 1788-1824

## EDUCATION AND TRAVEL
### 1788-1812

## FAME AND CHANGING FORTUNE
### 1812-1816

## IN EXILE FROM ENGLAND
### 1816-1818

## GREAT LITERARY PRODUCTIVITY
### 1818-1824

# THE INIMITABLE POET

## THE MAN AND HIS ART

The name of Byron is a signpost in English literary history. It has served both critics and admirers to take the measure of the age. If Byron did not fully understand himself, it is easy and natural enough for us to misunderstand him. But he knew his art, the objective work of his own mind; and that part of him anyone can comprehend clearly enough to derive pleasure from knowing it and to form an opinion of it. For Byron is one of the most concretely objective of all our poets. Probably only Chaucer equals him in the gift to see the thing itself, to set the idea out before the reader, at arms length where it may be examined as something released from the poet's mind and so be given form and made ready to become the possession of another. Like Chaucer, in brief, Byron succeeds in communicating his thoughts and feelings.

## PLEASURABLE READING

As we read *Childe Harold,* for example, we are made aware that he is not brooding on his ideas but writing them out; and the reader is given the pleasure of the creative experience with the poet. No poem of his haunts us, beyond reach, like Wordsworth's *Ode on Immortality.* The divine mystery of things, if it waylaid Byron, has found no deep channel through his writings to us. Such major works as *Manfred* and *Sardanapalus* deal with their problems as enigmas rather than as mysteries.

Yet one cannot read the best Byron has written and ever forget the pleasurable experience of learning lines like these:

> She walks in beauty, like the night
> Of cloudless climes and starry skies;
> And all that's best of dark and bright
> Meet in her aspect and her eyes:
> Thus mellowe'd to that tender light
> Which heaven to gaudy day denies.

Such poetry was not often being written in Byron's day; nor had it been popular since the time of Collins and Gray. It was a specimen of classical art, the sign of a return to style in English poetry, and to the Greek masters. And it therefore marked Byron as belonging, with Shakespeare and Keats, to a particular group of Romantic poets.

## THE VERDICT OF CRITICS

It is to be expected that opinions about Byron, both as man and poet, should vary greatly. His brilliant and passionate imagination eludes all but the most careful critics. The poet Swinburne held that "Byron, who rarely wrote anything either worthless or faultless, can only be judged or appreciated in a mass; the greatest of his works was his whole work taken together." Matthew Arnold regarded Byron as a brilliant, puissant personality but lacking the artist's "finely touched and finely gifted" nature. By the side of Milton with whom Sir Walter Scott favorably compares him, Byron, says Arnold, is vulgar and affected—in short, a barbarian. The German poet Goethe, by whom Byron was admired for his "daring, dash, and grandiosity," admitted that he was not a poet of thought but of action. "The moment he reflects," said Goethe, "he is a child." Swinburne's verdict sums up one attitude toward the distinctiveness of Byron's personality when he says that it has its source in "the splendid and imperishable excellence which covers all his offenses and outweighs all his defects: *the excellence of sincerity and strength.*" Another verdict is that Byron was a skeptical self-pitying egoist, restless, unsteady, without faith in God or man. The truth to be inferred from his letters and his poetry is that he was a man of conflict, of faith and doubt, both gentle and fierce, sympathetic and satirical, a fatalist and a lover of liberty, a guilty man wanting to be an innocent child, a prodigal wanting to come home, an embattled "pilgrim of eternity"— in short a person of strongly contradictory qualities which never became wholly reconciled. He felt most at peace amid the crash of the ocean wave against the rocky shore, or on a high mountain among the cold silent stars, as he says of *Childe Harold* in his exile pilgrimage:

> Where rose the mountains, there to him were friends;
> Where roll'd the ocean, thereon was his home;
> Where a blue sky, and glowing clime, extends,
> He had the passion and the power to roam;
> The desert, forest, cavern, breaker's foam,
> Were unto him companionship.

Byron's place in the Romantic movement is specialized and distinct. He is its dynamo—its energizing force converting life's raw and ready materials into a vigorous, flowing current of verse. He is curiously himself—a double self—in all that he writes: a blended mixture of the romancer, the satirist, the lover, the adventurer, the melodramatic egoist, and the voice of freedom at large, for a short time in England, then on the Continent, chiefly in Italy, between the years 1816 and 1824. The list of his literary works is kaleidoscopic. In ranges in vari-colored fashion from the lyrical and romantic to the critical and satirical, and more widely, to the historical, the Oriental, and the transcendental. The flash of change is everywhere apparent.

# EDUCATION AND TRAVEL

## BYRON'S ANCESTRY

Byron was born in London, in 1788, in a lodging place of the city, his mother being then on the journey from France to Scotland in the hope that his birth might take place in the country of her ancestors. Byron's mother had been Catherine Gordon, and she proudly claimed descent from the Scottish royal family. Her marriage to Byron's father was hasty and, from all appearances, unwise. She was herself undisciplined in self-control, and her husband was an altogether careless fellow, a rover, a spendthrift, violent and proud, but handsome. He had become known as "Mad Jack", was a captain in the guards, and had been previously married to a marchioness, the mother of Augusta, the poet's half-sister. The grandfather had distinguished himself as a seaman. Englishmen of the navy had picturesquely called him "Foul-weather Jack." The Byrons were well known in England's military history. Seven of them had been cavaliers for King Charles; and Newstead Abbey, the ancestral estate at Nottingham had felt, but withstood, the fire of Cromwell's cannon. The Abbey, at the time of the poet's birth, was in the possession of his granduncle from whom the boy George Gordon inherited it at the age of ten, and with the estate, then mortgaged, the title of Lord Byron, Sixth Baron. Of this granduncle William, fifth Lord Byron, the poet later wrote in the First Canto of *Childe Harold's Pilgrimage:*

> One sad losel soils a name for ay,
> However mighty in the olden time;
> Nor all that heralds rake from coffined clay,
> Nor florid prose, nor honied lines of rhyme,
> Can blazon evil deeds, or consecrate a crime.

## BOYHOOD DAYS

The education of young Byron was at first irregular—typical of what his entire life was to be. As a child he was extremely impressionable and, unfortunately, very ill taught by his temperamental mother. The father died when the child was but three, and the mother and son lived in rather shabby respectability in Aberdeen. There, herself miserable, she was violent toward him, doted on him, chided him for his lameness, nurtured and injured his pride, and, as a net result, made him gradually indifferent to her and independent of her care. But she, and his first tutors, did for him two things of enduring worth: they acquainted him, unforgettably, with the austere and colorful scenery of Scotland, and with the equally colorful and austere beauty of the stories of the Bible. From this early background he learned, in time, to look on nature with exultant wonder; on life with open, if not always discerning eyes; and on humanity with the skeptical misgivings of the Calvinist. Of the stately poetry of the Bible he learned much he was never to forget, notably the story of Cain and Abel; and we are told that the Psalms in the Scottish metrical version were especially pleasing to him as his nurse half chanted such words as these to the boy:

> That man hath perfect blessedness
> Who walketh not astray
> In counsels of ungodly men,
> Nor stands in sinners' way.

## EDUCATION AT HARROW

These were influences he carried with him into maturity. Meanwhile the chief effect of Byron's early environment was to stir in him his latent passions, his anger, his pride, his self-pity;

and besides these also a devouring desire to read, a love of the English poets, and a hunger for the solitariness to brood on them. His education at home, we have said, was neglected and irregular. When, at thirteen, he entered the preparatory school at Harrow, he was deficient in Latin and Greek. But he was happy there—happier than he was to be at any time afterwards. He excelled in swimming, boxing and cricket, despite his lameness. He was personally popular, gallant, gentle with the younger boys, their defender against the arrogant and, even then, defiant toward all tyrants. For education by the rule and page of the textbook he felt an early contempt. But he filled his mind with the pages of Chaucer and Shakespeare. Once, Thomas Medwin tells us in his *Conversations*, during a rebellion at Harrow, young Byron saved the schoolroom from being set on fire "by pointing out to the boys the names of their fathers and grandfathers on the walls." And, in the poem *Childish Recollections*, published when Byron was nineteen, he recalled in simple rhyming lines the record left there by these youths for posterity to read:

> No splendid tablets grace her simple hall,
> But ruder records fill the dusky wall;
> There, deeply carv'd behold! each Tyro's name
> Secures its owner's academic fame;
> Here mingling view the names of Sire and Son,
> The one long grav'd, the other just begun . . .
> And, here, my name, and many an earthly friend's
> Along the wall in lengthen'd line extends.

## THE YEARS AT CAMBRIDGE

In 1805 Byron left Harrow and entered Trinity College at Cambridge. He was now seventeen, an accepted lord, not a good scholar, but a brilliant speaker, a generous friend, idolized, handsome. His education continued irregularly. He read with abandon, and with insight, into the night. But he also gambled, recklessly, into the morning. Embarrassed by debts, he went to the money-lenders, who harassed him into drinking. He was in and out of Cambridge, restless under instruction, lonely after the joyous years at Harrow, increasingly temperamental, irritated by his creditors, yet somehow getting scholastic information, knowing the classics and the world of men. No longer happy, he chose to be gay, surrounding himself with gifted young men like John Hobhouse, afterwards Lord Broughton, his life-long friend. Himself intellectual, he delighted in everything intellectual.

## THE FIRST POEMS

In July, 1808 he received from Cambridge the M.A. degree. A year before then he had published a little volume of poems entitled *Hours of Idleness*. It had been indulgently received by almost everyone except the editors of the Edinburgh Review. They attacked the precocious poet mercilessly, cutting him, as he said, "to atoms." But by then Byron was coming of age and he was burnishing his weapon of satire by reading the stinging and brilliant *Dunciad* of Pope. In 1809 he replied to the *Review* with *English Bards and Scottish Reviewers*, his first significant poem. Byron was unjust in it toward the poets Wordsworth and Coleridge. But the reply was effective. It was a warning and a masterly poetical performance. His tribute to the style of Dryden and Pope indicated, as these lines show, that in literature his tastes were thoroughly classical:

> Time was, ere yet in these degenerate days
> Ignoble themes obtained mistaken praise,
> When Sense and Wit with Poetry allied,
> No fabled Graces, flourished side by side;

From the same fount their inspiration drew,
And reared by Taste, bloomed fairer as they grew,
Then, in this happy Isle, a *Pope's* pure strain
Sought the rapt soul to charm, nor sought in vain;
A polished nation's praise aspired to claim,
And raised the people's, as the poet's fame.
Like him great *Dryden* poured the tide of song,
In stream less smooth, indeed, yet doubly strong.

## TRAVEL AND ROMANCE

In the same year, being now twenty-one, Byron occupied
Newstead, restored the noble old Gothic structure, and celebrated the event with his friends with a feast on bacon and
eggs and ale. Then, having already taken his rightful seat in
the House of Lords, he set out on a journey with Hobhouse,
going first to Portugal, and thence, by way of the Mediterranean, to Turkey. En route he visited Spain, Malta, and Al-
bania. He spent two months in Athens, and was received in
Constantinople by the Sultan. For the novelty of the experience,
and to study Greek, he lived for a while in a Franciscan monas-
tery. The most popularly remembered thing he did on the
journey was to swim across the Hellespont. Of it he wrote,
remembering Leander who swam nightly from Abydos to
Sestos to visit Hero, and one night was drowned:

If, in the month of dark December,
    Leander, who was nightly wont . . .
    To cross thy stream, broad Hellespont!
If, when the wintry tempest roared,
    He sped to Hero, nothing loth,
And thus of old thy current poured,
    Fair Venus! how I pity both!
For *me*, degenerate modern wretch,
    Though in the genial month of May,

My dripping limbs I faintly stretch,
 And think I've done a feat today.
But since he crossed the rapid tide,
 According to the doubtful story . . .
 And swam for Love, as I for Glory;
'T were hard to say who fared the best;
 Sad mortals! thus the gods still plague you!
He lost his labor, I my jest;
 For he was drowned, and I've the ague.

## LOVE AND ADVENTURE

Greece, for its classical tradition and its current struggle for liberty, particularly appealed to him. Love of beauty, especially when it could be joined with a sense of danger, temperamentally brought out the best in him. A sophisticated and beautiful woman was Byron's life-long weakness. Yet he held pure loveliness and innocence, wherever he found them, in high regard; and we have in the poem *Maid of Athens, ere We Part,* written in Athens in 1810, one of the earliest examples of that tenderness of which he was capable, side by side with an acrid taste for satire. He had, we know, already shown in verses dedicated to Mary Chaworth, how the pangs of first love could by his genius be compressed into pure poetry like this;

 Away! away! my early dream
 Remembrance never must awake:
 Oh! where is Lethe's fabled stream?
 My foolish heart, be still, or break.

# FAME AND CHANGING FORTUNE

## POETRY AND FAME

Now, after two years, the great gift was maturing in him. His note-book of travels, written chiefly in verse after the pattern of Spenser, became his literary self-proclamation to the world. It was published, in 1812, as the two first cantos of *Childe Harold*. And the result was, as Byron himself said: "I awoke one morning and found myself famous." He was compared to the great poets, to Coleridge and Wordsworth, more especially by those who idolized him as an English lord without as yet fully evaluating him as a poet. He himself could have taught them better; for, while he accepted, and made the best use of his lordship, he consistently refused to place a high estimate on his own art. As a matter of fact, though, he was a better success as a poet than as a man. When he was actually traveling, and at work writing *Childe Harold* his thoughts were fresh and his imagination took great delight in objects that were classical or in pictures of daily life. By contrast, the society that made so much of him, imitating his foibles and expressing its doubtful concern for his moral behavior, irked and annoyed him, provoking him to melancholy brooding and to frequent cynical utterance. His behavior, admittedly, was an enigma alike to London dudes, adoring ladies, and moralists; and it is to be noted that he did nothing whatever to dispel the illusions they had of him. Instead he seems to have abetted these illusions peculiarly to please himself.

## BYRON'S CHARACTER

During the years from 1813 to 1816 Byron's moral conduct was open to serious and deserved criticism. He drank to excess and lived as a libertine. He was gallant toward ladies, but exhibitively contemptuous toward women. He posed, as it suited him, sometimes as a rake, at other times as a hero. He became infatuated with his half sister Augusta, and seemed to exploit the fact by his elaboration of the theme of incest in the poem *The Bride of Abydos*, which was published in 1813.

He married Anne Isabella Milbanke, hoping, or pretending to hope, that she would reform him. When, in 1816, events came to a crisis, and Lady Byron, outraged by her husband's conduct, left his house and returned to her parents, his disillusionment was shocking and sudden. Adulation turned to hate against him; he was ostracized from London society; and for the first time in his career he stood defenseless. Friends, like Scott, stood by him but could do nothing. The result was that he left England, never to return.

## HIS PRIDE AND HUMILIATION

The shock was indeed a severe one for Byron. Its effect on his injured pride was reflected in the Third Canto of *Childe Harold* in which he wrote:

> Long absent Harold re-appears at last;
> He of the breast which fain no more would feel,
> Wrung with the wounds which kill not, but ne'er heal;
> He would not yield dominion of his mind
> To Spirits against whom his own rebelled;
> Proud though in desolation.

And though in this crisis he sought and soon found consolation in the historic and natural scenery of the Continent, it was evident that his spirit was crushed, as he himself confessed in the lines composed in March, 1816, shortly after the deed of separation had been drawn between Lady Byron and the poet:

> Every feeling hath been shaken;
> Pride, which not a world could bow,
> Bows to thee—by thee forsaken,
> Even my soul forsakes me now.

## THE BYRONIC TEMPERAMENT

Byron's personal conduct is so closely tied up with his literary career that we cannot keep the two apart. The poet, moreover, makes it difficult for us by his refusal to separate them. Besides all this, he was too often glib and garrulous regarding his intimate associations with men and women. He was no less alluring than lured in brilliant company. And his poetry was mainly written for those who could find in it the sort of companionship suited to their sophisticated social circle. Byron did not strain or train himself to become a universal poet. He often expressed universal truths; but he belonged .to a clan. Rank and fame, passion and gossip, were recurring themes with him, in his conversation, in his letters, in his poems. He contributed toward almost everyone's misunderstanding of him by such uninhibited utterances as, for example, this about women: "I regard them as very pretty but inferior creatures, who are as little in their place at our tables as they would be in our council chambers . . . I look on them as grown-up children . . . The Turks shut up their women, and are much happier; give a woman a looking-glass and burnt almonds, and she will be content."

## HIS DEFENDERS AND CRITICS

Byron had his defenders. Scott, fond of Byron, confined his compliments of him to the attractiveness of his person and his gifts as a poet. Though rivals for fame, the two men managed, as Scott said, to be "good-natured fellows together." The Irish lyrist Thomas Moore was as good-natured as anyone, and Byron's friendly defender. But the women whom he influenced held more radical views of him. Frances Anne Kemble, the actress, confessed herself fascinated by his poetry, observed its effect on herself, and then "resolved to read that grand poetry no more, and to break through the thraldom of that powerful spell." Lady Caroline Lamb was driven from passion to madness by her infatuation for him. Anne Milbanke, married to Byron by an ill fate, was too shocked to shower comment on her husband, until after his death, when she gave vent to pent up and extravagant hallucinations about him. Augusta Leigh, Byron's half-sister, of all living persons, alone overlooked his faults, loved him unselfishly, and forgave him everything. She dared to hope that Byron's marriage would be successful. Instead, it failed dismally. The oft-quoted words of Fletcher, Byron's valet, that "any woman could manage my lord, except my lady," are perhaps comment enough on the poet's character. Byron perceived all this, felt himself to be both loved and hated, knew well the good reasons for these attitudes toward him, made no open apology for his conduct, but expressed himself in verses that reflected a moment's sincerity but an unhealthy mood, as, for example, in these written in final farewell to Lady Byron:

> All my faults perchance thou knowest,
>     All my madness none can know;
> All my hopes, whe'er thou goest,
>     Wither, yet with *thee* they go.

> Fare thee well! thus disunited,
>     Torn from every nearer tie,
> Sear'd in heart, and lone, and blighted,
>     More than this I scarce can die.

## HIS COMPETENCY AS POET

Meanwhile, during the three crucial years of Byron's rise and fall in personal fame, his power to write grew in him. Inwardly, the experience of power was explosive rather than gradual and growing; and it was disillusioning. The writings between 1813 and 1816 did not have in them the freshness, the "rush as of morning air," the rich but offhand description, of the first two cantos of *Childe Harold*. The indifferently clever, pleasure-loving years of his youth were gone. The romantic melancholy of the years between 1807 and 1812, too, had given way to a passion for melodrama. The well of sorrow had become, in the poet's imagination, a river of blood.

## THE TURKISH TALES

The important poems of the period were, all of them, tales: *The Giaour, The Bride of Abydos, The Corsair, Lara, The Seige of Corinth,* and *Parisina.* As narratives they show Byron's force, his competency, which was less structural than fanciful. He took his materials for them from sources close at hand: from maritime stories about Columbus, Gibbon's *Antiquities,* Pope's *Iliad,* Coleridge's *Christabel,* anecdotes about American buccaneers, and from allusions to truth and gossip about himself. Of gossip there was enough to keep his writings popular, even though in London the Byron fever was fast dying down. The *Corsair,* for example, was immensely successful: ten thousand copies of it were sold on the—carefully planned—day of publication. The story is about a Mediterranean pirate or privateer who, it is said, "had many vices and one virtue—a certain sense of chivalry." Like Byron, he lived by his passion as fighter and lover. The plot is exciting. The characters, Conrad, Medora, and Gulnare are well sketched in heroic verse, and we remember especially the *Lines To A Lady Weeping* which Byron added over his own signature in the second edition of the poem. The *Lines* provoked a fury of Tory attack on Byron for daring to criticize the Prince Regent in his quarrel with his Whig ministers. Advised not to republish them, Byron scorned the advice, saying; "I care nothing for consequences on this point." He gallantly recounted the tears shed by the young Princess Charlotte over her father's quarrel:

Weep, daughter of a royal line,
A Sire's disgrace, a realm's decay;
Ah! happy if each tear of thine
Could wash a father's fault away!

Weep—for thy tears are Virtue's tears—
Auspicious to these suffering isles;
And be each drop in future years
Repaid thee by thy people's smiles!

But the gallantry, accepted in 1812, was misspent in 1814. Byron was becoming socially unpopular. English society was deciding to resist "the triple insolence of beauty, genius, and free speech" with which he had ruled it. The *Lines* produced an uproar, the prelude to his tragic downfall.

## GENIUS AND TRAGEDY

The *Bride of Abydos* is fairly pleasant reading. It is a Turkish tale, typically romantic. In it Zuleika, a Turkish maiden dies of grief over her slain lover, slain by her father's sword: "She dies, to slow music." The tragic theme suited Byron's temperament; the octosyllabic measure, after the pattern of Scott, had in it "a kind of fiery facility of his own;" and lines appeared in it that fitted him, or were applied to him, exactly and autobiographically. There are two such lines in stanza twenty-seven that read like an epigram of his spiritual history during these painful years:

Thrice happy! ne'er to feel nor fear the force
Of absence—shame—pride—hate—revenge—remorse!

## POEMS OF CHARACTER AND ACTION

Among the Tales, *Lara* and *The Siege of Corinth* deserve additional notice. In *Lara* the story is thin and unimportant.

**139**

The heroic couplets are didactic; the troubled mood is typical of Byron; the figure of Lara is somber and grandiose. The poem is best read for its character study and its insight into the poet's mind where thoughts of "fiery passions" move in "hurried desolation" toward a predestined end. Readers of *Lara* see in it Byron's own portrait, that of a man of an extremely complex nature:

> In him inexplicably mix'd appear'd
> Much to be loved and hated, sought and fear'd;
> Opinion varying o'er his hidden lot,
> In praise or railing ne'er his name forgot . . .

> Yet there was softness too in his regard,
> At times, a heart as not by nature hard,
> But once perceived, his spirit seem'd to chide
> Such weakness, as unworthy of its pride  . . .

> There was in him a vital scorn of all:
> As if the worst had fall'n which could befall,
> He stood a stranger in this breathing world,
> An erring spirit from another hurl'd  . . .

## HISTORICAL TURKISH TALE

In *The Siege of Corinth* it is the action that predominates. The poet returns to the use of the octosyllabic stanza, interspersing it with an occasional anapest or dactyl to suit the theme which has an historical nucleus. The hero of the story is Alp, the renegade, a "protoplastic ruffian", an exiled Venetian leading the Turks against the city. He is introduced to us in the poem, with deft Byronic irony, as invested

> With deeper skill in War's black art,

Than Othman's sons, and high of heart
As any Chief that ever stood
Triumphant in the fields of blood.

## THE HEBREW MELODIES

The years 1814 to 1816 were lived by Byron as in a tempest.
His infatuation with Augusta, his marriage to Anne Milbanke,
and his separation from her, were the events; and they cut
deep into the poet, severing and drying the roots in him. In
1815, in the midst of the storm of scandal about his unfaithful-
ness to his wife, he turned to Biblical themes for new poems,
perhaps because they had become familiar to him in childhood. Of the *Hebrew Melodies* composed, two of the best
known are *The Song of Saul Before His Last Battle* and *The
Destruction of Sennacherib*. In them resignation and strength
meet to create a stirring effect. In the first King Saul, expecting
death on the battle field, calls his men to fight:

> Warriors and chiefs! should the shaft or the sword
> Pierce me in leading the host of the Lord,
> Heed not the corpse, though a king's, in your path:
> Bury your steel in the bosom of Gath!

In the second of these poems, especially, Byron's genius is
evident in the fine sweep of the anapest, the swift events, the
graphic picture of justice, the underlying pathos, the sudden
ruin of a great hostile power. The last stanza reads like a verse
of oratory in the book of Isaiah:

> And the widows of Ashur are loud in their wail,
> And the idols are broke in the temple of Baal;
> And the might of the Gentile, unsmote by the sword,
> Hath melted like snow in the glance of the Lord!

**141**

# IN EXILE FROM ENGLAND

## THE DIVIDING YEAR

The year 1816 began dismally for Byron. In January Lady Byron left him to go to her parents. In April he left England, exiled by an indignant London. His friend Hobhouse, who saw another side in Byron, accompanied him to Dover, and, seeing Byron sail away, wrote in his journal: "God bless him for a gallant spirit and a kind one." Others, looking on the scene in London, were less kind. At a farewell ball given by Sarah, Countess of Jersey, the icy coldness toward Byron was apparent. It was a sign to him that he was no longer welcome in English society, and he braced himself—as he had a gift to do on such occasions—to meet the inevitable outcome. André Maurois has described Byron's reaction to it in these words: "Great had been his fall; and the very grandeur of the crash gave him exactly what he needed—a great role to play, satanic though it might be . . . So be it. If England declared it time for him to go, he would set forth again on his pilgrimage."* On the morning of his departure, while the ship that was to take him from England, never to return, lay in unquiet anchor, Byron wrote these lines to his devoted friend:

> My boat is on the shore
> And my bark is on the sea;
> But before I go, Tom Moore,
> Here's double health to thee!
>
> Here's a sigh to those who love me,
> And a smile to those who hate;
> And whatever sky's above me,
> Here's a heart for every fate!

*André Maurois; *Byron,* P. 327, D. Appleton and Company, 1930.

## THE GREATER BYRON

There was indeed another Byron, known to the select few in England, though now temporarily and popularly ignored. He was the poet already come to recognition in the famous travel poem *Childe Harold's Pilgrimage*. Cantos I and II had previously appeared. But now, in Canto III, the poet's star rose in the firmament, and remained there to outshine everything he had written. His pride shaken, helpless in his anger at England, yet in love with it, exiled and disgraced, yet defiant, he was, in fact, rising to immortality in his art. Partly, perhaps, it was the sense that he was again free; partly, also, the majestic scenery of the Alps; partly, his awareness of Europe's dramatic history—that produced in him the emotions that make the Third Canto great. But chiefly it was the mind of Byron, beating his thoughts against the prison of the world, striking at the iron bars of injustice, intolerance, the mustiness of a smug morality, and the popular, shortsighted and intimidating ideas on religion. Byron was, of course, not writing a treatise on these topics; he was compelling himself to overcome grief by the resolute use of time. Of the actual state of his mind during the composition of the Third Canto Byron himself says: "I was half mad . . . between metaphysics, mountains, lakes, love unextinguishable, thoughts unutterable, and the nightmare of my own delinquencies." If it was freedom he sought, he now found it. Yet if the poem *The Prisoner of Chillon*, also written in 1816, the year of his exile, was an index to Byron's own deeper feeling—even more than to that of Bonivard—he was not happy in it. For, in contrast to Bonivard, he had "learned to love despair." And, as he ends the poem, he says:

> My very chains and I grew friends,
> So much a long communion tends

> To make us what we are:—even I
> Regained my freedom with a sigh.

## CHILDE HAROLD'S PILGRIMAGE

The Third Canto, begun in May, was completed in July, and published in November, in 1816. It contains 1102 lines: 118 Spenserian stanzas, and a lyric of four ten-line stanzas. The unity of the poem depends on Byron's travels, first, south from the scene of Waterloo, then up the Rhine, and finally, into Switzerland. The Fourth Canto, written in Venice late in 1817, is longer, has 186 stanzas, traces Byron's journey through Italy from Venice to Rome, and completes the poem. Places and people dot the pages in picturesque fashion: Napoleon and Waterloo; Coblenz, Ehrenbreitstein, the Alps; Rousseau; Lake Geneva with its "crystal face", the stars above it, and the solemn intense silence; Venice, St. Mark's cathedral and the "Bridge of Sighs"; Petrarch's tomb; Tasso, Ariosto, Dante; Florence, rich in commerce, luxury, learning; the statue of Venus de'Medici that makes the poet stand delirious with a sense of its beauty; Santa Croce where lie the bones of Galileo and Machiavelli; the Apennines, long ago described by Horace; Rome, the mother of dead empires, weeping, "childless and crownless", a marble wilderness—altogether, the two Cantos are a noble gallery of history depicting all fame and fortune under the edict of decay and time. The Coliseum, seen by moonlight, stands majestic, overshadowing time; seen by daylight, it symbolizes all Rome, and the world, temporal, transient and crumbling. The lesson is that our life is short. But there remains the power to feel and to think to which the poet gives voice in one of the closing stanzas of the journey,

> There is a pleasure in the pathless woods,
> There is a rapture on the lonely shore,

There is society, where none intrudes,
By the deep Sea, and music in its roar;
I love not Man the less, but Nature more,
From these our interviews, in which I steal
From all I may be, or have been before,
To mingle with the Universe, and feel
What I can ne'er express, yet cannot all conceal.

## PLAYFUL SATIRE

By 1818, Byron then living chiefly in Venice, had written,
besides *Childe Harold,* also *The Prisoner of Chillon,* the philosophical drama *Manfred,* and a genially satirical tale called
*Beppo.* In *Beppo* we get a foretaste of the later *Don Juan,* show-
ing us the poet as he is, superficially, at his happiest moments
and in his best style—in contrast to his deeper sense of sin and
his desperate drive against it—half innocently playful and half
lustily cynical, as for example in these lines written in the
Italian *ottava rima* made famous by Tasso and Ariosto:

"England! with all thy faults I love thee still,"
    I said at Calais, and have not forgot it;
I like to speak and lucubrate my fill;
    I like the government (but that is not it);
I like the freedom of the press and quill;
    I like the Habeas Corpus (when we've got it);
I like a parliamentary debate,
Particularly when 'tis not too late;

I like the taxes, when they're not too many;
    I like a sea-coal fire, when not too dear;
I like a beef-steak, too, as well as any;
    Have no objection to a pot of beer;
I like the weather, when it is not rainy,
    That is, I like two months of every year,
And so God save the Regent, Church, and King!
Which means that I like all and everything.

# LORD BYRON

## THE DEEPER BYRON

But beneath this playful mood there lurked a demonic spirit. His poems and letters in which, since his exile, he had found refuge and let go his barbed shafts of wit, exhibit a vast resourcefulness and an indefatigable zest for life. Passion and bitterness and self-pity rankled in him, tearing his spirit. Love and scorn burned in one flame to consume him, together with the world's sham and injustice. Pleasure-loving though he was, and skeptical of those who too loudly praised virtue, Byron's republican and aristocratic tastes were remarkably sound. Conservative men like Hobhouse held to him against popular distrust; by now, also, there were persons on the Continent who saw something more than the dramatizing egoist in the man. To them, Byron stood as the representative and defender of man's free spirit, his innate worth and human individuality. Europe's most significant literary voice of the time, we recall, was that of Goethe who heralding the arrival of Byron said of him: "His daring, dash, and grandiosity: do these not comprise everything, setting before us everything in splendor at the moment we are aware of it? Such a *personality*, for its eminence, has never yet been, and is not likely to come again." Though these words do not strike at the root of Byron's malady, or of the world's, they offer sufficient praise of the impetuous and daring spirit in him.

## POETRY OF POWER

What Byron did for poetry was revolutionary. Like Scott, he was a popularizer, but a more mature one. He added sophistication to emotion, satire to melody, criticism to humor, disillusionment to grandeur. At the same time, he made his meaning clear and easy to follow. Byron did not penetrate to the mystery of the truth by which we live with Wordsworth's religious insight or soar with Shelley's vision. Vistas of the depths and heights of theology, however, were not beyond him; and his early education, we know, served to keep his conscience troubled throughout his life about questions of ethics and religion. Comparatively speaking, while Shelley wrote hopefully of self-realization in an ideal society, Byron allowed himself no such a fond dream of Utopia, but held, though greatly troubled, to orthodox conceptions of sin, wilful evil and divine justice. This fact is evident in the poem *The Prisoner of Chillon* in which Bonivard, the patriot and hero of the poem, known to have been a profound student of theology as well as of history, speaks for the poet:

> Oh, God! it is a fearful thing
> To see the human soul take wing
> In any shape, in any mood:
> I've seen it rushing forth in blood,
> I've seen it on the breaking ocean
> Strive with a swoln convulsive motion,
> I've seen the sick and ghastly bed
> Of Sin delirious with its dread.

To say that this experience of Bonivard is the poet's own invention is to relate it immediately to Byron's own mind; and the added fact that the entire poem shows a marked resemblance to the poetry of Coleridge further substantiates the evidence of a religious strain in Byron's thinking. Its metrical construction, too, conveying the poet's vivid sensations and mood of noble and tender pathos, is in strong contrast to most of his earlier declamatory narrative verse styled after Scott. The *Prisoner of Chillon* thus marks a distinct trait in Byron's art and thought.

## CONFESSIONAL AND MEMORIAL POETRY

Two poems, written in 1816, and less often observed in surveying Byron's work, are *The Dream* and the *Monody on the*

*Death of Sheridan.* The contrast between them could hardly be greater: the *Dream* is confessional to the verge of exposed privacy; the *Monody* has the objectivity of a public and stately memorial. The first of the two poems centers in the person of Mary Chaworth, the object of Byron's youthful love, who is pictured by the poet as forcibly separated from him by a cruel fate which has led her to madness and him to an existence of relentless misery; the second poem, recited, in the absence of Byron, by Mrs. Davison at the Drury Lane Theater, is now famous for these last lines closing with the fine metaphor of Ariosto:

> Long shall we seek his likeness—long in vain,
> And turn to all of him which may remain,
> Sighing that Nature formed but one such man,
> And broke the die—in moulding Sheridan.

## MANFRED: THE HUMAN DILEMMA

The dramatic poem *Manfred,* published in London in June, 1817, was Byron's major attempt to deal with a philosophical theme. It is a poem of conflict. Manfred, the hero, is neither angel nor villain, but a man of a large and agonizing mind, resembling Marlowe's Faustus, terrified with remorse and the sense of sin. The problem is the dual one of guilt and expiation. How shall Manfred free himself from sin and rid the world of the evil his act has brought? His first answer is, by seeking death and hoping for oblivion. But it is his destiny to live. The seven spirits cannot give him oblivion. They are themselves immortal beings and know nothing of death. When he tries to throw himself from the cliff of the Jungfrau, saying,

> Farewell, ye opening Heavens!
> Look not upon me thus reproachfully—
> You were not meant for me—
> Earth! take these atoms!

a chamois hunter seizes him, saves his life, and takes him to his cottage in the Alps. Manfred is doomed to live and to suffer; his evil life is not his own; and forgetfulness is denied him, except on the witch's terms which he scorns to accept. He must live, brooding on death. All this is come upon him because he refuses to bow to any master but his own imperious mind. At this point in the poem we see Byron's Calvinism shattered on the reef of man's inordinate desire. Divine destiny and the sovereign will of man confront the poet with an irreconcilable dilemma. The road to divine reconciliation is closed to Manfred who calls himself his own judge.

## THE POEM'S CHARACTER AND STYLE

The dark night of the soul of Byron hovers over Manfred, foreshadowing its fuller expression in the drama *Cain*. The theme of *Manfred* suggests that of Goethe's *Faust* of which Byron had had portions translated to him by his friend Lewis, but from which it differs, for example, as the man of action differs from the philosopher. Compared to Marlowe's *Faustus,* which Byron denies ever having read, it is wanting in the sustained grandeur which gives to that Elizabethan drama its lasting fame. As *Faustus* represents the final surrender of the human will, so *Manfred* exhibits its ultimate breakdown. It is not repentance, at last, but death that Manfred seeks; death self-willed, self-accomplished. Yet these are his dying words to the abbot:

> 'Tis over—my dull eyes can fix thee not;
> But all things swim around me, and the earth
> Heaves as it were beneath me. Fare thee well!
> Give me thy hand.

The best parts of the poem are those in which the troubled

mind of the poet enters into the dark mysteriousness enveloping man's earthly life, as for instance in the climactic scene in which the Sisters of Destiny, looking down on the world from their summit in the Alps, chant together this cold song of their cruel power:

> Our hands contain the hearts of men,
> Our footsteps are their graves;
> We only give to take again
> The Spirits of our slaves!

# GREAT LITERARY PRODUCTIVITY

## THE LATER YEARS

The period from 1818 to 1824, the year of Byron's death, began in degradation. But it ended in a kind of triumph. Three events especially characterize the poet of these last years: his submission to the finally helpful influence of the Italian countess Guiccioli; the publication of *Don Juan;* and his gallant expedition to Greece. There were other things he did. One might make a long list of them: he escaped from one love affair into another; he made new friends and mostly kept his old ones; he wrote letter after letter, easily, healthily, naturally; he stood up intrepidly against insult and gossip; he fought to assuage his incurable melancholy; and, most significantly, he wrote, besides *Don Juan,* such varying poetical works as *Mezeppa, The Prophecy of Dante, Marino Faliero, The Two Foscari, Sardanapalus, The Vision of Judgment,* and *Cain.* Each of these works has character, shows genius, reveals Byron's power of satire; his pre-occupation with the fact of evil, his demonology, his doctrine of self-realization; his bold love of nature, his fondness for everything Oriental and magnificient; his sense of a relentless fate; his racy, ribald, and yet delicate art of telling a good story.

## PASSION AND FREEDOM

Most of these poems were written at Ravenna and at Pisa, in the year 1821. Byron was then living with the Countess Guiccioli whose influence, as we have said, had a good effect on his literary life. On July 5, 1821 he wrote to Thomas Moore from Ravenna: "I am now in the fifth act of 'Foscari,' being the third tragedy in twelve months, besides proses; so you perceive that I am not at all idle." Occupied Byron certainly was; and preoccupied. His chief preoccupation was a zealous passion to set free enslaved persons and peoples. The Countess Teresa was freeing herself from Count Guiccioli without much help from Byron, except that the two fell in love at first sight. But there was Italy chafing under Austrian rule. Something must be done, with Teresa's help. The result, in 1819, was the *Prophecy of Dante,* a tirade against tyranny, typical of Byron's gift to dissolve sweat and dust in the splendor and passion of love. And, later, there was Greece, chafing under Turkish rule, and calling for the best that was in Byron, which he gave, willingly, against great odds, and at the cost of his life. Besides, there was Shelley, then living at Pisa, toward whom Byron felt the desire of a friendly attachment; more, it must be said, than Shelley felt toward him. The two poets met and arranged to publish a periodical, called *The Liberal.* It was in the last year of Shelley's life; for on July 8, 1822, Shelley was drowned. A month later Byron officiated at the body's cremation on the beach. Hunt and Trelawny were there with him. They solemnly watched the fire, and saw how the oil and wine and salt "made the yellow flames glisten and quiver." When Shelley's ashes had been gathered up in the urn, Byron walked to where the breakers rolled upon the sand and swam into the sea.

# LORD BYRON

## INTENSE LITERARY CREATIVITY

It is of interest to note how during these last years Byron's mind was set on writing. He wrote, it appears, incessantly. In *Cain: A Mystery* he gave vent to rebellious thoughts about the justice of God which had long been fermenting in him. In the poem *Heaven and Earth* he wrote less sensationally, more nobly and with control, of nature, of human suffering, and of the characters of Noah and his sons and daughters. In the *Vision of Judgment* he skillfully basted the poet laureate Southey and King George III together on his grill of satire.

## BYRON AND ITALY

Something further may be said of two poems of Italian setting, indicating Byron's versatile style. The first of these, already mentioned, is *Beppo*. It is a lightly ironical poem making use of the *ottava rima* and illustrating the "nimble impudence" to which Goethe referred in speaking of the poet. Its theme is the now tritely conventional one of the long-absent husband who comes home to find his wife contented with another lover. Instead of the usual resort to daggers, there is the call for coffee, "a beverage for Turks and Christians both;" the wife overcomes the husband with talking: "Beppo! what's your pagan name? Bless me! your beard is of amazing growth!" and all ends well. In the *Ode on Venice* Byron returns to the loftier theme and succeeds in its use, making the orthodox distinction between the venial sins of Venice, those of "the softer order, born of love," and Austria's mortal sin of tyranny and oppression, and adding the hope that the spirit of freedom, having lately crossed the Atlantic, may

> O'er the deep
> Fly, and one current to the ocean add,

One spirit to the souls our fathers had,
One freeman more, America, to thee!

## THE POETS DANTE AND TASSO

Byron's power to seize the high moments of great men is a gratifying trait in him. In *The Lament of Tasso* he pictures the author of *Jerusalem Delivered,* whom someone has called "the genius of the transition from the Renaissance to the Counter Reformation", as imprisoned in the hospital of St. Anna, his over-sensitive mind deranged, but speaking in lucid intervals of the transcendent light that still shines upon his work, and adding,

> I stoop not to despair;
> For I have battled with mine agony,
> And made me wings wherewith to overfly
> The narrow circus of my dungeon wall,
> And freed the Holy Sepulchre from thrall;
> And revelled among men and things divine,
> And poured my spirit over Palestine.

Similarly, in *The Prophecy of Dante,* written as he says "to gratify the Countess Guiccioli," Byron pictures Dante as exiled in Ravenna and, after the completion of the *Divine Comedy* and awaiting death, as moved to this lamentation over Italy:

> Oh Florence! Florence! unto me thou wast
> Like that Jerusalem which the Almighty He
> Wept over, "but thou wouldst not;" as the bird
> Gathers its young, I would have gathered thee
> Beneath a parent pinion, hadst thou heard
> My voice.

## HISTORICAL TRAGEDIES

In 1821 Byron wrote a tragedy called *Sardanapalus* which he dedicated to the German poet Goethe. The story of this last

Assyrian king who lived in extreme sloth and effeminate luxury very naturally did not escape Byron; and he made his own use of it, pressing the events of a long war into an explosive rebellion of one day. The dramatic effect is striking when, for example, at Byron's prompting the effeminate king censured for his sloth answers:

> 'Tis true I have not shed
> Blood as I might have done, in oceans, till
> My name became the synonym of Death—
> A terror and a trophy . . .

> I leave such things to conquerors; enough
> For me, if I can make my subjects feel
> The weight of human misery less, and glide
> Ungroaning to the tomb; I take no license
> Which I deny to them. We are all men.

But in the end the play loses much of its power to hold us. The king's farewell words—spoken as the torch is about to be put to the pile setting fire to the monarch on his throne—are unheroic and rhetorical, ending in a whimpering confession of regret. The king is a pulpy character, and the play, as we might expect, is without much grain of moral fiber.

## THE TWO FOSCARI

This is a better play, having a more solid core of tragedy. The father, the Doge of Venice, is forced to decree the banishment of his son, only to find that the *Ten* of Venice have decreed to demand the Doge's retirement. Both son and father are men of a sensitive spirit, suffer because they love, and die of broken hearts. The scene of the Doge's death, just as the clock at St. Mark's strikes the hour of his successor's elevation, has the poignant setting of a true climax:

*Doge.* The bell tolls on!—let's hence—my brain's
on fire!

*Barbarigo.* I do beseech you, lean upon us!

*Doge.* No!
A Sovereign should die standing.

## CAIN: A MYSTERY

Byron dedicated the drama *Cain* to Sir Walter Scott who made this fitting comment on it: "The great key to the Mystery is, perhaps, the imperfection of our own faculties, which see and feel strongly the partial evils which press upon us, but know too little of the general system of the universe, to be aware how the existence of these is to be reconciled with the benevolence of the great Creator." The remark sometimes made that in the play Lucifer talks like a Manichean can only mean that evil, unable to destroy good, tries to appear in seeming equality with it—a deception not shared by the poet. The drama suggests a comparison with *Paradise Lost;* but the argument in it is not assimilated as it is in the great work of Milton; and neither the meter nor the thought rises to Milton's height, except in the few rare passages in which the choppy and disputatious dialogue is left behind and the measure smooths itself out in august and pure pathos. Of the pervading thought of the play we get our best glimpse, perhaps, in Act III, Scene I, in which Cain and Abel offer their morning sacrifice: Abel, kneeling, spreads his thank-offering before the altar, bowing his own face "Even to the dust, of which he is—in honour of Thee;" Cain, standing erect, addresses the Almighty with a succession of thoroughly rationalistic "Ifs", as for example: "If thou must be propitiated," "If thou must be induced," "If thou lovest blood;" and he ends his discourse in the true manner of a Shopenhauer saying that the World-Ground is inexorable *will,* and adding,

> And whether that be good or ill I know not,
> Not being omnipotent, nor fit to judge
> Omnipotence—but merely to endure
> Its mandate.

Cain argues that it was by the will of God that Adam was created. Why should Cain be punished for the sin be inherits, and so be predestined to be damned *before* the crime? He will endure the punishment, but deny the guilt. Yet when the deed is done, and Abel lies dying at the altar, slain at his brother's hand, Cain cries out:

> My brother, awake! . . .
> Abel! I pray thee, mock me not! . . .
> Oh, God! Oh, God! . . .
> My brother!—No:
> He will not answer to that name; for brethren
> Smite not each other.

## HEAVEN AND EARTH

Of this Mystery, written late in 1821 at Ravenna, we have the key given us by Byron himself in the quotation from *Kubla Khan:* "And woman wailing for her demon lover". The announced theme of the drama is found in the verse in the Biblical book of *Genesis* which records the mating of the sons of God with the daughters of men. Here Byron finds the wide range he desires for his poetical performances, and he has made the expected use of his liberties. Trivial dialogues and monologues of high sentence intermingle with lyrics of grandiose proportions involving the ancient Noah, the daughters of Cain, and the heavenly Spirits who, despite Raphael's warning, stand on the brink of the abyss into which Satan has fallen. Byron quite properly concludes that the created world is best allowed to be what it is, that angels and men alike cease their unholy striving, that heavenly Spirits content themselves with their immortality, and that earthly mortals, after life's pain, accept the boon of a natural death.

## MAZEPPA

It is with relief that one turns from the reading of *Cain* to *Mazeppa*, written two years earlier. The story belongs to Voltaire. It is the swift episodic tale told by Mazeppa about himself, remembering when as a youth he was caught in an intrigue with a nobleman's wife, lashed naked to the back of a wild stallion that was driven off in galloping terror into the wilderness toward the open steppes of the Ukraine, where the horse fell dead. Mazeppa was rescued by the sympathetic peasants, given hospitality, and in time became a hero and captain of a band of Cossacks. Told in the first person the story has the immediacy of direct experience. A tender subdued account of the lovers' tryst is followed by the rush of ensuing events, letting the reader of the poem share the delirium of the youth tied fast to the galloping horse:

> My breath was gone,
> I saw not where he hurried on:
> 'Twas scarcely yet the break of day,
> And on he foamed—away!—away!
> The last of human sounds which rose,
> As I was darted from my foes,
> Was the wild shout of savage laughter,
> Which on the wind came roaring after
> A moment from that rabble rout:
> With sudden wrath I wrenched my head,
> And snapped the cord, which to the mane
> Had bound my neck in lieu of rein,
> And, writhing half my form about,
> Howled back my curse; but 'midst the tread,

> The thunder of my courser's speed,
> Perchance they did not hear nor heed:
> It vexes me—for I would fain
> Have paid their insult back again.
> I paid it well in after days.

## THE POET'S MASTERPIECE

Finally, in *Don Juan* all of Byron's talents coalesced in the telling of an adventurous, sentimental and satirical story. Everything that Byron had thought, and of which he still wished to think, went into the story: comedy, tragedy, mystery, ribaldry, beauty, sweet innocence, sordid guilt; thoughts touching on history and theology; exposures of public manners and of private morals. And the end he achieved gives us the impression that man is a strange mortal who finds consecutive thinking distasteful, and action, by contrast, pleasurable; is easily given over to fashion and folly, to intermittent rapture and disillusionment, realizing little besides things immediate, and finding in the end that life, when examined, offers more cause for lusty laughter than for pure praise.

## POET'S PHANTASMAGORIA

That, of course, is not all there is in *Don Juan*. It is a Byron's Encyclopedia of Manners. But it is also a poem. The parts are adroitly montaged together to form a work of art. "Its greatness," one critic says, "lies in the magnificent vital fusion of its varied elements." Another calls it a "gigantic torso overlaid with a crust of rich humor and satire." Blackwood's Edinburgh Magazine regarded it as a "thorough and intense infusion of genius and vice." It is inadvisable to read the poem only here and there and so to judge it. Its dedication begins, for example, by offering insult to the Lake Poets, to Wordsworth and Coleridge, quite foolishly saying:

> You're shabby fellows—true—but poets still,
> And duly seated on the immortal hill.

Then, in the First Canto, it turns to burlesque in treating the characters of Donna Julia and Donna Inez. The shipwreck section of the first half of the Second Canto is not for readers of a delicate digestion. Then suddenly, with about the hundredth stanza, the scene changes, and we are in a paradise. Haidee, the lovely maiden, is nursing Juan to health after his shipwreck. The scene is a tender one, the mood idyllic. Even here, though, the intruding hoof of Pan is detected when Byron, breathing through the reed of his verse as it pleases him, now sweetly and now impishly, continues in stanza 148:

> And she bent o'er him, and he lay beneath,
> Hush'd as the babe upon its mother's breast,
> Droop'd as the willow when no winds can breathe,
> Lull'd like the depth of ocean when at rest,
> Fair as the crowning rose of the whole wreath,
> Soft as the callow cygnet in its nest;
> In short, he was a very pretty fellow,
> Although his woes had turn'd him rather yellow.

And so the poem *Don Juan* continues, through seventeen cantos, to a total of nineteen hundred and seventy two stanzas, amounting altogether to more than sixteen thousand lines. Through Byron's consummate mastery of it, the *ottava rima* becomes the "Don Juan Stanza," eloquent, versatile, memorable. The poem's major tone is distinctly mock-epic. Its treble note of tender sentiment is almost always drowned in the basso voice of the poet's laughter—or stopped dead still by his sudden surprising pause of suspicion. An ultra-critical approach to the poem is, at last, disarming and useless. It is, in short, a magnificent disguise of the poet—of Byron dressed in the self-spun garb of his own versification.

**159**

# LORD BYRON

## SOLDIER AND CAVALIER

Byron died of a fever at Missolonghi in 1824. The expedition into Greece proved costly, taking him from his friends, and using up his money to equip the troops he had rallied around the cause with him. An unmerciful fate now turned his much used irony against him, denying him the honor of dying gloriously on the field of battle. Nevertheless this last chapter of his life deserves to be proudly written. The mutiny of his troops, the incessant rain, and the fever that burned away his hopes and his life—these he endured, as he had before endured his exile, with gallant fortitude. He was, after all, a cavalierly soldier, eager to find some exacting and exalting cause to which to give his life. Morally, his life had gone to atoms, and he seems now to have wished to find a way to redeem it. On his thirty-sixth birthday, he had written:

> My days are in the yellow leaf;
> The flowers and fruits of love are gone;
> The worm, the canker, and the grief
>     Are mine alone!
> If thou regrett'st thy youth, *why live?*
> The land of honorable death
> Is here:—up to the field, and give
>     Away thy breath!
> Seek—less often sought than found—
> A grave, for thee the best;
> Then look around, and choose thy ground,
>     And take thy rest.

Poetry had been his avocation, he once intimated; fighting, his vocation. And when he died the Greeks who knew him only as a soldier asked to be allowed to bury him with their nation's honor; but the request was not granted and his body was brought to England and placed in the village church near Newstead Abbey. But his heart lies buried in Greece.

## MAN AND POET

The flood of superficial criticism of Byron has now subsided. The facts about him are all, or almost all, known; and it is clear that he understood himself well enough, better perhaps than we do. In his *Epistle to Augusta* he wrote:

> Mine were my faults, and mine be their reward.
> My whole life was a contest, since the day,
> That gave me being, gave me that which marr'd
> The gift,—a fate, or will, that walked astray;
> And I at times have found the struggle hard,
> And thought of shaking off my bonds of clay:
> But now I fain would for a time survive,
> If but to see what next can well arrive.

But, to check against this confession, we have his poetry. Much of it, we may say, is commonplace; some of it is extraordinary; a considerable portion of it is great. All of it reflects the man, his view of life, his peculiar and idiosyncratic art. On the most obvious side of his nature Byron was a sensual realist, and what he knew of men and women did not inspire him to much trust in them. He believed human nature to be generally corrupted, having no sufficient strength to redeem itself. As it was his inherited Calvinism that made him skeptical of a current rationalistic humanism, so it was his love of the Old Testament that gave to his best thoughts a positive moral grandeur.

## DIVINE JUSTICE

But that was as far as Byron's spirit could go. He could "strike against the bars of flesh," as in the poem, *The Bride of Abydos;* he could call on the Alps to witness his remorse, loathe mankind and himself, as he does in *Manfred,* longing for oblivion; he could worship a hero like Childe Harold, express outrage against injustice, and go to the extreme length, as in *Cain*, of questioning the just providence of God. But his search ended there. He pictured a world in sin and without any certain knowledge or hope of escape. Divine justice was real to him, as we can see in the "Hebrew Melodies," particularly, in such an admirable poem as *The Destruction of Sennacherib*. But on the themes of Christian grace and faith Byron has left us no representative poem. Perhaps his single contribution to religious thought was that he kept clear of confusing Romantic ideals with Christian doctrine, and that he held fast to the classical and orthodox conception that man lives in two worlds—those of Nature and of Spirit—and that, being essentially a creature of soul, he is a "pilgrim of eternity."

## THE FINAL ESTIMATE

Byron's passionate desire, as someone has said, was "to hurl down oppression, hypocrisy, shams, avarice, cowardice, sloth, and to strike a blow for freedom ere he died." To this end he used his poetry, rather as a weapon than a fine art; and a grand weapon of rhetoric it was, at its best—a brandishing, bejeweled blade of satire. His boldness in using it, in defying literary taste, is illustrated by lines like these in *Don Juan*:

> But—oh! Ye lords of ladies intellectual,
> Inform us truly, have they not hen-pecked you all?

Here the rime is certainly slurred, yet just as certainly sophisticated. Again, the mere listing of place names like Salamis, Thermopolae, Athens, Venice, Florence, and Rome, gave the poet solid pleasure. Finally, his antitheses are always masterly, having in them some definite quality taken from the structure of his thought. Yet his verses are equally notable in their power of synthesis. It is, perhaps, this dual power of building and destroying that is most remarkable about Byron. Thoughts high and low meet in him; sometimes to enrich and give magnitude to the scene of life's drama; at other times, as in some mighty Armageddon, to root up and tread down the chaste truth and beauty of the ancient cause for which he strives. But in all that Byron writes the issues are clear. They take on the pattern of his decisive thought; and the poet succeeds in communicating to the reader the peculiar and pungent essence of his mind.

# Percy Bysshe Shelley
## 1792-1822

## THE RISE OF GENIUS
### 1792-1810

## FORMATIVE YEARS
### 1810-1814

## PERIOD OF TRANSITION
### 1814-1818

## GOLDEN YEARS OF POETRY
### 1818-1822

# THE RISE OF GENIUS

## BYRON AND SHELLEY

The opinions which men, in his time, had of Lord Byron were outright and decisive. Quite generally, they were of two sorts: Byron was a bad man; or, Byron was a good poet. Such were the summary verdicts. Other things said of him, whether of praise or blame, were of the nature of a lively argument obviously designed to convince the reader. But the name of Shelley, from the first, presented a problem. Here was not a man only, but the symbol of a man, an Idea called Shelley, and so a name with which to conjure. For Shelley was indeed, to quote a recent biographer, "a highly penetrating and sympathetic intelligence" let loose in the world; and the thought which issued from this intelligence was a globe of fire—as if some meteor had broken from Absolute Truth and was now a wandering planet, incandescent and moving in its perpetual orbit of light.

## MAN AND POET

We are not to infer from this rather dazzling glimpse of him that Shelley lacked the ingredient qualities of mother earth in his own human nature. He was indeed very human—the man being sometimes too frail to endure the light of truth to which he opened his own mind and which sent the poet Shelley in constant pursuit of that idea of "intellectual beauty", or perfect love, of which he was the dedicated voice. Shelley the poet and

Shelley the man were in almost life-long conflict with each other, so distinct were their individualities. Yet it was out of the desire of the man to be identified with the poet, and this desire's periodic fulfilment, that the poetry of Shelley may be said to owe its origin and nature. It is necessary, therefore, in reading Shelley, to assimilate into our formative judgment of the poet, the conflicting views by which he has been diversely called an atheist, an angel, a madman, a child, a liar, a monster, and a prophet or seer of the truth that lies beyond all common reason. This task will be made easier by remembering that the Shelley we wish to know is Shelley the poet, that the man apart from his poetry is mostly hidden from us, that the relatable story of his life is only the moving shadow of his thought, and that he himself regarded the life he lived as but a symbol of a day made "solemn and serene" by the passing beauty of the hours, by a "luster in the autumn sky", provoking him to this prayer to the Spirit of Beauty:

> Thus let thy power, which like the truth
> Of nature on my passive youth
> Descended, to my onward life supply
> Its calm—to one who worships thee,
> And every form containing thee,
> Whom, SPIRIT fair, thy spells did bind
> To fear himself, and love all human kind.

## LIFE'S REALITY

Love was a fiery passion to Shelley, and suffering a reality. His life was a succession of disappointments and sorrows. His expulsion from Oxford; his attempt to reform Ireland; his disappointing marriage to Harriet Westbrook, his first wife, and her suicide; the tragic death of Fanny Imlay; the loss of the guardianship of his and Harriet's children; the death of two of his and Mary Godwin's children; Mr. Godwin's sordid ill treatment of him; the literary reviewers' caustic criticism of his poetry and the public's ignorant indifference toward it— these and other experiences, and the disillusionment they brought, were Shelley's lot during the last ten of the thirty years he lived. They do not prove him a mere dreamer, or a sentimentalist, or a mad theoretical reformer. That Shelley's was a sensitive and idealistic nature we know. But his poetry is essentially intellectual and philosophical—a metaphysical poet's answer to the summary question: What is man's life? We find clear evidence of the poet's subordination of his own feeling to philosophical discipline and to the achievement of literary form in the *Hymn to Intellectual Beauty*, written when he was twenty-four. It is a mature and masterly work. Mrs. Mary Shelley, writing at a later time, remembered in connection with it Shelley's self-abnegation and "the worship he paid to Love". But we have, in Shelley's own translation, a substantiating passage from Plato's *Symposium* on the discipline of love and its "power to enable the lover to penetrate through the forms of beauty to the one eternal beauty." Plato had said:

He who has been disciplined to this point in love, by contemplating beautiful objects gradually, and in their order, now arriving at the end of all that concerns love, on a sudden beholds a beauty, wonderful in its nature. . . . It is eternal, unproduced, indestructible.

## THE IMPERISHABLE IDEAL

That fragmentary passage is the clue to our understanding of Shelley. From it the poetry of the introductory *Hymn* is clearly derived. Shelley, we see immediately, is the poet of ideal beauty. To him this beauty, ultimately, is Spirit, and so divine. It visits this world, transforming it and giving it life, loveliness, and joy. To it Shelley vows a poet's allegiance, calling it by endearing names and, as the shadow falls on him, exclaims in ecstasy:

> With beating heart and streaming eyes, even now
> I call the phantoms of a thousand hours
> Each from his voiceless grave:—
> They know that never joy illumed my brow
> Unlinked with hope that thou wouldst free
> This world from its dark slavery,
> That thou—O awful *Loveliness*,
> Wouldst give whate'er these words cannot express.

## POET AND MAN

It is not enough to call Shelley a poet's poet—though such indeed he is—or an ethereal lyrist, an abstract artist. Nor may we repeat, without reservation, Arnold's classic verdict: "In poetry, no less than in life, he is a beautiful and ineffectual angel, beating in the void his luminous wings in vain." We can no more simply accept these current judgments of him than take literally Mary Shelley's domestic praise of her poet-husband or, in contrast, his father's obtuse notion that he was an immature spoilt son, or the rabid opinion of the editor of *The Gentleman's Magazine* who, after Shelley's death wrote: "We ought as justly to regret the decease of the devil (if that were possible) as of one of his coadjutors." Doubtless to each of these persons Shelley was such a being. Perhaps men and women have looked on him so variously because of the light or the darkness in their own eyes. His essential genius, his growth as a poet and the obsessive ideas so compellingly at work in him are difficult to analyze. It is about as easy to catch the wind in a net, or to imprison the song of the skylark in a cage, as to put a restricting label on the mind of Shelley. Yet his thoughts are the variously familiar ones represented in the teachings of Locke, Rousseau, William Godwin, Bishop Berkeley, the Bible, and Plato. Whoever has a knowledge of these sources adds immeasurably to his understanding and enjoyment of Shelley's poems.

## EVENTS AND YEARS

Shelley was born on August 4, 1792. He died on July 8, 1822, by drowning, at the age of thirty. He was twice married: first, to Harriet Westbrook, aged sixteen, who drowned herself in 1816; later, to Mary Godwin who survived him. Harshly misjudged, he left England in March 1818, never to return. His greatest year of poetic activity was the year 1819. In that year he completed the writing of *Prometheus Unbound,* a work of triumph, of genius, of literary immortality. Shelley attributed the poem to the "blue sky of Rome"; but it was, in truth, the work of his rebirth from a materialistic to a spiritual view of the world.

## POETRY AND MEANING

During the ten creative years between 1812 and 1822 Shelley wrote, successively, *Queen Mab, Alastor, Laon and Cyntha, The Cenci, Epipsychidion, Adonais* and *Hellas,* besides the odes and lyrics by which he is best known, a masterly work of literary criticism entitled *A Defense of Poetry,* and important letters. These works, in addition to his trials at Eton, his joys at Oxford, until his expulsion from the University, his friendships with Hogg, Byron and Hunt, Williams and Trelawney, and his residence in Switzerland and Italy, sum up Shelley's career. But among these facts and literary works, the monuments of his fame, walks Shelley himself, the peculiar living being, secure in his immortality. Merely listing the facts of

Shelley's life and itemizing the poems gives one no assurance of finding the poet. The poet himself lives in the *meaning* of what he has written, in the immortal spirit that broods over all that he has composed. We commonly call it the poet's fantasy. It is a spirit so sensitive that in reading the poems one is haunted by visions of the *Divine Comedy* in which Dante pictures the agonizing spirits speaking from the bleeding wounds of trees. It is this immediacy of perception in Shelley that captures and holds us in its grip. By it we rise with him through the contemplation of sorrow to the ecstasy of joy, while he guides our thought, as for example in the poem *The Sensitive Plant:*

> It is a modest creed, and yet
> Pleasant if one considers it,
> To own that death itself must be,
> Like all the rest, a mockery.

> For love, and beauty, and delight,
> There is no death, nor change: their might
> Exceeds our organs, which endure
> No light, being themselves obscure.

The poem is a parable. *The Sensitive Plant* is Shelley himself. The seasons bring the birth, growth, and death of things. But it is a mockery that the garden of the world should produce and propagate only mandrakes and toadstools:

> Thistles, and nettles, and darnels rank,
> And the dock, and henbane, and hemlock dank.

Death—as men generally speak of it—is the greatest of illusions. And beauty does not die.

### AT ETON

For Shelley life actually began when, at twelve, he was sent to Eton. There he was stabbed awake by the cruel system of fagging and the cold insensitivity to anything but material success. He endured what he could, finding refuge in his own fancy and in the experiments of science. Once he exploded gunpowder in the school yard to express his protest against social tyranny. At another time he seemed to be fumigating his room when the master entered. Surprised and deep in his experiment, Shelley said, "Please sir, I am raising the devil." At Eton he read the romances of Mrs. Radcliffe, and found a trusted friend in Master Lind. Fancy, curiosity and a spirit of rebellion worked in him like a fermenting leaven. There also he began to read the *Political Justice* of William Godwin. Before long his extreme daring had earned for him the title of atheist. It was not his disbelief in Deity but his opposition to the tyranny of the accepted household gods—for example, all domestic and religious institutions—that was implied in the nickname "Shelley the Atheist". All it meant was that he reverenced what he thought was divine in man but hated what was inhuman—a simple humanitarian trait of all reformers. Only in Shelley who was young and impatient it took a radical turn. The new necessitarian disciple of William Godwin had yet to learn of the ideal of liberty taught by Plato.

# FORMATIVE YEARS

## AT OXFORD

In the summer of 1810, while still at Eton, he began to write verses and stories. They remind one of eaglets designed for high flight, but not yet ready. No anthology contains them now; their slight thoughts are the pin feathers of the future poet's wings. Meanwhile Shelley fell in love, or nearly so, with his cousin Harriet Grove, to whom his parents appear to have wanted him to be engaged. But his daily companion, during the summer, was his sister who helped him with his writing. In the autumn of 1810 he entered Oxford, and met his first important friend, Thomas Jefferson Hogg. At this time, strangely enough, Shelley's chief interest was not poetry but science, or, should we say, philosophical chemistry, by means of which he hoped to disclose the secret of creation. He hoped with the chemist's magic wand to remove the veil from life's mystery, and after that to reconstruct the social fabric of a better world. He found his ideal, or the stimulus to attaining it, in the rationalism of three men; Locke, Hume, and Voltaire. Here, he thought, were men who lived by the rule of reason of which the age was in need. Hogg and Shelley read together in their rooms, far into the night, Shelley sometimes falling into a deep sleep before the fire; then awakening suddenly, as if the leopard rug had come to life, he launched into a fierce argument that threatened to last until morning. Discussion led to the urge to write, and Shelley put it all down, so he then thought, in a pamphlet called *The Necessity of Atheism*. It was not about Deity, but about the feeling men have for Deity, a feeling based solely on sense perception, that he was thinking. In a letter to Elizabeth Hitchener, written in 1811, he says:

Locke proves that there are no *innate* ideas. In consequence, there can be no innate speculative or practical principles which might overturn all appeals of *feeling* in favor of Deity, since that feeling must be referable to some origin. There must have been a time when it did not exist; in consequence, a time when it began to exist. Since all ideas are derived from the senses, this feeling must have originated from some sensual excitation. Consequently the possessor of it may be aware of the time, of the circumstances, attending its commencement. Locke proves this by induction too clearly to admit of rational objection.

It is obvious that the revolutionary ferment was at work in

him. Because it was close at hand, the Established Church was especially blamed for being tyrannical, for making gods of convention, bigotry and intolerance, for outraging reason and so deserving to be overthrown. Had Shelley had a better understanding of history, he would have known how to appraise the usefulness of bishops and the value of convention. Being young, he resolved to be intolerant of intolerance. The Oxford authorities took the case in hand; Hogg asked for clemency; but before the year ended the two young men together found themselves expelled from the university.

## DOMESTIC SITUATION

Shelley was now free of church and school, but he had yet to deal with the domestic wishes of his father. Timothy Shelley was a man of property; and money and respectability were the household gods of this Sussex squire. He expostulated and pleaded with his son. If young Shelley would be less free with his own ideas he might be allowed to be more free with his father's money. He might sow wild oats socially, but not intellectually. With this view his cousin Harriet Grove seems to have agreed, fearing — with fundamental good reason — the young man's heresy more than his immorality. This parental tyranny outraged Shelley even more than the tyranny of the state, the university, and the church. He was still the egotistic spirit which could yield only to the discipline of time.

## IN LONDON

Early in the summer of 1811 Shelley and Hogg went to London. Timothy Shelley was withholding his son's allowance; but the needed shillings found their way from the father's hands, through devoted sisters, to the hands of the brother. At the school for girls outside London there lived, besides Shelley's sisters, also Harriet Westbrook, a girl of sixteen, whose father, now retired, had owned a thriving coffee-house; and she too, under Shelley's influence, now began to feel that she had been born to be free from the schoolgirl discipline which was tyranny to her. It was not love that attracted Shelley to her, but idealism. He resolved to oppose tyranny wherever he found it; to act on principle; to scorn expediency. He advised Harriet to resist. She did, and being undisciplined, and besides disliked by some of her former friends, called on Shelley for help. The young couple eloped to Edinburgh and there were married.

## SHOCKING EXPERIENCE

Events now began to take a disillusioning course for Shelley. He had come to Harriet's rescue out of principle, and then had married her out of chivalry; for, fundamentally, he believed the institution of marriage to be a form of tyranny. But now, scarcely married, he found that his friend Hogg had, in Shelley's absence, made love to his wife. Shelley forgave Hogg, but could not forget the shock of the experience. He moved with Harriet to the Lake Country, met Southey there, respected him for his character, but found him disappointingly conservative. He went to see his father, was received by him and offered an annual income of 2,000 pounds, but was shocked to know that Timothy Shelley would all but disinherit his wife and daughters in order, on required conditions, to bestow primogeniture on him. He travelled to Ireland to give himself to the cause of Catholic Emancipation, wrote there, in 1812, his *Address to the Irish People,* and was disappointed that he was not even persecuted. His gospel of brotherly love and universal tolerance was being ignored; and that, till now, was to Shelley an untasted bitter medicine.

## DISILLUSIONMENT

To fill the measure of his disappointment there was added the disillusioning association with Elizabeth Hitchener whom Shelley had met in Wales, who was then 29 when he was 19, and who further stirred his enthusiasm for his necessitarian ideas. Mature and cleverly intelligent, she seemed to Shelley the "image of intellectual beauty." She came—armed with her own designs—to live with Harriet and Shelley as "the sister of his soul." But between July and December of 1812 he sadly and wisely discovered her to be, as he later said, a "Brown Demon." The spirit of Necessity was indeed driving him into a wilderness. The supposed principle of order was betraying him into more and more confusion—something for which he paid dearly, taking from him his will to stand up against hard circumstance, and causing him to fall too easily into acquiescence of his fate, as we see, for example, in these later lines from *Stanzas, Written in Dejection, near Naples:*

> I could lie down like a tired child,
> And weep away the life of care
> Which I have borne and yet must bear,
> Till death like sleep might steal on me,
> And I might feel in the warm air
> My cheek grow cold, and hear the sea
> Breathe o'er my dying brain its last monotony.

## TIME OF GRIEF

Among things now sadly disappointing to Shelley was his relationship with Harriet. Of open or hidden hostility in the mind of Shelley there was never the barest sign. He may have been unintentionally cruel; but he was by nature incapable of hating anyone. But there was in him the deep hunger to be understood, and the desire for intellectual companionship; and Harriet could not satisfy them. Marriage, to Shelley, to be meaningful, needed to be a richly spiritual companionship, amounting to an affinity of souls between two mutually endearing persons. Harriet's willingness, at first, to help and encourage him was comforting. But what she could give was not enough; his talents found no continuing stimulus in her presence. This state of things was for Shelley the deep tragedy of the world; its sensations—on which Locke had taught him to depend—did not fulfill the dreams of his ideal of perfection. He sought but could not find in it any lasting joy or peace. Like a bird at sea he must follow every passing ship till it vanished out of sight, leaving him forlorn and disconsolate. The truth is that desire and restraint in him were never evenly balanced. He did not know, as Keats knew, how to look on the world as "a vale of soul-making," to see its bare use to man and so to be reconciled to it. To Shelley, from first to last, the world was but a fit theme for a poet's lament. It was such to him when he wrote, bidding it adieu, in the poem *A Dirge:*

> Rough wind, that moanest loud
> Grief too sad for song;
> Wild wind, when sullen cloud
> Knells all the night long;
> Sad storm, whose tears are vain,
> Bare woods, whose branches strain,
> Deep caves and dreary main,—
> Wail, for the world's wrong!

## THE DUAL SHELLEY

This poem written near the end of Shelley's life reflects a maturity beyond his earlier formative years, ending in 1814. But we note that even during this revolutionary time for him the poet's thought began to undergo a change, gradually bringing together the two Shelleys as we now recognize them in his poetry: the one, the philanthropic prophet of *Prometheus*

*Unbound;* the other, the melancholic individualistic soul of the lines,

> When the lamp is shattered,
> The light in the dust lies dead;
> When the cloud is scattered,
> The rainbow's glory is shed.

Sometimes, as Professor Oliver Elton tells us, these two moods in the poet "clash and fall into confusion," as in *Laon and Cythna;* now and then they "coalesce in a wonderful harmony," as in the *Lines Written Among the Euganean Hills* through whose lyrical couplets runs the repeated refrain,

> Other flowering isles must be
> In the sea of life and agony.

## THE GREAT CHANGE

Of the two Shelleys the revolutionary idealist, with his passion to reform the world, appeared first; the lonely dreamer followed, born of bitter sorrow. Between these two "master-feelings" in the poet most of the poetry written by Shelley may be said to have its origin. The reformer, at first materialistic in his outlook, underwent a gradual change into a metaphysical idealist; and the dreamer, we observe, also changed in his solitary search for the complete Self, passing from disillusionment in *Alastor,* through a momentary ecstasy of fulfillment "under the roof of blue Ionian weather" in *Epipsychidion,* to the larger consummate vision of "sustaining Love" in *Adonais.* Of these stages, if they may be called such, we may now get a clearer picture by returning to the events of Shelley's life.

## QUEEN MAB

These early disappointments, personal and painful as they were to Shelley, contributed to his growth as a poet. Perhaps the great and unconscious desire in him was to be made perfect through suffering. More of it was to come. But there was by now enough of song in him to join together the unrest and the vision he experienced into the pattern of a poem. The first significant piece Shelley wrote was *Queen Mab*. It was published early in the year 1813. To anyone now reading it, the poem presents two aspects: the one is its lawlessness; the other, its idealism. To Shelley they formed one united conclusion: all institutions were the expressions of tyranny, and so the source of existing evil; and the source of evil, he held, was not in the soul, but in society. That was the early rationalistic conclusion to which Shelley came through an over-confidence in human nature, a reasoning from natural sensations, a belief in the doctrines of necessity and perfectibility, and an immature knowledge of the history and tradition of our culture. In a later day he was to be his own severest judge when he called *Queen Mab* "villainous trash". The poem was written while the poet was taking his first deep draught of the wine of freedom. It will temper our judgment of him to remember that Shelley's thought at this time was passionately humanitarian. Materialist that he still thought himself to be, he was counting on the Spirit of the universe to crush tyranny everywhere among men. We can imagine how at the age of twenty the doctrine of Necessity still possessed his mind, moving him to write:

> Spirit of Nature! all-sufficing Power,
> Necessity! thou mother of the world!
> Unlike the God of human error, thou
> Requirest no prayers or praises.

Six years later, humbled and wiser, he was to cry out in *The Indian Serenade:*

> Oh, lift me from the grass!
> I die! I faint! I fail!

## PERIOD OF TRANSITION

### A NEW WORLD

A turning point in Shelley's life came in 1814 when he met Mary Godwin. In her he found the love that was to him both a passion and an ideal. Mary, the gifted daughter of William Godwin, fell deeply in love with Shelley; and the two presently lived together in a world of transcendent ideas enriched by a strong and enduring affection. Godwin had invited Shelley to his house in London; Shelley had responded by praising him as the author of *Political Justice;* and Godwin had accepted the money that Shelley had found it possible to lend him. The Godwinian doctrines of reason, necessity and perfectibility had before then already taken deep root in the young poet. Mary, then seventeen, was attractive and intellectual. Godwin, aware of the effect of his own teaching, protested against the romance, and Harriet, when she came to realize the truth, reproached Shelley. But the thing was done; there was now no going back; and, in July 1814, Shelley and Mary eloped to the continent. In September they were back again, needing money.

### ALASTOR

In January, 1815, the death of Shelley's grandfather provided him with a legacy, and he now turned earnestly to poetry and the writing of *Alastor.* The poem owes its occasion to a summer excursion on the River Thames in the company of his friend Thomas Peacock. In composing it he indicated that for him the social utopia could wait while he "turned his eyes inward" in a poet's quest for an ideal love. Shelley gave the poem the subtitle "The Spirit of Solitude"; and he himself wrote a preface to it dated December 14, 1815, the essence of which is that the

**179**

external world does not satisfy the soul which seeks an image of itself in some Being it can love. The poem contains seven hundred and twenty lines of blank verse, and falls into five parts: (1) the poet's introduction; (2) Alastor's journeyings and searchings till the vision comes to him; (3) his following after the blissful vision; (4) his death; (5) the poet's conclusion. The poem is important mainly because it is a prelude to Shelley's later and greater works. It is as if he were entering the strange wilderness called life, nurtured by visions of earth's beauties, looking to find a meaning in them, and so were carried away enamored and moonstruck, but doomed to disillusionment; and then, as if he were left there standing on the brink of wonder, saying:

> O, for Medea's wondrous alchemy,
> Which, whereso'er it fell, made the earth gleam
> With bright flowers, and the wintry boughs exhale
> From vernal blooms fresh fragrance! . . .
> But thou art fled,
> Like some frail exhalation; which the dawn
> Robes in its golden beams,—ah! thou hast fled!
> The brave, the gentle, and the beautiful,
> The child of grace and genius.

The poet's wanderings, his love of nature, of solitude, even his yearning for an ideal mate and his desire to be united with her through death, are symbols of the ebb and flow of his thoughts —thoughts of evanescent beauty haunting and waylaying him, as if he felt in the air he breathed the fanning of angel's wings. For their descriptive value, and the poem's overtone of symbolism, we may select especially lines 369-492, in which Alastor's boat finds its way through a cavern into a deep canyon, after which it passes a whirlpool and at last enters a quiet stream leading into a beautiful valley where, even at midday,

> One darkest glen
> Sends from its woods of musk-rose, twined with jasmine,
> A soul-dissolving odor, to invite
> To some more lovely mystery. Through the dell,
> Silence and Twilight here, twin sisters, keep
> Their noon-day watch, and sail among the shades,
> Like vaporous shapes half-seen . . .
> Hither the Poet came . . . He heard
> The motion of the leaves, the grass that sprung
> Startled and glanced and trembled even to feel
> An unaccustomed presence, and the sound
> Of the sweet brook that from the secret springs
> Of that dark fountain rose.

## TRANSFORMATION

But Shelley was not long allowed to live in dreams. Reality, grim and stark, confronted him. It was in the year 1816. The Shelleys were then living in Switzerland. First, like an avalanche of ice, came the news of the suicide of Fanny Imlay, Mary's half-sister; then, in the autumn, as the leaves began to fall, the news that Harriet too had taken her life. It was as if the world were disintegrating before his eyes. There was more than a change of viewpoint in what Shelley now experienced. His mind, subdued by grief and by the majestic scenery which the Alps afforded, underwent a structural transformation. Something was dying in him, and something being born—as if his brain were a chrysalis in which a new dream was waiting until it could take wings. Influences traceable to several sources were at work in him. One of them was personal and active in the friendship of such men as Thomas Love Peacock and Leigh Hunt. Another was classical and represented in the Greek poets. Another was philosophical. It was at this time that Plato began to displace Hobbes and Hume, and that the idealism of Bishop

Berkeley was gathering strength against the materialism of Godwin.

## INTUITION

But most important, because nearest to him, was the influence of Wordsworth and of his ideas. Two of them were particularly important and formative in Shelley's mind: one was the elder poet's idea of intuition, or imagination; the other was his nature-taught doctrine of love. Wordsworth owed them both, indirectly to the neo-Platonists, more directly to Spinoza. Intuition, Spinoza declared, was a direct and divine way of knowing truth. It was a surer guide than the Aristotelian logic recommended by the Scholastics, or the principle of solving all problems by common sense, so over-praised by the English Deists who imitated Voltaire. By intuition, Shelley learned, man learns because he already knows. It was the old truth of paradox brought to light again; but in it now lay the greater truth that like begets like and that the soul of man has an affinity for God. To Shelley it was as though these months of 1816-1817 were acting as the agents of an alchemy in him, purifying through the solvent of bitter tears those thoughts which had from the beginning stirred in him as a rebel, a humanitarian, and a lover of beauty. Wordsworth's influence and the alchemizing effect of Platonism are reflected in the poem *Mont Blanc*, composed at this time. The law of nature indeed rules in it, solemnly and mightily. But there is a sublime mystery in the power that rules:

> The wilderness has a mysterious tongue . . .
> Power dwells apart in its tranquillity
> Remote, serene, and inaccessible.

After likening the dizzy ravine, on which he looks, to his own mind filled with a

> Legion of wild thoughts, whose wandering wings
> Now feast above thy darkness, and now rest
> In the still cave of the witch Poesy,—

the poet concludes with lines comparable to sections of Wordsworth's *Prelude* and Coleridge's majestic *Hymn Before Sunrise:*

> The secret strength of things
> Which governs thought, and to the infinite dome
> Of heaven is a law, inhabits thee!
> And what were thou, and earth, and stars, and sea,
> If to the human mind's imaginings
> Silence and solitude were vacancy?

## MARY SHELLEY

All this had taken place in Shelley's mind early in 1818 when
he left England, never to return. The year 1819, the *annus
mirabilis* for him, was yet to come. Meanwhile, distraught
though he was by recent domestic troubles involving the cus-
tody of Harriet's children, there was Italy, the land of romance,
repository of a rich culture, offering him congenial ground for
his deep-rooted passion for liberty and justice. Italy, too,
promised better health for Shelley who had suffered much, had
been all his life "as much sinned against as sinning", and was
now happily married to Mary Godwin whose devotion to the
poet had ripened into a gentle maturity and wisdom. How
greatly indebted Shelley was to her is shown in the poem *To
Mary*, in which he dedicated the completed poem *The Revolt
of Islam* to her with this initial stanza:

> So now my summer task is ended, Mary,
> And I return to thee, mine own heart's home;
> As to his Queen some victor Knight of Fairy,
> Earning bright spoils for her enchanted dome;

> Nor thou disdain, that ere my fame become
> A star among the stars of mortal night,
> If it indeed may cleave its natal gloom,
> Its doubtful promise thus I would unite
> With thy beloved name, thou child of love and light.

## LYRICAL DRAMA

In the years 1818 and 1819 Shelley completed *The Revolt of Islam* which the year before had been composed under the title *Laon and Cythna,* and then wrote *Prometheus Unbound.* The latter over-shadowed the former in lyrical genius, dramatic symbolism and power. Both works were on the theme of liberty, the universal, age-old hunger of man. In the *Revolt* the vision is still blurred: the golden age is seen in glimpses through dark clouds; the poet's passion and serenity are yet in conflict; good and evil divide the world between them, equally and with equal dominion, as the poet says:

> Two powers o'er mortal things dominion hold,
> Ruling the world with a divided lot,
> Immortal, all pervading, manifold,
> Twin Genii, equal Gods—when life and thought
> Sprang forth, they burst the womb of inessential
> Nought.

# GOLDEN YEARS OF POETRY

## UNDER ITALIAN SKIES

Shelley himself tells us that he wrote the lyrical drama *Prometheus Unbound* under "the bright blue sky of Rome". There, shut in by "the mountainous ruins of the Baths of Caracalla", alone with the past and his own thoughts, he felt himself visited by the spirits of the ocean, the earth, and the moon, and by the gods who were themselves ruled over by Demogorgon, the spirit of revolutionary justice. It seemed to Shelley that the stars that drenched the heavens with light were drenching his spirit, filling it with awful and beautiful objects, each representing some force in the cosmos and in him. He found himself in a universe, first, of physical force, then, of reason, and its opposite, unreason, and at last, of love, overcoming its opposite, relentless hate.

## HEROIC POETRY

The poem is magnificent. Its point of view is essentially Greek, placing man at the center of the world order, and the gods above and around him to test his sense of justice, to invoke him to passionate activity, and to stir in him those compulsive thoughts of rebellion, freedom, beauty and love that are deep and ineradicable in Shelley's mind. At the outer orbit of the poet's thought is Cronus, fabled god of the golden age, known also as Saturn, encircled by his rings of time, the symbol of physical and moral law. His executor of fate, which may be identified either with eighteenth century *reason*, or with the "ultimate omnipotence of Good", is Demogorgon. All things happen as he decrees. Prometheus is man or, more accurately, the mind of man chained and suffering until it can forgive and love. Jupiter symbolizes tyranny. Asia represents nature; Panthea, faith; Ione, love. Shelley desires Prometheus to be united with Asia: suffering man, rebellious and revolutionary, must be joined by love to Nature to be free. In this union with man Nature, too, will be transformed. Mother Earth will be regenerated, and life on our planet will again be fair in the glory of a new day. Until that day comes, Shelley's hero must speak through patient endurance, though held in chains. So, while the earth listens and the spirit of the hour, waiting propitiously,

**185**

holds time in check, and Panthea and Ione utter dithyrambs of apocalyptic prophecy, Demogorgon, the arbiter of all life in heaven and on earth, speaks the final word:

> To suffer woes which Hope thinks infinite;
> To forgive wrongs darker than death or night;
> To defy Power, which seems omnipotent;
> To love, and bear; to hope till Hope creates
> From its own wreck the thing it contemplates;
> Neither to change, nor falter, nor repent;—
> This, like thy glory, Titan, is to be
> Good, great and joyous, beautiful and free;
> This is alone Life, Joy, Empire, and Victory!

## ANALYSIS AND AIM

*Prometheus Unbound* is a long poem of four acts, presenting us with eleven separate scenes and a literary composition of 2610 lines. The speeches—for such they are—of the principal characters are in blank verse: that of Prometheus, beginning the drama with "Monarch of gods and daemons", suggesting the epic of Milton. The lyrics interspersed among the scenes are imageful and rhythmic, as, for example, these lines of Ione:

> My wings are folded o'er mine ears:
> My wings are crossèd o'er mine eyes.

And the choruses have in them the Aeschylean slow motion and mood shown, for instance, in Semichorus I of Act I, referring to Prometheus' suffering:

> Drops of bloody agony flow
> From his white and quivering brow.

Shelley himself declared that his purpose in writing the poem was,

"to familiarize the highly refined imagination of the more select classes of poetical readers with beautiful idealisms of moral excellence; aware that until the mind can love, and admire, and trust, and hope, and endure, reasoned principles of moral conduct are seeds cast upon the highway of life which the unconscious passenger tramples into dust."

## SUDDEN GRIEF

While living at Este among the Euganean Hills as Lord Byron's guest, Shelley wrote, besides the first act of *Prometheus Unbound* and the already mentioned *Lines on the Euganean Hills,* also the poem *Julian and Maddalo* which holds a special interest to us for its striking description of Byron's personality. Shortly afterward, on their return to Rome, the Shelleys were suddenly stricken with grief by the death of their seven-year-old son William. It was at this time that the poet laid plans for the writing of the tragedy *The Cenci,* and the family presently moved to Leghorn where the poem was completed.

## REALISTIC TRAGEDY

Conceived in a Shakespearean mood, *The Cenci: A Tragedy* moves directly to its goal. It is to place the higher law of the mind above external circumstances in the character of Beatrice in whom, as Shelley desired it, "energy and gentleness dwell together without destroying one another". The dramatic action takes place in an atmosphere surcharged with "restlessness and anatomizing casuistry." The story is that of an old debauchee whose murder is plotted by the gentle Beatrice for his incestuous crimes. The poetry in the play, without being strongly lyrical, is lucid and revealing, as for example in these words spoken by Beatrice after she has avenged herself and been sentenced to death:

> The deed is done,
> And what may follow now regards not me.
> I am as universal as the light;

> Free as the earth-surrounding air; as firm
> As the world's centre. Consequence, to me
> Is as the wind which strikes the solid rock
> But shakes it not.

## ATTEMPT AT PARODY

From this mood of tragedy and his reading of Sophocles and Shakespeare, Shelley turned to write the playful *Peter Bell the Third,* a parody in ballad form directed—perhaps through Byron's influence in composing *Don Juan*—at Wordsworth. In good-natured jest and intending, as Mary Shelley said, no personal reflection on Wordsworth whom he admired and read continually, Shelley identifies the great poet with his own Peter Bell and, remembering at the same time the immortal *Tintern Abbey,* writes this verse:

> At night he oft would start and wake
>      Like a lover, and began
> In a wild measure songs to make
> On moor, and glen, and rocky lake,
>      And on the heart of man.

## THE GREAT ODE

But this poetry was not like Shelley. It was but a diversion for the poet and a relief from the overstrain of his intense emotions. The actual Shelley returned with the writing of his shorter and much more famous poem, the *Ode to the West Wind.* In it his spirit rose, as if with the sudden flight of an arrow, above the fog and noise of this transitory world to that region which was to him the symbol of reality. The air, the cloud, rain and lightning, and the deep mysterious sea—in these he discovered his own identity. In them he lived his cherished

life of freedom, communing with nature's counterparts, the
spirits of the universe, and dreamed his intense dream of self-
dedication in imploring words like these:

> Drive my dead thoughts over the universe
> Like withered leaves to quicken a new birth!
> And, by the incantation of this verse,
> Scatter, as from an unextinguished hearth
> Ashes and sparks, my words among mankind!
> Be through my lips to unawakened earth
> The trumpet of a prophecy! O, wind,
> If Winter comes, can Spring be far behind?

**LIBERTY**

This ode, written in *terza rima*, is typical of Shelley's maturest poetry. It illustrates the perfect blending of lyricism and
idealism by which the poet is best known. At about this time
Shelley also wrote a prose essay entitled *A Philosophical View
of Reform* in which he criticized Europe's system of government, deplored violence and counselled human sympathy and
moderation. He commended the extension of political liberty
to the citizenry after the pattern of a modern democracy, show-
ing thereby that his utopian dreams were not confined to the
airy regions of pure thought. And he further substantiated his
capacity to do practical thinking in the poem *Mask of Anarchy,*
written in 1819, on the occasion of the massacre at Manchester.
In it the poetry vibrates with piston strokes of passion and
satire as he calls on the people of England to

> "Rise like lions after slumber
> In unvanquishable number!
> Shake your chains to earth, like dew
> Which in sleep had fallen on you—
> Ye are many, they are few!"

# PERCY BYSSHE SHELLEY

## PATRIOTISM

Mrs. Shelley, writing twenty years later, said that the "Peter-loo Massacre", as it was called, roused in Shelley "violent emotions of indignation and compassion"; and Shelley himself declared that in such an hour as that it was a hard but great thing "to hold the balance between popular impatience and tyrannical obstinacy; to inculcate with fervor both the right of resistance and the duty of forbearance". That he succeeded is a tribute to him. His passion for freedom was matched by his love for England. This strong feeling toward his own English people was equal to his theoretical concern with political and economic principles, as is again shown in the now famous *Song to the Men of England* which comes to this climax:

> The seed ye sow, another reaps;
> The wealth ye find, another keeps;
> The robes ye weave, another wears;
> The arms ye forge, another bears.
>
> Sow seed,—but let not tyrant reap;
> Find wealth,—let not imposter heap;
> Weave robes,—let not the idle wear;
> Forge arms,—in your defense to bear.

## AT PISA

The year 1819 ended in comparative happiness for Shelley and Mary with the birth of their son, Percy Florence Shelley. Early in 1820 the family took up residence at Pisa where the poet found a small colony of acquaintances near at hand. Here he was visited by Lord Byron, learned to know the Williamses and talked often with Captains Medwin and Trelawney. Here also, later in the year, he wrote, among other poems, *The Witch of Atlas*, the *Ode to Liberty*, and the felicitous *Letter to Maria Gisborne* in which he indicated his longing for the society of his friends and fellow poets in England. And, as the winter approached, he composed *The Sensitive Plant,* a delicately inwrought poem dedicated to the beauty of the garden and the lady who tended it. The lady dies and the flowers wither, leaving the garden an unsightly place; and the Sensitive Plant— symbol of the poet's spirit dying for want of love—weeps, folding its tears within its closing leaves, so that,

> When Winter had gone and Spring came back,
> The Sensitive Plant was a leafless wreck;
> But the mandrakes, and toadstools, and
> > docks, and darnels,
> Rose like the dead from their ruined charnels.

## THE CLOUD

The level to which Shelley felt himself exalted during the summer of 1820 is suggested to us in two particularly happy and popular poems, *The Cloud* and *To A Skylark.* It seemed to him at times that the heavens had drenched his spirit and were dissolving his past years of hardship into pure laughter. He looked upon the world with a new exhilaration, with a sense of joy bursting upon him in an amazing and sudden freshness in which he perceived his thoughts unfolding before him as sweet buds after the rain. Four times, in *The Cloud,* Shelley lets his verse break forth into laughter: once, in the cloud's voice of thunder; then again, in the stars' vast whirl and flight, "like a swarm of golden bees"; for a third time, in the moist earth's grateful answer to the rain; and at last, in the serene heavenliness of the blue sky that owes its existence to the storm. The poem's theme seems to be expressed in these words:

> I am the daughter of Earth and Water,
> > And the nursling of the Sky;
> I pass through the pores of the ocean and shores;
> > I change, but I cannot die.

## TO A SKYLARK

This same spirit of joy is expressed in *To A Skylark;* only here it rises to the height of a mystical experience. It is the hidden reality behind all phenomena in nature that the poet invites us to see. Shelley gives this reality the wings of song; and from it, as from an eternal source, come perfect love and happiness, untouched by pain or death. It is in such poetry as this that we see Shelley translating his own spiritual vision into enduring art. Perhaps—by their contrast to the skylark's song—the lines of the poem most remembered are these:

> We look before and after,
>     And pine for what is not:
> Our sincerest laughter,
>     With some pain is fraught;
> Our sweetest songs are those that tell of saddest thought.

## POETRY DEFINED

The poet himself wrote of this exalted state of the imagination in his critical essay, the *Defense of Poetry.* In it he declared that

"poetry lifts the veil from the hidden beauty of the world, and makes familiar objects be as if they were not familiar; it reproduces all that it represents; and the impersonations clothed in its Elysian light stand thenceforward, in the minds of those who once contemplated them, as memorials of that gentle and exalted content which extends itself over all thoughts and actions with which it coexists."

By his lofty view of the poet and of his mission Shelley places him in a position to see, in one revelatory moment, both the present intensely and the future in the present. In this position he becomes both the historian and the prophet of his age. "Poets," Shelley concludes, "are the unacknowledged legislators of the world." Without them, and that translated picture of the world which we see written in their eyes, our weaker spirits languish and sink into lassitude, and the actualities of life gradually assume a pattern of incoherence and, at last, of chaos. Through poetry we are compelled "to see that which we perceive, and to imagine that which we know", and so to live creatively and divinely, as Shelley intends to have us understand him when he quotes Tasso who said: "No one deserves the name of creator except God and the poet."

## THE NEW AGE

Mention should here be made of *Hellas*, Shelley's political drama, notable for its hope for Greek freedom. It is valuable to us chiefly for its group of songs that express, more concretely than those in *Prometheus Unbound*, the quickening pulse of the poet who was ever in love with the voice that signalized the doom of tyrants and heralded the day of which he wrote in the the poem's concluding chorus:

> The world's great age begins anew
> The golden years return,
> The earth doth like a snake renew
> Her winter weeds outworn;
> Heaven smiles, and faiths and empires gleam,
> Like wrecks of a dissolving dream.

## VISION OF LOVE

In the same year 1821, in which Shelley published the *Defense of Poetry*, he wrote the two remarkable poems *Epipsychidion* and *Adonais*. Both were written in Pisa, the one in January, the other in June. *Epipsychidion* is an intimate poem, having, so to speak, two natures: the one, its body; the other, its soul. In the garb of the first, Emilia Viviani to whom the poem is dedicated appears as a lovely woman, an earthly being, the actual incarnation of visible beauty; in the guise of the second, "Emily" is a vision of pure loveliness, white as the moon, golden as the sun, an object of "intellectual" love, a symbol of heavenly beauty, and an expression of the ideal world which the soul builds for itself in the realm of the infinite. Between the two axes which we may call the intimacy and the infinity of the poem there is a realm open to critical speculation. Is the poem the story of Shelley's experience in love? Probably the best answer to the question is found in the poet's own concluding statement that "love's . . . reward is in the world divine which . . . it builds beyond the grave"; and in the comment which he made less than a year later: "The poem should not be considered my own . . . It is a production of a portion of me already dead . . . and to be published simply for the esoteric few." The ideas in the poem are related to those in Alastor, and are important to the student of Shelley because they reflect his debt to Plato's *Symposium*. However a distinction is here appropriate. While Plato is concerned with the *idea* of beauty, Shelley is in pursuit of *ideal* beauty as represented in a human being he can love. Plato, a philosopher, remains serene in the contemplation of beauty's essence; Shelley is disillusioned in love's experience. In the poem *Epipsychidion* Emilia is called "this soul out of my soul"; by June 1822, in a letter to a friend, Shelley says: "the *Epipsychidion* I cannot look at; the person whom it celebrates was a cloud instead of a Juno."

## TO JOHN KEATS

In *Adonais* Shelley turned to the pastoral elegy. The poem was written in the month of June, in 1821, in memory of the poet Keats who had died in Rome in February. Throughout its fifty-five Spenserian stanzas it gives evidence of Shelley's literary genius. The thought and the art in it are of one piece: poetry and philosophy are joined together in a supreme achievement. In its theme and structural progress the poem focuses the reader's attention, first on the earth darkened with grief, then on the poet as a "Spirit beautiful and swift—a Love in desolation masked—a Power girt round with weakness," and at last on "that Light whose smile kindles the Universe," and forever shines while earth's shadows fly. Keat's pathetic illness, his too little appreciated genius, his untimely death, and Shelley's own thoughts of himself—a year and a month before his own death—gave that occasion to the poem of which, while composing it at Pisa, he wrote: "I have dipped my pen in consuming fire for his destroyers"—referring to the critics and reviewers of Keat's poetry.

## CRUEL CRITICS

Two spirits are driving actively in Shelley as he writes *Adonais:* the one, the fierce active spirit of the avenger of injustice; the other, the contemplative spirit of the poet brooding on the truth of eternal beauty and on the bold reality of death. Keats had been cruelly attacked by obtuse critics, expressly by J. W. Croker in the April, 1818 issue of the *Quarterly Review;* and, being ill, the young poet was believed to have been fatally hurt by this criticism. If ordinary social injustice always deeply stirred Shelley, it is easy to imagine how his spirit was outraged at what he felt Keats suffered. The myth of Adonis loved by Venus and warned by her to keep clear, in the hunt, of the rending tusk of the wild boar, gave Shelley the symbolism he needed to carry the charging weight of his thought. The beloved Adonis had been too noble to be timid, and so was slain. For a moment Shelley dwells on the thought, himself half in love with death, and says of Keats:

> Now thou art dead, as if it were a part
> Of thee, my Adonais! I would give

> All that I am to be as thou now art!
> But I am chained to Time, and cannot thence depart!

But Adonais is not dead; nor is he simply and at last asleep; rather, he has "awakened from the dream of life." By such an awakening, Shelley concludes, is the grief of those who mourn the loss of lovely things turned into the exaltation of the soul.

## THE POEM'S STRUCTURE

Outwardly the poem, like Milton's *Lycidas,* has the somewhat artificial structure of the English elegy. It follows the classical pattern of these steps: an invocation to the heavenly Spirit; an appeal to pitying nature; the scene of earthly mourners; the poet's personal digression; the climax of his sorrow; his change of mood; and the closing exultation. But within this framework Shelley builds, stanza by stanza, his "dome of many-colored glass," until at last the whole poem stands there all lofty and luminous before the reader. Then, as the piercing light of the poet's vision falls on it, this outward structure seems to melt away, exposing to our view the "white radiance" of Shelley's thought. At that moment we are aware that poetry is life: the poet has built as high as human hands can build; as for the rest, he must await death to reveal it. The poet Keats, he declares, is now among those to whom this revelation has come. He is, at last, one with

> that sustaining Love
> Which through the web of being blindly wove
> By man and beast and earth and air and sea,
> Burns bright or dim, as each are mirrors of
> The fire for which all thirst.

In *Epipsychidion* Shelley had lingered dreamily under "the blue roof of Ionian weather," yielding to the ecstasy of an ideal love. In *Adonais,* now completely drawn out of himself, beyond nature and all earthly things, he concludes the poem, and says:

> My spirit's bark is driven
> Far from the shore . . .
> I am borne darkly, fearfully, afar;
> Whilst, burning through the inmost veil
> of Heaven,
> The soul of Adonais, like a star,
> Beacons from the abode where the Eternal
> are.

## FULFILMENT

If this was the poet's foreboding of his death, it was actually soon to come true. For in the next year, on July 8, 1822, he set sail in his yacht, the *Ariel,* on the Mediterranean and was drowned. On the tenth day the sea gave up his body to the beach; and a month later Trelawney, Hunt, and Byron made a funeral pyre of it on the sand and carried the ashes to Rome. Nothing could have served as a more fitting close of Shelley's life than his death by drowning and the cremation of his body on the shore of the Mediterranean: nothing more Grecian than this absolute dissolution of every corporeal element in him and its return to those primary essences of water and fire from which Thales and Heraclitus believed all life to have originated. To see his life so ended was in fact a prescient gift in him; and his death, therefore, was the perfect symbol of his life, a living through dying, or a kind of apotheosis, or manifestation, of the doctrine of eternal recurrence which lay behind his ethereal conception of man's life in an eternal universe. We note again the almost triumphant manner in which, in the climactic stanza 52 of *Adonais,* he says:

> Life, like a dome of many-coloured glass,
> Stains the white radiance of Eternity,

> Until Death tramples it to fragments.—Die,
> If thou wouldst be with that which thou dost seek!
> Follow where all is fled!

## SUMMARY

In our final appraisal of the poetry of Shelley, we find our attention drawn to three obvious traits in it. The first is his comprehension of abstract beauty, the power to view it transcendentally, and to see it as one with goodness and truth. The second is his ability to give this conception magnificent embodiment in pure lyrical poetry, in the creation of objects of his exquisite fancy and in visions of superterrestrial life. The third is his all-embracing interest in humanity, his recognition of moral good and evil, of man's supreme worth, of the need of reason to control passion, of the still greater need of intuition to discover and exalt the soul, and finally of the power of love to effect the regeneration of mankind and to open the way to a more universal freedom and happiness in the world.

## CRITICISM

Perhaps it was a fault in Shelley to allow himself to be so fully pre-occupied with abstract truth and ideal humanity. For, judged by this ideal, the world, man, and life itself stood not only condemned but in hopeless contrast to the chief direction of his thought. It has been said that he had great faith in ideal love but little faith in actual man. What he saw of men's behavior caused him to turn from them in contempt rather than to them in pity. He was, in last analysis, an aristocratic humanist and not a Christian humanitarian. The concept of Christian redemption for sinful man was foreign if not abhorrent to him. As a result he found life too much even for his conscientious spirit to bear and looked to an escape from it as the end of his striving. Neo-Platonism and not the Bible was his guide to man's deliverance.

## CONCLUSION

In reading Shelley, therefore, we must not try to discover what is not there. Rather we should content ourselves with his high devotion to those "beautiful idealisms of moral excellence" in which his poetry so richly abounds. If we go to him in order to find and treasure them, we shall study Shelley with never-ending pleasure and profit.

# John Keats

*1795-1821*

## TIME OF PREPARATION

*1795-1816*

## FIRST CREATIVE PERIOD

*1816-1817*

## YEAR OF TRIAL AND VICTORY

*1818*

## THE MIRACULOUS YEAR

*1819*

## REMAINING DAYS

*1820-1821*

# TIME OF PREPARATION

## HIS POETRY

The name of Keats has a winsome sound to one who reads good poetry. Like Mozart's name in music, it recalls pleasing sensations, behind which lie the imaged forms of pure truth and beauty, and beyond which one gets some glimpses of the poet's "realms of gold." Keats' life was short. The body of his writings is not massive; but it has a significance as recognizable as sunlight, and as penetrating. His poems have the strength of character, the solidity and the texture of chiseled marble. One concludes, after reading one of his odes or sonnets, that the poet took seriously his own advice to Shelley to "fill every rift with ore." Then presently, on learning more of Keats, one is astonished at the willful genius of the young man who forsook a career in surgery for poetry and, in five short years, fulfilled the promise of the early lines he wrote on being introduced to George Chapman's translation of Homer:

> Then felt I like some watcher of the skies
> When a new planet swims into his ken;
> Or like stout Cortez when with eagle eyes
> He star'd at the Pacific—and all his men
> Look'd at each other with a wild surmise—
> Silent, upon a peak in Darien.

## FAMILY BACKGROUND

John Keats was born in 1795, in London. His birthplace was the upper room of a livery stable of which his father was the manager. His mother, Frances Jennings, was the livery owner's daughter, given to Thomas Keats in marriage for his faithfulness and ability in the business. She was as sensitive as her husband was steadfast. There were in the Keats family, besides John who was the eldest, two brothers, George and Tom, and a sister Frances. Another child, Edward, died in early infancy. The Keats ancestry went back either to Devon or Cornwall; that of the Jennings to Wales. Some students of the poet have, for this reason, found in him more evidence of Celtic traits than of English.

## EARLY EDUCATION

The elder Keats had an ambition for his children's education. John, with George, was sent to the preparatory school at Enfield, ten miles out of London. It was a good school, and John was happy there. But it was, at first, not his studies that made him so, but the friendships he made through his generosity and his love of fighting. He was a small, sturdy, sensitive boy, fond of laughter, often in tears with intense passion, tenacious, quick to feel an offense and quick to right one. But, almost suddenly, near the close of the Enfield period when he was fifteen, Keats became engrossed in reading. Poetry, especially, became his consuming interest. The cause of the change lay partly in his adolescence, but more particularly in the death of his mother, which occurred in 1810, and in the close friendship he had formed with Charles Cowden Clarke, the son of Enfield's head-master. For one year the school's library entirely claimed him; books were his world. He read the *Aeneid*, made a translation of it, and delved into books of history and travel and fiction. He became acquainted with Leigh Hunt's magazine, the *Examiner*—later he was to meet the "mighty man" himself, to revere him, and to be influenced by him beyond the power of a full recovery. But it was the library's books of ancient mythology that he read most avidly and learned by heart. Their effect on him was like magic and pervaded his thought during every free creative year that followed. He began to feel the insatiate thirst for poetry, of which he later wrote in a letter to his friend John Reynolds:

"I find I cannot exist without Poetry—without eternal Poetry—half the day will not do—the whole of it—I began with a little, but habit has made me a Leviathan."

## CAREER OUTLINED

Then came the change in the career of young Keats. Before the year ended, the year 1810, his guardian, Mr. Abbey, decided that Keats should study medicine, and apprenticed him to Dr. Hammond, a surgeon at Edmonton, for a term of five years. The periods of Keats' life, as we see them from this point of time, are here clearly outlined for us: (1) the first eight years of his childhood in London; (2) the next eight years in the preparatory school at Enfield; (3) the five years, from 1811 to 1816, of apprenticeship to surgery at Edmonton; and (4) the five remaining years of his life given entirely, and in self-dedication, to poetry.

## INFLUENCE OF SPENCER

The five years of training in surgery were, in reality, not wasted. If the duties were irksome, they were not slavish, and Keats found time for literature. During three of the five years he was not far away from Enfield, and his visits there were frequent. One of them, when Keats was seventeen, proved to be an epochal event. It was the day when with his friend Cowden Clarke he first read the poet Spenser. They sat down together in an arbor while Clarke read the *Epithalamion,* the wedding hymn with its final refrain in which "all the woods make answer and their echoes ring". It was evident that Keats was moved. After that he was as one enamored of poetry and dedicated to it. His first stanzas were written in imitation of Spenser. His effort at mastering the Spenserian measure, while at the same moment paying respect to Shakespeare and Virgil, is nobly shown in these lines written when Keats was not yet eighteen:

> Ah! could I tell the wonders of an isle
> That in that fairest lake had placèd been,
> I could e'en Dido of her grief beguile;
> Or rob from aged Lear his bitter teen:
> For sure so fair a place was never seen,
> Of all that ever charmed romantic eye:
> It seem'd an emerald in the silver sheen
> Of the bright waters; or, as when on high,
> Through clouds of fleecy white, laughs the coerulean sky.

Meanwhile he read the Spenserian poets, among them chiefly Fletcher and Browne and the young Milton. Besides them, he read and admired also Burns and Wordsworth. Among his friends, it was said, he had the gift of making apt and cheerful rhymes. His apothecary training and his surgery were not neglected. But literature was gradually and inevitably claiming him.

## TRIBUTE TO HUNT

It was during this time that Hunt was imprisoned for being so outspoken in his *Examiner* as to call the Prince Regent "a fat Adonis of forty". Keats was stirred by this act of liberal political leadership and, on Hunt's release, wrote one of his first sonnets containing the worshipful lines:

In Spenser's halls he stray'd and bowers fair,
Culling enchanted flowers; and he flew
With daring Milton through the fields of air:
To regions of his own genius true
Took happy flights.

The poetry was not yet significant. Nor was the tribute to Hunt final and just. But the note on Milton and Spenser was vibrant and sound; and already the suspended cadence of his verse—the so-called enjambment or overflow—and its air of enchantment, appeared as noticeable traits.

## FAREWELL TO SURGERY

But the sonnet was written in 1816, and at the end of the five-year period of his training for surgery. Of the slow-passing months till then we know, mainly, that he was not lax in taking careful notes of the lectures on anatomy; that he read incessantly and often out loud with Cowden Clarke; and that, in 1814, after a sharp disagreement with Dr. Hammond, he resigned the apprenticeship and went to live in London. By 1816 he had made the acquaintance of the artist Haydon, the poet Shelley, and the essayists Hazlitt and Lamb. But more important than all these was his literary acquaintance with the ancient poet Homer through the Elizabethan translation of George Chapman. After that event, which we learn occurred in October, 1816, he made his peace with the men in authority at Apothecaries' Hall and gave himself to poetry. Of his last surgical operation, performed when he was twenty-one, he later wrote to his friend, Charles Brown: "I did it with the utmost nicety, but reflecting on what passed through my mind at the time, my dexterity seemed a miracle, and I never took up the lancet again."

# FIRST CREATIVE PERIOD

## READING SHAKESPEARE

It is difficult to say to whom Keats owed most, whether to the great literary masters he systematically studied, or to himself and his own persistent self-discipline, or to his faithful friends. It is certain that he began his career as a poet wisely by making the best use of these resources. Among writers he chose the master of them all, Shakespeare, whom he studied not to imitate but to be taught what it was to be a poet. And since to Keats, from the very start, poetry was life, the poet was regarded by him as the entire man, with all his sensations and thoughts intact, a man immersed in imagination, delighting in life, apprehending the meaning of pain and sorrow, thirsting for beauty, excited in its presence as in the presence of a lovely and passionate woman, and haunted by the mystery of the world and of his own being. It was from this consciousness that Keats wrote: "I never quite despair, and I read Shakespeare." In March, 1816, in a mood of such continuous selective reading he composed this section of a sonnet:

> How many bards gild the lapses of time!
> A few of them have ever been the food
> Of my delighted fancy,—I could brood
> Over their beauties, earthly, or sublime:
> And often, when I sit me down to rhyme,
> These will in throngs before my mind intrude:
> But no confusion, no disturbance rude
> Do they occasion; 'tis a pleasing chime.

## HELPFUL FRIENDS

Next to Shakespeare Keats read Milton, and his own now famous contemporary, Wordsworth. Among his friends, five were immediately helpful. Shelley found a publisher for the

*Poems* of 1817. Hunt praised the little volume in his *Examiner.* The artists Haydon and Severn introduced him to the Elgin Marbles brought from Athens by Lord Elgin to the British Museum. And Benjamin Bailey, the young Oxford undergraduate, a lover of good books and an admirer of Wordsworth, gave to Keats his warm affection and friendship. As for himself, Keats decided that he must work incessantly, live by himself, read, write, and test the temper of his soul.

## POEMS

The volume of 1817 was not a public success. Its publishers, the brothers Ollier, regretted that their opinion of its talent had led them to print it; and they had, besides, been insulted by some customer's remark that the book was "no better than a take in." And they passed the insult on to both John and George Keats. But the volume contained such poems as *Sleep and Poetry* and *Chapman's Homer,* and these were sufficient to encourage the poet's friends. Themselves good critics, they saw in him signs of immaturity, even of crudity; but the freshness was there, the exhilaration and charm, the sensitivity to experience, the rich and fine fancy; and these contained the promise of the future poet. Keats himself gives us the best glimpse of the vision and the struggle to make good this promise, in these lines:

> O Poesy! for thee I grasp my pen
> That am not yet a glorious denizen
> Of thy wide heaven . . . If I can bear
> The o'erwhelming sweets, 'twill bring to me
> the fair
> Vision of all places: a bowery nook
> Will be elysium . . .
> O for ten years, that I may overwhelm
> Myself in poesy; so I may do the deed
> That my own soul has to itself decreed.

The poem was not the "flash of lightning that will rouse men from their occupations, and keep them trembling for the crash of thunder that will follow", that the over-robust Haydon declared it to be. But Haydon's advice to Keats was a good one. He prescribed solitude to the poet.

## TRAVEL

Accordingly, in April, 1817, Keats left London. He went, first, to the Isle of Wight, then to Margate; and, after that, to Canterbury, and, in the summer, back toward London and to Hampstead. He found the island reminiscent of King Lear, and the pounding of the sea was half poetry to him, and half misery. Margate, in May, was better; not new to him, but intimate and restful, releasing his spirit from an innate melancholy and preparing his mind for the task to which he had set himself. That task was the composition of the poem *Endymion*. In it he gave release to his passionate desire for intense esthetic experience and his soul's search for ideal beauty. The myth of Endymion, nightly visited by the beautiful Moon-Goddess, delighted the poet's fancy and fitted the theme. The poem was to be, first of all, a festival to Pan, a celebration of nature in its idyllic and passionate mood, a narrative of adventure, half of it earthy and luxuriant, the other half aerial and philosophical. It was to "surprise by a fine excess" and at the same time to be a trial of the poet's creative and assimilative imagination. It was, in short, to be both Gothic, or romantic, and classical, or Greek.

## ENDYMION

As it turned out, and very naturally, the poem's passion and dizzy bewilderment were not matched by an equal power of controlling structural imagination. The literary self-discipline

Keats needed and sought was sure in coming; but it came slowly. His passion for poetry was great, and he read even the Elizabethan poets with too much abandon to be easily tamed into servitude to them. That *Endymion* was full of the breath of poetry, everyone with sympathetic judgment knew. Nor did the poem lack the signs of that greater search for ideal beauty whose divine essence is the hidden reality of all this earthly show. Keats was aware of it even then, and it lured his fancy and awakened in him visions of the clear bright stars in the midst of his youthful and feverish sighing for a poetry that was akin to sleep, a pillowy rest in some "leafy luxury", an interval with "cups of old wine", a dream of love and of death. It was this early struggle between the poet's sensations and visions that caused him, close to the end of Book I in *Endymion* to write

> Wherein lies happiness? In that which becks
> Our ready minds to fellowship divine,
> A fellowship with essence; till we shine,
> Full alchemiz'd, and free of space.

We see in the poem that Keats was not content to rest his case in passionate nature. He sends Endymion in pursuit of the Moon-Goddess, symbol of the poet's quest for ideal beauty; but though the youth finds himself in earthly love with the Indian Maiden who says, "We are here! What wouldst thou ere we all are laid on bier?" Endymion answers, "Sister, I would have command, if it were heaven's will, on our sad fate." And the poem ends with Endymion's taking flight with fair Cynthia, leaving Peona alone wandering "home through the gloomy wood in wonderment." To us the bereft Peona's mood is real and a cause for pity. Earth's loves and fancies fade. But the poem endures. Its blemishes cannot destroy it; and the opening sixty-two lines contain the poet's creed and are his monument.

The first five demand to be quoted.

> A thing of beauty is a joy for ever:
> Its loveliness increases; it will never
> Pass into nothingness; but still will keep
> A bower quiet for us, and a sleep
> Full of sweet dreams, and health, and quiet breathing.

# YEAR OF TRIAL AND VICTORY

## TAKING ACCOUNT

With *Endymion* completed within the year, edited, and ready for publication, Keats rested his case with those who would, he knew, criticize it. Concerning his own view of the poem, he said: "It is as good as I had power to make it by myself". He resolved to be serene and ready and to trust his gifts. And he added: "I will write independently. I have written independently *without judgment*. I may write independently *with judgment* hereafter." As for the future he was determined, he said, to follow Solomon's advice to "get learning—get understanding."

## HARSH CRITICISM

But, more immediately and urgently, he felt that he must accept his friend Brown's invitation to take a summer's walking tour through Scotland. The two men started from London in June, 1818. The journey was, at first, exhilarating to Keats. But the weather was often rainy, and the daily walks were long, and, in August, he became ill, and was forced to return home alone. It was this illness that marked the beginning of the disease of tuberculosis that was later to lay its dreaded hand on him. Now scarcely settled at Hampstead, he was greeted by the harsh criticism of the reviewers. Both *Blackwood's* and the *Quarterly* appeared with attacks which accused him of belonging to Hunt's "Cockney School of Poetry"— of expressing "the most incongruous ideas in the most uncouth language"— and descended to the rude level of alluding to him as Johnny Keats, and saying: "so back to the shop, Mr. John, stick to plasters, pills, and ointment boxes." And, in full measure of insult, *Blackwood's* added: "But for heaven's sake, young Sangrado, be a little more sparing of soporifics"—inducing heavy sleep—"in your practice than you have been in your poetry". Bailey interceded for Keats in a conversation with Lockhart; but no one moved to retract the insult. Yet Keats, though naturally hurt, was not broken by these criticisms; and we find it unnecessary to assume with Shelley in the elegy *Adonais* that the stupid critics killed the young poet. On the contrary, he judged himself, ably and rightly, in these words: "I begin to get a little acquainted with my own strength and weakness . . . The attempt to crush me in the *Quarterly* has only brought me more into notice . . . I think I shall be among the English poets after my death."

## DARK DAYS

Meanwhile there were worries enough of consequence for Keats. First among them was his brother Tom's illness which weighed on him as the months passed by. In September, 1818, he wrote: "I am obliged to write and plunge myself into abstract images to ease myself of his countenance, his voice, and feebleness—so I live now in a continual fever." The facts revealed that Tom was dying of consumption, and his death followed in December. Besides now being himself undermined in health, Keats was lonely. His brother George had gone to live in America. At this time, against his wish, and contrary to his avowed philosophy about women, the poet fell in love with Fanny Brawne.

# JOHN KEATS

## MEN AND WOMEN

How bitter was the irony that was added to his passion may be seen from one of Keat's early letters in which he said, "When among men . . . I feel free to speak or be silent . . . When I am among women . . . I cannot speak or be silent; I am full of suspicion, and therefore listen to nothing; I am in a hurry to be gone." And he had expressed this attitude even earlier in verse, remembering a certain lady whom he had often passed while walking in Vauxhall Gardens, but to whom he had never spoken:

> Fill for me a brimming bowl
> And let me in it drown my Soul;
> But put therein some drug, designed
> To banish Women from my mind.

But he was even then at war with love; for he added,

> In vain! away I cannot chase
> The melting softness of that face.

## LOVE'S SWEET PAIN

And now that love had come to him in all its wonder and sweet pain, accompanied by a foreboding of his own fate, he began to feel that strange dividing and reuniting of thought of which in 1818, thinking perhaps of Fanny Brawne, he was compelled to write:

> And when I feel, fair creature of an hour,
>     That I shall never look upon thee more,
> Never have relish in the faery power
>     Of unreflecting love;—then on the shore
> Of the wide world I stand alone and think
>     Till love and fame to nothingness do sink.

How like Shakespeare in form and theme, and how like Milton in quiet grandeur, these lines are, is evident. This like-

ness indicates to us the startling growth toward maturity—
toward what Keats had called "understanding"—and toward
a mastery of his artist's technique, now so evident in his writing. He was even then "among the English poets" among whom
he knew his death would number him. How he felt the delight
of this fellowship with poets, living and dead, is hinted to us
in the buoyant *Lines on the Mermaid Tavern* in which he pictures himself tippling in the wine of poetry with comrades of
his art, and saying:

> Souls of Poets dead and gone,
> What Elysium have ye known,
> Happy field or mossy cavern,
> Choicer than the Mermaid Tavern?

## HEALING LABORS

It was indeed a fever in his brain, this passion contending
fiercely with his desire to get understanding and to write better
and enduring poetry—all this inner drive coming hard on
the heels of his enervating Scotland journey, the harsh criticism of his poetry, and his brother's death. As the year ended,
following "the black autumn" of 1818, he began to assuage in
him the passion for poetry, and the disturbing anguish of his
love for Fanny Brawne, by writing some of his best poems.
Among them were *The Eve of St. Agnes, Lamia, Isabella,* the
famous odes *On a Grecian Urn, To a Nightingale, To Autumn,*
and the two versions of *Hyperion.* These pieces, and others,
appeared together in Keats' third volume published in 1820.
The years, the two short years, between 1818 and 1820, were
Keats' greatest and best. Genius, the fire in his blood, the
hunger for knowledge, and the death-driving stress of time
worked mightily in him toward attaining the wisdom necessary to the creating of a work of art of lasting substance and
form. How these powers grew in him, together with his insight

into their use, is suggested to us in a letter of Keats written to John Reynolds in May, 1818. After alluding to Milton's comparative freedom from "anxiety for Humanity" and Wordsworth's martyrdom "to the human heart," and saying that we all come to wisdom through sorrow, he compares "human life to a large Mansion of Many apartments . . . The first we step into we call the infant or thoughtless Chamber . . . The second Chamber I shall call the Chamber of Maiden-Thought." In it, all is at first light and full of "pleasant wonders." But the very light helps one to see the many doors "all leading to dark passages," sharpening one's vision "into the heart and nature of Man," and into the world that is "full of Misery and Heartbreak." It was from these dark passages leading out of the "Chamber of Maiden-Thought" that the mind of Keats was now emerging.

# THE MIRACULOUS YEAR

## YEAR OF GRACE

Nothing concerning Keat's life demands now to be stressed except that he was becoming a true and mature poet. He wrote, he studied to perfect himself in his art and he lived in the ecstasy of his creative imagination. But in all this expenditure of vital energy he suffered the intense anguish of the sensitive brooding mind. Then, by the time the year ended, to fill the cup of suffering, the disease of tuberculosis was fastening itself on him with its sentence of an early death. The sentence indeed was not long delayed. Meanwhile the year 1819, the Miraculous Year, was a year of grace. It offered him an Indian Summer of joyous activity on the early *Hyperion*, the *Eve of St. Agnes*, and the *Odes*. Like a true "bard of passion and of mirth," "double-lived," he left one soul on earth, as he writes, and, led by his other soul, wandered off to commune with the music of the spheres, listening, through the day, to the trees' whisper, imagining himself on "Elysian lawns, Browsed by none but Dian's fawns"; and, as he continues, living

> Where the daises are rose-scented,
> And the rose herself has got
> Perfume which on earth is not;
> Where the nightingale doth sing
> Not a senseless, tranced thing,
> But divine melodious truth;
> Philosophic numbers smooth;
> Tales and golden histories
> Of heaven and its mysteries.

## ROMANCE

In the poem *St. Agnes's Eve* Keats not merely browsed in romance, but revelled in it. He allowed himself, with the mature poet's sure touch, to go where he wished his fancy to lead him. By means of the melody and grace of the Spenserian stanza he built an altar to beauty and loveliness in the midst of a grey cold house of stone, and peopled it with creatures of warmth and friendliness, with lovers, who, by their dream and daring, transformed the objects and effigies of cold stone into living and feeling things. By his poet's trusted hand, he leads Porphyro, the lover, to his sleeping bride and, in the thirtieth stanza, draws for us the picture on which we now can look forever with entrancing joy:

> And still she slept an azure-lidded sleep,
> In blanched linen, smooth, and lavender'd
> While he from forth the closet brought a heap
> Of candied apple, quince, and plum, and gourd;
> With jellies soother than the creamy curd,
> And lucent syrops, tinct with cinnamon;
> Manna and dates, in argosy transferr'd
> From Fez; and spiced dainties, every one,
> From silken Samarcand to cedar'd Lebanon.

# JOHN KEATS

## TEXTURE OF POETRY

One can see how Keats' spirit has distilled itself into the poem. Luxury and sensous passion are interfused with exquisite and delicate skill. The poem is inwrought with arabesque detail, suggesting Keats' own words when he called it "the embroidery of a dream." The medieval, the classical, and the Oriental are seen side by side in the figures of the pious beadsman, the carved angels, and the enchanted Madeline; and the entire poem is overshadowed by the spirit of romance and held together by the masterly use of the Spenserian stanza. The sensuous atmosphere of Boccaccio is perceivable in its imagery; but even more evident are the chaste sensibility of Spenser and the melodious felicity of the Elizabethan lyric. We see these characteristics intertwined, as if in lovers' embrace, in the oft-quoted lines:

> Full on this casement shone the wintry moon,
> And threw warm gules in Madeline's fair breast,
> As down she knelt for heaven's grace and boon;
> Rose-bloom fell on her hands, together pressed,
> And on her silver cross soft amethyst,
> And on her hair a glory, like a saint.

## THE POEM'S ARTISTRY

No one can read *The Eve of St. Agnes* carefully without noting that it is more than a winsomely sensuous poem. The poet's critical faculty is as evident in it as in the great *Odes*. It is at work in the controlled diction, the precise imagery and the faultless metrical structure beneath the colorful drapery. The mind of Keats is here seen wearing the garment of the outer world. The word in him is become flesh; and what it says is that at the birthplace of the natural world, as of a poem, there is unveiling beauty and warm love, and that these are a high reason for "argent revelry," for an invitation to a soul's feast. In Keats' mind, as he writes, is Fanny Brawne, and with her are Dante's Beatrice and Shakespeare's Romeo and Juliet. But in the fallen world, outside the castle walls, all is bitter cold—cold with age and ready for death. The wise owl sits there chilled in ruffled feathers, the naturally nimble hare limps "trembling through the frozen grass"; the obedient sheep, symbol of the faithful, wait through the night, silent, protected and together. The beadsman, symbol of Christian devotion, tells his rosary with "frosted breath" pitying, in a mood suggesting Dante in the *Purgatorio*, the "sculptur'd dead . . . Emprison'd in black, purgatorial rails," while the silver snarling trumpets proclaim the hour of the worldly lord's feast. The contrast is not merely the poet's artistic device; it expresses Keats' underlying conception of life.

## LOVE AND REASON

In the poem *Lamia*, written during the summer of 1819, Keats dealt with the age-old theme of happiness. The story in it was Greek; and the meaning which the poet attached to it was that it was better to live by love and illusion than by reason's intrusive scrutiny. Keats had obviously been reading Robert Burton's *Anatomy of Melancholy* — in a mood that was congenial also to his composition of the *Odes*—and he had found in it the ancient tale of Philostratus about the youth of Corinth who had fallen in love with a beautiful woman who, by her magical art, had built a palace of delight for him. But, as the story continues, the beautiful lady was a *lamia*, that is, a serpent in disguise. Recognized in this disguise by the youth's teacher, a philosopher who had come to the feast of the wedding, the serpent-woman—whose "furniture was no substance, but mere illusions" — suddenly vanished. So — in the poem — the spirit of critical science, the unwelcome

**217**

guest, intrudes on the feast of man's passions, his intellect is at war with his feelings, as we note in this familiar passage:

> Do not all charms fly
> At the mere touch of cold philosophy?
> There was an awful rainbow once in heaven;
> We know her woof, her texture; she is given
> In the dull catalogue of common things.
> Philosophy will clip an angel's wings,
> Conquer all mysteries by rule and line,
> Empty the haunted air and gnomed mine—
> Unweave a rainbow, as it erewhile made
> The tender-person'd Lamia melt into a shade.

## AFTER THE DREAM

It is the intensity of the poem that one feels most while reading *Lamia*, and remembers longest. Whether the thought of Keats was on the pain of loving a false and unworthy object, or on the rude awakening that comes after every beautiful dream, we are not quite sure. The effect is the same. It is the fact that life is cruel to every sensitive spirit. And Keats, by his use of the Dryden couplet in the poem, drives that piercing truth home to the reader's imagination and heart.

## SKILL IN COMPOSITION

Begun early in 1819, *Lamia* was composed in two parts between which, during the interval, Keats was hard at work on the dramatic composition of *Otho*, a character tragedy of Shakespearean proportions in scope, intensity, and imagery. He undertook *Lamia* with unusual vigor, writing resolutely and objectively, filling, according to his own counsel to Shelley, every rift with the ore which he took from the mines of Renaissance poetry, using with fine skill such telling compound words as *lute-fingered, vermilion-spotted, green-recessed, pur-*

*ple-lined, tress-lifting, silent-blessing,* each of which, as Charles
Lamb remarked, was "a poem in a word"; and he made, besides
this, such assimilative use of Christian and classical mythology,
clothing the story in such rich language of romance, as both
to excite the reader and soothe him in one moment—as when,
for example, he presses together the opposite ideas of beauty
and deformity, the symbols of good and evil, in this description
of Lamia:

> She was a gordian shape of dazzling hue,
> Vermilion-spotted, golden, green, and blue;
> Striped like a zebra, freckled like a pard,
> Eyed like a peacock, and all crimson barr'd; . . .
> She seem'd, at once, some penanced lady elf,
> Some demon's mistress, or the demon's self . . .
> Her head was serpent, but ah, bitter-sweet!
> She had a woman's mouth with all its pearls complete:
> And for her eyes: what could such eyes do there
> But weep, and weep, that they were born so fair?
> As Proserpine still weeps for her Sicilian air.
> Her throat was serpent, but the words she spake
> Came, as through bubbling honey, for Love's sake.

## TENDER TRAGEDY

In the poem *Isabella,* surnamed *The Pot of Basil,* written
in 1818, and so earlier than *Lamia,* Keats took a story from
the *Decameron* and wrote it over to please himself. In it the
terror of the medieval tale is turned to delicate and tender
pathos. Isabella, whose lover is slain by her brothers, secretly
bears away his head and places it in a pot of earth with fragrant
herbs, plants a sprig of sweet basil in the ground above it,
and waters it with her tears. The facts of the story are grim.
But the poet's hands, like those of the heroine, are gentle and
assuring. By its pure feeling and the felicity of its diction the

poem re-enacts before our eyes the scene of love's sweet and bitter sorrow in a world in which those nearest to us in blood may often give us greatest pain. At first unmolested, Isabella's suffering is assuaged by the tender passion with which she touches the basil springing green and fragrant from the earth.

> And so she ever fed it with thin tears,
>   Whence thick, and green, and beautiful it grew,
> So that it smelt more balmy than its peers
>   Of Basil-tufts in Florence; for it drew,
> Nature besides, and life, from human fears,
>   From the fast mouldering head there shut from view:
> So that the jewel safely casketed,
>   Came forth, and in perfumed leafits spread.

When, presently, the basil-pot is discovered by the cruel brothers and taken away, her grief knows no bounds,

> And so she pin'd, and so she died forlorn,
>   Imploring for her Basil to the last.
> No heart was there in Florence but did mourn
>   In pity of her love, so overcast.
> And a sad ditty of this story born
>   From mouth to mouth through all the country pass'd:
> Still is the burthen sung—"O cruelty,
>   "To steal my Basil-pot away from me!"

The poem was written in the Italian form known as the *ottava rima* consisting of stanzas of eight lines with a rhyme scheme of a b a b a b c c. Byron had used it the year before in writing *Beppo,* a mock-heroic story based on his knowledge of Venetian life. Keats worked so successfully with the "whip-crack" closing couplet of this stanza that it altogether lost its sting and quietly prolonged the strain of the stanza's intense action and passion.

## HYPERION

At this time — during the "black autumn" and bleak winter of 1818, and into the golden spring of 1819 — Keats was occupied with the writing of *Hyperion*. He had planned that it should be his great work, an epic poem of large design. Its subject was to be the overthrow of the Titans, the gods of brute force, and the establishment, in their stead, of the rule of Apollo, god of poetry and symbol of an age made wise through divine insight and sorrow and pity. The poem's theme was thus plainly Homeric. But its epic pattern and style were in imitation of Milton's *Paradise Lost*. It was the early *Hyperion* of which this was true; for there were two parts, or versions, of the poem: one bearing the sub-title *A Fragment,* the other the sub-title *A Vision.*

## THE POEM'S COMPOSITION

Scholars hold divergent views of the history and composition of *Hyperion*. The view generally held is that we have here two originally separate poems, both of them fragments. The first *Hyperion* is direct, of an even composition, and of one piece. Someone has called it the poet's purest artistic endeavor. The second *Hyperion,* by contrast, is held to be a work of poetic vision—the difference between them being the difference between the reaches of the unaided human imagination and a reliance on supernatural insight. In September 1819 Keats wrote, in a letter to Reynolds: "I have given up *Hyperion;* there are too many Miltonic inversions in it. Miltonic verse cannot be written but in an artful, or, rather, artist's humor. I wish to give myself up to other sensations." But a few months later, it appears, he was rearranging the composition of the poem to represent the growth of a poet's mind — its growth

JOHN KEATS

in two directions: in revealing, unveiling spiritual insight; and in a deeper understanding of human life. So viewed, the second *Hyperion* rises above the first, from a dream of idealized nature to a vision of the poet's soul. Keats himself — if we accept this distinction—lets us see into the difference between them. In *Hyperion: A Fragment,* for instance, he pictures the palace of Hyperion in the grand Greek manner,

> Bastioned with pyramids of glowing gold, . . .
> And all its curtains of Aurorian clouds
> Flushed angrily: while sometimes eagle's wings,
> Unseen before by Gods or wondering men,
> Darkened the place; and neighing steeds were heard,
> Not heard before by Gods or wondering men.

In *The Fall of Hyperion: A Vision* he lets us look at the poet himself, and not only at his tantalizing dream. Mnemosyne, or memory, gives place in the poem to Moneta, or future experience. Moneta chides the poet:

> Art thou not of the dreamer tribe?
> The poet and the dreamer are distinct,
> Diverse, sheer opposite, antipodes.
> The one pours out a balm upon the world,
> The other vexes it.

The poet in Keats is exhausted by the fever of his youthful dreams. He longs to escape from the unreality of a past grandeur, and from a sensual death. We read in Canto I, lines 20-110, that he has had visions. He has slumbered in the scented, trellised garden of sensuous delight, but has awakened out of his slumber to find "the fair trees gone," and "the mossy mound and arbor are no more." Presently, before him stands a temple, "an old sanctuary." It is the temple of knowledge. He remembers "none the like upon the earth": there his curious

222

eye may explore the wonders of science, philosophy and art.
Awe-inspired he looks at the "embossed roof, the silent massy
range of columns north and south—ending in mist of nothing."
At last his eyes light upon the altar in the temple's distant west;
it is the altar of self-knowledge and self-dedication, to be
approached by toilsome steps and "patient travail." And he
hears the Voice:

> If thou canst not ascend
> These steps, die on that marble where thou art.
> Thy flesh, near cousin to the common dust,
> Will parch for lack of nutriment.

It is plain that Keats is now more deeply influenced by Dante
than by Homer, and more directly moved by Wordsworth's
neo-Platonic thinking than by the style of Milton and the
theme of *Paradise Lost*. Accordingly the story of *Hyperion*
takes a new turn. Apollo ceases to be the revolutionary god
of the reformer and becomes the contemplative god of the
poet who with the aid of the goddess Memory is now able to
endure all things, even the death of all things beautiful, and
so attain self-knowledge and find peace. It is in this mood that
Apollo, looking into the face of silent Memory, reads there
Keats' maturest thoughts:

> Mute thou remainest—Mute! yet I can read
> A wondrous lesson in thy silent face:
> Knowledge enormous makes a God of me.
> Names, deeds, gray legends, dire events, rebellions,
> Majesties, sovran voices, agonies,
> Creations and destroyings, all at once
> Pour into the wide hollows of my brain,
> And deify me, as if some blithe wine
> Or bright elixir peerless I had drunk,
> And so become immortal.

## THE ODES

To the year 1819, the Wonderful Year of Keats' life, belong also the great *Odes*. Five of them are famous. A tender melancholy spirit overshadows them. They are composed with utmost classical restraint; yet within the poet's self-imposed limitations the thoughts in them move with exciting and strangely touching variations of beauty and strength. In the *Ode to Psyche* it is the young goddess' priest that the poet wishes to be. His poem is an altar built "To let the warm Love in." The story of Cupid and Psyche, as told by the ancient Apuleius, is before Keats. He remembers Cupid's love for Psyche and her long search for him, the jealousy of Venus, the great Jupiter's taking pity on the lovers and his gift of immorality to Psyche, the daughter of a king. The thought of the soul so touched by love and made immortal moves the poet to say:

> O latest born and loveliest vision far
> Of all Olympus' faded hierarchy!
> Fairer than Phoebe's sapphire-regioned star,
> Or Vesper, amorous glow-worm of the sky;

and we go with him as he enters the "wide quietness" of the woods to build the "rosy sanctuary" of this leisurely *Ode*.

## THREE GHOSTS

In the *Ode of Indolence* Keats lives momentarily in a world of shadows. Three figures pass with their faces turned toward him. They are the fair maid Love, pale-cheeked Ambition and his "demon Poesy." It is an English May in the year 1819 and the poet is in a wholly indolent mood; his hour of sleep has been "embroidered with dim dreams"; his soul, he says, has been "a lawn besprinkled o'er with flowers." He bids the three Ghosts adieu in language that is as languorous as sleep itself, in words that fade "Into the clouds, and nevermore return."

## SONG TO DEATH

The *Ode To a Nightingale* is weighted with the opulent imagery of such sets of double words as "light-winged Dryad," "deep-delved earth," "purple-stained mouth" and "leaden-eyed despairs." Double word sets like these are not found only in the Odes; the sonnets are replete with them. But their weight in the Odes is singularly compounded with intense, yet restrained emotion. One feels that language is here extended to the utmost, that "every rift is filled with ore"; yet even with so great a cargo the flight of the poet's fancy is not impeded, as we note in the fourth stanza of this Ode:

> Away! Away! for I will fly to thee,
>   Not charioted by Bacchus and his pards,
> But on the viewless wings of Poesy,
>   Though the dull brain perplexes and retards:
> Already with thee! tender is the night,
>   And haply the Queen-Moon is on her throne,
>   Cluster'd around by all her starry Fays.

Yet Keats' thoughts bring him back to earth as he compares his fate with that of the Nightingale, the "immortal Bird." The reference to the Biblical Ruth standing "in tears amid the alien corn" expresses the complex feelings of the poet who finds melancholy closely linked with joy, pain so close a brother to pleasure and art so near to but not identical with life. It is in the *Ode On Melancholy* that this mood is most succinctly expressed. It is a brief *Ode*, compact and intense. Melancholy "dwells with Beauty—Beauty that must die," and it is neighbor to "Joy, whose hand is ever on his lips, Bidding adieu." And the poet concludes,

> Ay, in the very temple of Delight
>   Veil'd Melancholy has her sovran shrine,
> Though seen of none save him whose strenuous tongue
> Can burst Joy's grape against his palate fine.

The Ode *To Autumn*, written in September, 1819, is mellow in diction and blithe in spirit. It is free and relaxed in composition and style, and delightful to read. One feels pleasurably in accord with the poet as he thinks of the warm days of summer now past, and of the cool clear days of autumn in the country, with the rich harvest completed, the granary filled, the plowing begun; and there is little surprise on seeing Autumn herself, like a maid, her "hair soft-lifted by the winnowing wind," sitting "on a half-reap'd furrow sound asleep." The sweet sensuousness of the poem and the poet's classical control of the forming stanzas are held in a fine balance. Nothing more needs to be said than that to a mature mind an acquaintance with such poetry as this is pure pleasure.

## THE GREAT ODE

The *Ode On a Grecian Urn*, too, was written in the month of May, in 1819. To give it background there were, besides the season's pastoral setting, the Elgin Marbles deposited in the British Museum, with their brocaded story of the classical culture of the Greeks. The soft springtime and the solid marbles offered Keats the strong contrast he needed to set forth the Ode's central idea already, before then, expressed in *Endymion* — the idea that "A thing of beauty is a joy for ever," and "will never pass into nothingness." Here in the *Ode* the urn is the symbol of Eternity. The warm pastoral scene of ardent youthful life has crystallized into the solid substance of what endures, and is the ultimate object of all our knowing. The urn bears the story beautiful of this our earthly life; it defies time, the wear and tear of the hours, the days and years.

The Joy is not destroyed. It is preserved, with "brede of marble men and maidens overwrought." The "happy, happy boughs" cannot shed their leaves. It is forever Spring. All this is implied in what Keats means when he says that what is at a climactic moment so melodious and bright and warm does not die, but endures, "forever young, All breathing human passion far above." It is joy's instant made eternity. Perhaps the highest pleasure which such a work of art as this can give is best illustrated in the Ode's second stanza:

> Heard melodies are sweet, but those unheard
> Are sweeter; therefore, ye soft pipes, play on;
> Not to the sensual ear, but, more endear'd,
> Pipe to the spirit ditties of no tone:
> Fair youth, beneath the trees, thou canst not leave
> Thy song, nor ever can those trees be bare;
> Bold Lover, never, never canst thou kiss,
> Though winning near the goal—yet, do not grieve;
> She cannot fade, though thou hast not thy bliss,
> For ever wilt thou love, and she be fair!

The style of the Ode is that of maturity. The mood is tense without being feverish; the double words are few but well chosen; the description is superb; and the essence of the Greek myth — though the Elgin fragment did not tell Keats its whole story — is preserved to us alive, as only poetry can preserve it.

# REMAINING DAYS

### TIME'S CHANGES

Though beauty and truth endured, Keats knew that for him time did not wait. The hard period of grave illness was before him, and he must have had premonitions of it. Although by late 1819 there had been no hemorrhage, one was impending;

and the exhilaration of the year was soon to take its toll. Meanwhile, as he had appraised his life, he had come to a mature conclusion regarding its meaning to the world. In a letter to his brother George he had written:

A man's life of any worth is a continual allegory, and very few eyes can see the Mystery of his life—a life like the Scriptures, figurative— which such people can no more make out than they can the Hebrew Bible. Lord Byron cuts a figure—but he is not figurative—Shakespeare led a life of Allegory: his works are the comment on it.

Keats wished his poetry to be a commentary on the hidden mystery. In this mood the Odes had been written; and so also the sonnets. Particularly among them were the two on *Fame*, in which fame is called a "wayward Girl . . . a Gipsey . . . and a Jilt," that to *Fanny*, in which he poured out his heart to the girl he loved, and this perhaps his loveliest and most enduring sonnet:

> Bright star, would I were steadfast as thou art—
>     Not in lone splendor hung aloft the night
> And watching, with eternal lids apart,
>     Like nature's patient, sleepless Eremite,
> The moving waters at their priest-like task
>     Of pure ablution round earth's human shores,
> Or gazing on the new soft-fallen mask
>     Of snow upon the mountains and the moors—
> No—yet still steadfast, still unchangeable,
>     Pillow'd upon my fair love's ripening breast,
> To feel for ever its soft fall and swell,
>     Awake for ever in a sweet unrest,
> Still, still to hear her tender-taken breath,
> And so live ever—or else swoon to death.

In these sonnets we see the figurative unveiling of the man in whom the passions, delicately balanced, are at work—at work in the world which Keats called "the vale of soul-making." In

**228**

another letter to George Keats — then living in America — John makes one of his rare mentions of the relation between poetry and theology, and adds that a Soul is to be distinguished from an Intelligence. The latter is a "spark of divinity," but without identity until it becomes a soul, and intelligences become souls "through the medium of the Heart." Such were the thoughts coursing through the mind of Keats during this memorable year. Poetry, he now well knew, was ultimately not a record of natural sensations; nor a representation of unearthly phantasms; it was not experience only; it was experience that, through suffering, had undergone a sea change into something rich and strange. Poetry, he knew, was pain alchemized. It could make a heaven of hell. And it was doing this for him in these days of his prolonged farewell to Fanny Brawne — days in which he was finding the pain endurable by giving it utterance in transmuting forms of beauty, as in this sonnet written in the darkening autumn of 1819:

> The day is gone, and all its sweets are gone! . . .
> Faded the flower and all its budded charms,
> Faded the sight of beauty from my eyes,
> Faded the shape of beauty from my arms,
> Faded the voice, warmth, whiteness, paradise;—
> But, as I've read Love's missal through today,
> He'll let me sleep, seeing I fast and pray.

## FINAL ACHIEVEMENT

It was plain by the end of the year 1819 that for Keats mining the golden ore of poetry was almost at an end. It was not that the rift was exhausted, but that time for him was running out. Living in Winchester, and later in Hampstead, he had written, besides the *Odes* and *Lamia*, a melodramatic play in blank verse, entitled *Otho the Great*, of which the plot and characters had been generously supplied by his friend

Charles Brown. During November and December he worked at re-writing sections of *Hyperion*. It was at this time also that he left unfinished an unromantic fairy-poem, *Cap and Bells*, in which the poet had decided "to untether Fancy, and to let her manage for herself"; but the attempt was without satisfaction to him, and without worthy success. He managed, indeed, for a while, under Brown's genial influence, to be tranquil and happy, occupying his mornings pleasantly, as Brown later said, and writing with ease and facility. But deep within him now lodged a misery that only death could heal. As someone has said, "a triple flame was burning away his life: the flame of genius, of passion, and of disease." In January, 1820, the disease entered the first acute stage. His friend Brown helped to nurse him through it and, by May, his spirit was restored sufficiently to enjoy the summer's pastime, which was to watch the growth of the season's flowers. But late in June there occurred a relapse. He was attended this time by Fanny Brawne and her family, and was much comforted. In September it was decided that he should go to Italy for the winter, and Joseph Severn the painter whom he had known since 1815 accompanied him to Rome. They arrived in Rome, by the way of Naples, early in November, driving, we read, through a lane of autumn flowers. For a little while Keats revived, went riding, and found surcease from pain and distress in looking into books. Then, in December, came his last illness. Severn, at his request, read to him from Jeremy Taylor's *Holy Living and Dying*. He died on February 23, 1821, and was buried in the Protestant Cemetery in Rome.

## THE LETTERS

In summing up the work of Keats, we must not forget his letters. They let us see the man he was: sane and ready in his understanding of practical problems; sagacious in his judgment of men; straightforward and frankly honest, yet gentle, unselfish and forgiving; a man of keen wit and of a lively, sensitive, sympathetic spirit. We like, and remember the letters for their intimacy — not the daring exhibitive intimacy of Byron's letters, but the quiet intimacy of true confidence. They attest to the poet's genius for friendship; and they present us with his valuable comments on poetry — as, for example, when he says, "if poetry comes not as naturally as the leaves to a tree, it had better not come at all"; or again, "I think poetry should surprise by a fine excess." Concerning his own poetry he wrote to his brother George: "I think I shall be among the English poets after my death." It is so. And that is as it ought to be.

# Minor
# Romantic Writers

## SIR WALTER SCOTT
### 1771-1832

## JANE AUSTEN
### 1775-1817

## CHARLES LAMB
### 1775-1834

## WILLIAM HAZLITT
### 1778-1830

## THOMAS DE QUINCEY
### 1785-1859

## THE LESSER ROMANTICS

## THE LITERARY REVIEWS

# SIR WALTER SCOTT

## MAJOR AND MINOR POETS

The Romantic movement cannot well be defined without the help of its minor writers. In them the individual trends of an age are often more clearly seen than in a major writer in whom multiple forces are always creatively at work. A minor poet or novelist or essayist may as truly be an artist as a major one; but, compared to the major writer, he is like the flutist compared to the organist. A tuneful melody by Thomas Moore is more easily followed than an ode by Wordsworth, with its intermingling strains. An age's tendencies are usually many; and they are often diverse, or in conflict with one another. A major writer is one in whom this conflict is possible; there is room enough in his nature for antithesis and complexity. It is the virtue of a minor writer to strike one consistent note; his appeal to us is immediate and direct. He requires less effort to be understood. Genius in him does not obtrude on the age in which he lives. Instead, he reflects the age, submits himself to it and becomes, if he is a genuine poet, its tuned instrument of artful expression.

## LITERARY TALENT

Sir Walter Scott stands first among the writers to be here studied. He may be called a major novelist and a minor poet. His talent for writing was extraordinary. But it must be admitted that he wrote novels and poems in too great quantity to give to each the distinctive mark of excellence. We think of him today as author rather than artist. He thought of himself as a man writing, a gentleman of estate interested in history, fond of romance, with a gift and a great impulse to tell a story. He was not a stylist; he was not a philosopher; he had no great sense of the mystical. The characteristics that fit him best are implied in the term medievalism. Here was his forte; in it he excelled and revelled with the passion of an antiquary hidden in some remote place and surrounded, knee-deep, by precious historic relics. The battlements of an old castle, landscaped among Scotland's green hills, stirred his imagination to activity in lines like these from the Third Canto of *Rokeby:*

> And as I rode by Dalton-hall,
> Beneath the turrets high,
> A maiden on the castle wall
> Was singing merrily:—

> "O, Brignall banks are fresh and fair,
> And Greta woods are green;
> I'd rather rove with Edmund there,
> Than reign our English queen."

A historic setting; wooded hills; the reminiscence of an old ballad; a roving huntsman, a heroic fighter, and a gallant lover; the bagpipe's wild voice; galloping horses; lances shimmering in the sun; and at night the blazing hearth, the festive wassail, and talk of brave deeds, Scottish ancestry, or English honor — these things delighted Scott above all else; and to tell of them in song and story was his life's work.

## HEROES AND HISTORY

Scott liked the great Middle Age. And he liked it, not merely as a story book, full of tales of golden days, but as a world and a time in which he supposed men lived free from pseudoclassicism, from philosophical cant, and from the self-conscious fuss and cult of the esthetic. To him writing, like living, was a matter of integrity, of honesty, of honor. He hated sham and everything that was artifical. He extolled the hero; and the hero was the man who acted, who acted bravely and naturally. And, to Scott, a writer was one who recorded these heroic and natural acts. It was therefore to history that he turned for the facts upon which to exercise his romantic imagination. Here, especially in his own Scotland and in England, was material enough for his enchanter's wand. Here were ballads and lays already at hand, already charged with that mystery and appeal to heroism that stirs men's minds even while it inform them. The colors were there, ready to be put on canvas; and the landscape was awaiting the poet's and novelist's brush. How freely and vigorously, and with what strokes of health, bold color, and broad outline he covered his large canvasses, we can see from a more close study of his life.

## THE EARLY YEARS

Scott was born in Edinburgh in 1771. His ancestors had risen as raiders and clansmen to the position of Cavaliers in defense of the Stuart King Charles I. His father was a lawyer, honest and practical. His mother was a woman of excellent tastes and fond of reciting ballads, proverbs and tales. In childhood, he was often ill, developed a slight lameness, learned to read early and eagerly, fed his imagination on the ballads of Robin Hood, and delighted in retelling them. In his youth he made many friends and was, as he later said, "plunged into an ocean of reading" by a prolonged illness at fifteen, "becoming a glutton of books," but was saved from an excess of fiction by a turn to books of travel and history. At the age of twenty he fell in love with a nobleman's daughter, and passed, as he tells us, "through three years of dreaming, and two of awakening," leaving him dismissed by her and disappointed, but not cynical. It was of Williamina Stuart, his false love, that he was thinking when, at 25, he wrote the poem *The Violet:*

> The violet in her greenwood bower,
>     Where birchen boughs with hazels mingle,
> May boast itself the fairest flower
>     In glen or copse or forest dingle.
>
> Though fair her gems of azure hue,
>     Beneath the dewdrop's weight reclining;
> I've seen an eye of lovelier blue,
>     More sweet through watery lustre shining.
>
> The summer sun that dew shall dry
>     Ere yet the day be past its morrow,
> Nor longer in my false love's eye
>     Remained the tear of parting sorrow.

Lockhart, Scott's biographer, says that "he digested his agony." When he was twenty-six he married Charlotte Carpenter, a French royalist refugee's daughter who was, as John Buchan tells us, "witty, sprightly, and full of hard Latin good sense." The marriage was not unhappy.

## THE PERIOD OF POETRY

Scott was now a young Edinburgh lawyer. But literature was his hobby; and he proved it by collecting and editing ballads. In 1802-3, when he was in his thirty-second year, he published *The Minstrelsy of the Scottish Border*. The volume contained ballads never before printed, and it made Scott publicly known. Its publication brought him criticism, but also supporters and friends, and its composition did much to discipline and to purify his literary taste. This first book was followed, in 1805, by the *Lay of the Last Minstrel;* in 1808, by

*Marmion;* and, in 1810, by *The Lady of the Lake,* which breathed excitment through its lake and mountain scenery, its rush of activity, and its chivalric romance. Other poems followed, until 1813, but none again attained the level of that magnificent story. Like Duncan, in the famous Coronach, the poet in Scott was now a "summer-dried fountain." He could say of that magic gift in himself what he had said of that hero:

> Like the dew on the mountain,
> Like the foam on the river,
> Like the bubble on the fountain,
> Thou art gone, and forever!

He was to write lyrics after that, but no important long poem. In 1814 he published *Waverly,* his first novel.

## THE LADY OF THE LAKE

The poem is composed of six cantos. The scene for it is laid in the Loch Katrine area of the beautiful Scottish highlands. The hero of the poem is James Fitz-James, in reality the king himself. The heroine is Ellen, daughter of Douglas the outlaw. The fierce Roderick Dhu and young Malcolm Graeme are rival suitors for the hand of Ellen who is in love with Malcolm. Roderick, in a fight, is fatally wounded by Fitz-James who—at last recognized as King James—pardons Ellen's father and opens the way for her marriage to the man she loves. The Third Canto is remembered for its description of the Fiery Cross and the Coronach. Every reader remembers the poem's Introduction, opening with the lines,

> Harp of the North! that mouldering long hast hung
> On the witch-elm that shades St. Fillan's spring.

Most famous of all is Ellen's song in Canto I, section 31, sung

in the evening by the fireside after Fitz-James has related how
his horse has fallen in the hunt:

> Soldier, rest! thy warfare o'er,
>     Sleep the sleep that knows not breaking;
> Dream of battled fields no more,
>     Days of danger, nights of waking.
> In our isle's enchanted hall,
>     Hands unseen thy couch are strewing,
> Fairy strains of music fall,
>     Every sense in slumber dewing.
>
> Soldier, rest! thy warfare o'er,
> Dream of fighting fields no more;
> Sleep the sleep that knows not breaking,
> Morn of toil, nor night of waking.

## THE TURN TO FICTION

The year 1814 marked the beginning of the second literary
period of Scott's life. He was now in his forty-third year, a
man of good vigor, living, as his clerkship required in Edinburgh, but preferring country life, and so presently at work
building what was to be the great estate of Abbotsford on
the Tweed. His literary labors were intense. He must have found
them exhilarating; for novel followed novel in rapid succession. *Waverly* dealt with the Jacobite rebellion of 1745, the
attempt to place the Stuart pretenders on the throne. *Guy
Mannering*, published in 1815, with its setting in the time of
George III, is best known for its character study, especially that
of Meg Merrilies whose gypsy's curse on Ellangowan remains
a cherished memory to the reader. In the story the gypsies
have been expelled from the Ellangowan estate, seven families
of them, including aged persons and infants. Meg, her tangled
black hair falling in "elf-locks," resembles a "sibyl in frenzy"
as she cries out:

Ride your ways . . . ride your ways, laird of Ellangowan! This day have ye quenched seven smoking hearths—see if the fire in your parlour din burn the blyther for that. Ye have riven the thack off seven cottar houses—look if your ain rooftree stand the faster. . . . Ride your ways Ellangowan.—Our bairns are hinging at our weary backs—look that your braw cradle at hame be the fairer spread up.

The *Antiquary,* followed in 1816, a picture of the "idealism and hard practicality of the Scottish character" in a setting of the war against France. *Old Mortality,* also published in 1816, is an exciting story of the fight between the Covenanters and the Stuarts. *Rob Roy* was written in 1817, again on the theme of the Jacobite uprising. Then followed *The Heart of Midlothian,* in 1818. It was one of Scott's best novels. Its broad panorama and brilliant narrative, its racy characterization, its dialogue, its passion, its humor, its study of manners, made the novelist internationally famous. The setting of the story is in the time of George II and Caroline. No reader of the novel is likely to forget Jeanie Deans and her visit to the Queen and the plea she made, tutored by the Duke of Argyle, for her sister's life. As the story goes,

"Her majesty could not help smiling at the awe-struck manner in which the quiet demure figure of the little Scotchwoman advanced toward her, and yet more at the first sound of her broad northern accent. But Jeanie had a low voice and sweetly toned, an admirable thing in woman, and eke besought 'her Leddyship to have pity on a poor misguided young creature,' in tones so affecting, that, like the notes of some of her native songs, provincial vulgarity was lost in pathos."

It is in the fortieth chapter of *Midlothian* that we find the lyric *Proud Maisie,* the death song of Madge Wildfire, the mad daughter of old Margaret Murdockson. The lyric's condensed ballad style—terse dialogue, vivid drama and swift motion — makes it one of the most quotable in our language.

> Proud Maisie is in the wood,
>   Walking so early.
> Sweet robin sits on the bush,
>   Singing so rarely.
>
> "Tell me, thou bonny bird,
>   When shall I marry me?"
> "When six braw gentlemen
>   Kirkward shall carry ye."
>
> "Who makes the bridal bed,
>   Birdie, say truly?"
> "The grey-headed sexton,
>   That delves the grave duly.
>
> "The glowworm o'er grave and stone
>   Shall light thee steady;
> The owl from the steeple sing,
>   'Welcome, proud lady.' "

## MORE GREAT NOVELS

In *The Bride of Lammermoor* Scott achieved the height of tragic drama. Passion and catastrophe stand out against a background of history set in the time of William and Mary. The sufferings of Lucy Ashton, and the sight of young Ravenswood galloping wildly into the quicksand, were pictures of pathos well suited to make the novel the source of Donizetti's opera *Lucia di Lammermoor*. The novel *Ivanhoe*, belonging also to the year 1819, is purely English and medieval in its setting. The time is that of Richard the First; and the novel's combined elements of history and melodrama have given it a popularity which it has not lost. No reader of it can easily forget the event of the great tournament, or the storming of the castle of Torquilstone with its touching story of Rebecca nursing the wounded Ivanhoe whom she secretly loves but must leave to go with her father, saying, "And my father!—Oh, my father! evil is it with his daughter, when his grey hairs are not remembered because of the golden locks of youth!" The contrasting pictures of "chivalric glory" and the "demon of vainglory" are presented to us in Scott's best prose style. *Kenilworth,* written in 1821, has a sixteenth century setting, is remembered for its pictures of Elizabeth and Leicester and English court life, and for the story of the tragic fate of the beautiful Amy who, by the design of the evil Varney, is caused to fall through a trapdoor to her death. Other novels followed, good ones, a number of them, such works as *The Fortunes of Nigel, Quentin Durward, The Talisman,* and *Woodstock,* written between 1822 and 1826. Of these the last two are especially noteworthy: *The Talisman* for its capture of the spirit of the Crusaders and its vivid description of the Holy Land; and *Woodstock,* written against the great odds of the novelist's declining health, financial disaster and his wife's death. Of all that he wrote after that, *The Fair Maid of Perth,* published in 1828, is probably the best. In the last novel, *Castle Dangerous,* as the biographer John Buchan tells us, "the opression of his spirits is curiously reflected in the weather of the tale, for all the events take place under gray skies, in creeping mists and driving rain."

## DETERMINING YEARS

It was indeed the closing in of darkening skies for Scott. The traceable reason was the sad calamity that befell him late in the year 1826. That year, and the year 1814 when he bade farewell to poetry, were the determining ones of his career. Mr. Buchan, in his well known volume on Scott, refers to the years between 1821 and 1825 as the time of *high noon.* After that came a year of *dark days;* then five years of *servitude;* and at last, after September 1831, until his death in September, 1832, a year of gradual and welcome release. The years between 1810 and 1820, we note, were almost equally divided between poetry and fiction. Together, these items give us a broad outline of his literary life.

## THE COUNTRY GENTLEMAN

But Scott, besides being a poet and an author, was a lawyer, a landowner, a man of affairs. He enjoyed hard work, had a taste for all sports, especially for riding and hunting, and knew the pleasure of accumulating—as well as the pain of losing—large sums of money. He seems to have had two dominant desires, both natural and forgivable: one was to own Abbotsford and to bequeath it, with a family name, to an heir; the other was to become "the grand Napoleon of the realms of print." Both were fulfilled, despite the painful cost. Abbotsford was expensive to build and to maintain; but it brought its owner much joy. The castle was set in a large acreage on the Tweed, where on winter nights it was ablaze with lights in honor of some distinguished guest, perhaps some "celebrated scientist like Sir Humphrey Davy, or a poet like Wordsworth, or a man of letters from abroad like Washington Irving."

## TOIL AND HEROISM

Scott's venture into the partnership of publication with the firm of Ballantyne, first brought him personal disaster, then made a public hero of him. He had entered the partnership secretly, and, as he soon came to know, unwisely; but when the Ballantynes went into bankruptcy he resolved as a man of honor to pay the debt; and he almost did, by sheer hard work with his pen. Besides writing six novels in the remaining six

years of his life, he produced a nine-volume *Life of Napoleon*.
He lived, we can see, a crowded and strenuous life. He wrote
voluminously, occasionally with a certain magnificence; and
as we look at his work we note in it the marks of a well balanced
nature in which passion, sensation, reason, and imagination
were happily so combined as to assure him his extraordinary
literary success.

## BARD OF BATTLES

As a poet, Scott suggests a comparison with some ancient
epic bard whose thought is far away from much of the self-
conscious artistry of our modern times. To those who associate
poetry with rhythmic impulse, stately ritual, and the will to
action, his poems are sufficiently satisfying. On the other hand,
the more sophisticated reader may pronounce him shallow; the
scholar may regard him careless and diffuse; the exacting literary critic may find him defective in style and intellectually dull;
and the general reader of penetrating insight may declare his
poems moralizing and trite. Ultimately, like his novels, his
poetry "does not address the soul of man." It is clearly a trumpet
call to action, to life's battle, written "as if it were composed
in the saddle," reminding one, at its best, of the *Iliad*, to which,
for its appeal to heroism and human sympathy, it has been aptly
—though perhaps exaggeratedly—compared.

## THE LIVING PAST

Among our novelists Scott's fame seems secure. It rests, at
last, on two grounds: on the historical and fictional content of
the novels themselves; and on their great influence on subsequent fiction in other lands—in England, in Germany, in Russia,
in Italy, and in France. The first thing one notices in the novels
is their resemblance to history. They read as if they were of

the very substance of the historical events; and so they are, to a degree; except only that two other important elements are added: romance and fiction. The former acts on the history itself, on the historic characters and events, magnifying them and adding contrasting touches of color and light; the latter supplies the elements of characterization and incident necessary to give a picturesque setting and a literary framework to the story. The historical novel, of which Scott may be said to be the founder, has been adversely criticized as the "mortal enemy both of history and of fiction." This is stringent criticism. It should be remembered that for us who live in the present age the past has emotional as well as statistical value; and that, for human reasons, as Professor H. A. Beers has indicated, "it is treating the past more kindly to misrepresent it in some particulars, than to leave it a blank to the imagination."

## CHARACTER AND STORY

Scott made the bygone ages live again. That was his gift to literature. As every writer must, Scott wrote of what he saw. There were important aspects of life that all but escaped his notice: the deep inner conflict of man's soul; the penetrating reality of mystical experience; the pity and terror of Greek tragedy; the height and depth of the poetry of Dante and Milton—of these Scott had no awful blinding vision. He recognized simple goodness and other obvious virtues in men, saw them as commendable traits and facts in life, and represented them in strong and positive characters, in men of action generally depicted as types of passion tempered by good sense. The more subtle refinements of art, of scholarship, and of religion he wisely left to others of greater intellectual gifts. His forthright nature demanded a world of forthright virtues, met by their opposites, the openly recognizable vices. The people in his novels are therefore usually stock characters, living before us within a framework of vivid description, but themselves having little of the enchanting loveliness, the mystery of temperament, or the social passion of notable creations of art. Scott is, in last analysis, an inspiring entertainer—a "rose-colored chronicler of feudalism," as someone has said, rather than a writer of original thought who has some profound truth to give to the world. The present-day reader must appreciate and be content with what he aimed to do: to compare and square history with modern progress, to enrich contemporary life by bringing into it the wealth of an old tradition. He desired to see heroic action kept alive in an increasingly nonheroic and commercial age. His sentences, we admit, lack the subtlety and firm structure of good prose. But he makes up for this defect of style by telling a good story. The characters in his novels live, even the minor ones, at least momentarily; and it is worth noting that the novelist-poet's love of his native land is stronger in them than the romance of sex.

## BREADTH OF VISION

All of Scott's work has scope. The scene of action, in both his poems and novels, seems to move horizontally and massively across the pages, like some giant shadow across a sun-drenched landscape. At their best there is a striking Biblical quality in the stately measures of his songs as, for example, in Rebecca's Hymn in *Ivanhoe*, beginning with the well known stanza:

When Israel of the Lord beloved
Out from the land of bondage came,
Her fathers' God before her moved,
An awful guide in smoke and flame.
By day, along the astonished lands
The cloudy pillar glided slow;
By night, Arabia's crimsoned sands
Returned the fiery column's glow.

## THE FINAL ESTIMATE

To read Scott with pleasure requires adaptation: a setting bounded by the appropriate time and place, and a willing surrender to the romantic mood. So read, he overmasters and delights us; and in that mood we can see why he is most praised by those who know him best. Such praise as his peers have given him endures, and his fame endures with it. Saint Beuve called him "an immortal painter of humanity," and Goethe held him to be a delineator of great genius. Carlyle extolled Scott's mastery of the picturesque, and Leslie Stephen noted in particular his vivacity of description and the spirited manner in which he treated things antiquarian. One almost forgets his diffuseness, his habitual carelessness of language, his spread-eagle glorying in the silver escutcheons and lavish display of medieval upholstery, his anachronisms, his lack of philosophical insight, as one ponders the words of the French critic and historian Taine, who said: "By his fundamental honesty and broad humanity, Scott was the Homer of modern-citizen life." To sum up what has been said: from the appearance of *The Lay of the Last Minstrel,* in 1805, with its patriotic lines,

> Breathes there a man, with a soul so dead,
> Who never to himself hath said,
> This is my own, my native land!

to the publication of the last of the thirty-two Waverley novels, in 1829, over a span of twenty-five years, there extends a golden bridge of romance. Every section of it is dotted with scenes and characters from *The Lady of The Lake, Ivanhoe, Kenilworth, The Bride of Lammermoor, The Talisman* and the other important works. The list is imposing. It includes the readily recalled pictures of Loch Katrine in the Trossachs; of the gallant young Lochinvar,

> "So daring in love, and so dauntless in war";

of proud Maisie, listening to the presageful song of the robin; of Meg Merrilies, the gypsy, uttering her curse to the "laird of Ellangowan"; of Jeanie Deans pleading for her sister's life before the Queen in London; and of Ivanhoe, the imprisoned hero, tenderly watched over by the beautiful Rebecca during the siege of the castle. These scenes, and others, deserve a place in his gallery of fame. The poems and novels in which they are found establish Scott's reputation as a man of wide learning, of immense literary productivity, a great romancer, and as the fully accredited "wizard of the North".

# JANE AUSTEN

**TREASURY OF FICTION**

The novel as a literary form has an interesting history. No type of writing is so touched by the contemporary scene; and none is so free to follow its own course, to be what it wishes, to borrow and reject, to move from one area to another, from age to age, to follow and interpret history, to create characters and adapt them to the writer's purpose, to realism or romance, to art or criticism or philosophy. The writer, for instance, may go back to the Arthurian romance and its theme of Christian chivalry, or to the French *fabliau*, or the Italian *novella* for a moral lesson or humorous incident, or to Chaucer and Boccaccio for an example of the perfect story. The English novelist of the year 1800 might draw back the curtain of two centuries on scenes in *Don Quixote* to depict the modern forces of realism in their corrosive influence on medieval Europe. Or he might examine Sidney's *Arcadia* for its epic structure, its English scenes, and its creation of a fanciful world of ideal beauty. If he should read Lyly's *Euphues* or Thomas Lodge's *Rosalind* he might be influenced by these authors' artistry of words and himself be moved with the desire to write for style. Spenser's *Faerie Queene* would suggest to him the rich field of allegory beyond romance and teach his thought to move through history into philosophy; More's *Utopia* would show him how a story may be a work of profound social criticism; and in *Pilgrim's Progress* he would have the opportunity to see how a work of Christian teaching could be written in such a simple English idiom as to become a masterpiece in the language. Nor would the 19th century 'novelist escape knowing *Robinson Crusoe* whose author so skillfully turned the literary types of the journal and biography to the uses of fiction; nor *Gulliver's Travels* in which Swift, in the guise of composing entertaining fiction, wrote his stinging self-tormenting satires.

## MASTERS OF THE CRAFT

But is was particularly to Richardson and Fielding, to Smollett and Sterne, and to Goldsmith that a novelist like Jane Austen would go to acquire whatever knowledge her genius could glean from their novels. Jane Austen's distinctive gift was to portray English character, and she acquired the skill to do it by her mastery of an objective and incisive style. She knew what to respect in Richardson' *Pamela* and *Clarissa,* and what to contemn and avoid. Richardson's analysis of human character had been inwardly passionate and sentimental; hers was to be quietly detached, concrete and ironical. Her bent, like that of Fielding, was toward realism and satire, toward comedy and criticism. Her novels did not display the epic power of Fielding's *Joseph Andrews* or *Tom Jones* which were written, as someone has said, with the novelist's "eye upon Aristotle and the Greek drama." Jane Austen's world was England, and only a very small part of it came within the circle drawn by her controlling pen. Her characters appear as if cut in hard wood; and they are portrayed in the spirit of comedy to evoke the understanding smile. Compared, for example, to Smollett's *Peregrine Pickle* or *Roderick Random*, Miss Austen's *Pride and Prejudice*, or her *Mansfield Park*, suggests a miniature Parthenon set against a theater for harlequins. Both writers are realists. But while Smollett presents us with a work of his colossal wit, one might say, with the debris of a novel, Miss Austen, by her subtle astringent style, cuts through bombast and affectation to achieve distinction as a writer of pure prose.

## STYLE AND SENTIMENT

The novels of Sterne are similarly formless in contrast to those of Jane Austen. Sterne's *Tristram Shandy* is expressly soft and sentimental, an agglomeration of stories from all sources, including subtle jests, learned sayings, and quaint and sometimes salacious allusions. Now and then his delicacy of feeling and use of the pure English idiom captivate the reader, as in the passage in which the "recording angel drops a tear upon an oath of Uncle Toby's." But an almost Rabelaisian mask of mockery covers the delicate features of his story. He is saying to us that what he writes about is all very beautiful, that even the little sins are pleasant ones, but that it is after all nothing but a pretty jest that he is perpetrating on us. Against this show of pleasure in life's little ironies, Oliver Goldsmith presents us with an honest picture of life—a picture of realism touched with tender emotion. Though listed as of the school of sensibility, he endeavors, as for example in *The Vicar of Wakefield*, to give to human emotion an authentic status, to purify it by associating it with moral and religious truths and to find a determining place for it in a sane philosophy of life.

# MINOR ROMANTIC WRITERS

## SOLITARY LIFE WITH LETTERS

Jane Austen could hardly have been unaware of what these earlier writers of fiction had been doing. The popular claim that she owed nothing to any other writer is certainly a mistaken one; though it is true that she was not a literary scholar, or a devourer of other writers' books. She lived, we know, quite alone and wrote of what she saw. And she wrote as she lived: first of all, circumspectly and with neat care; and, after that, with a rare self-detachment and a sense of style as a novelist of manners and a writer of comedy. Her life was outwardly uneventful. She was born in 1775, the daughter of a clergyman who lived in the south of England. For the first twenty-five years of her life she lived in the Steventon rectory. In 1801 when Jane was twenty-six, the Austen family moved to Bath. In the next year, it is believed, while visiting in the west of England, she fell in love. In 1807 the Austens took up residence in Southampton; in 1809 they moved to Chawton, in Hampshire. Her novel *Sense and Sensibility* was published in 1811; *Pride and Prejudice* followed in 1813; *Mansfield Park* in 1814; *Emma* in 1816. *Persuasion* was finished, and the last part of it rewritten, in 1816. In May, 1817, Jane moved to Winchester where she died in July of that year. She was buried in the Cathedral at Winchester.

## THE GREAT NOVELS

Miss Austen's first complete novel was *Northanger Abbey* which she carefully revised and sold to the publisher in 1803. But it was not published until 1818. It was her initial venture into modern comedy, and turned out to be a convincing burlesque of the current Gothic romance. The Abbey, in the story, instead of being dreadful, is a cheerful and comfortable place for the heroine who, instead of being terrorized, day-dreams pleasantly of distant and harmless horrors. In *Sense and Sensibility* the satire, though mild, is articulate. It is directed against the excessive and false sentimentality represented in the character Marianne who acts on every impulse, finds pleasure in her misery, thinks it a crime to fall in love a second time, is jilted by a false lover, experiments rather dangerously in hysterics, and is finally cured of the fever of her emotions and becomes, like her sister Elinor, a wholesomely sane woman. In *Pride and Prejudice* the emotions of the lovers are allowed to come into direct conflict. The barriers are Elizabeth's prejudice and Darcy's pride. The lovers' passion reaches its proper intensity and then is, by degrees, assuaged by the purifying and restoring power of love. The fine wit, stylistic achievement and psychological insight of Miss Austen are well illustrated in this short passage of the novel in which William Collins, a pompous, silly and self-satisfied young suitor approaches Elizabeth in the following manner. She has, with all courtesy, but definitely, refused his hand. But he persists.

*Collins.* "When I do myself the honor of speaking to you next on the subject, I shall hope to receive a more favorable answer than you have now given me: though I am far from accusing you of cruelty at present, because I know it to be the established custom of your sex to reject a man on the first application; and perhaps you have even now said as much to encourage my suit as would be consistent with the true delicacy of the female character."

*Elizabeth.* "Really, Mr. Collins, you puzzle me exceedingly. If what I have hitherto said can appear to you in the form of encouragement, I know not how to express my refusal in such a way as may convince you of its being one."

*Collins.* "You may give me leave to flatter myself, my dear cousin, that your refusal of my addresses is merely a thing of course . . ."

*Elizabeth.* "I do assure you, sir, that I have no pretensions whatever to that kind of elegance which consists in tormenting a respectable man. I would rather be paid the compliment of being believed sincere. I thank you again and again for the honor you have done me in your proposals, but to accept them is impossible. My feelings in every respect forbid it . . ."

*Collins.* "You are uniformly charming! And I am persuaded that when sanctioned by the express authority of your excellent parents, my proposals will not fail of being acceptable."

The novel *Mansfield Park* is less dramatic, but rich in character study. Fanny Price is the heroine: honest and modest and faithful in love. She is, in the story, what we should expect her to be in actual life; except that her character is so aptly touched by Miss Austen's specialized skill at portraiture as to bring the situation of irony into pleasurable relief and to give us the critical effect of good comedy. The heroine in *Emma* is excellently portrayed. She seems to walk directly out of the rural England of the 18th century: trim, vain, ambitious, a matchmaker to the young and eligible, herself in love and hopeful of being loved, injudicious, duped, mortified at finding her own clever heart outwitted by love's strange ways, and at last repentent and made humble and happy by the proposal of marriage to the land-owning Mr. Knightley.

### SELF-REVELATION

Miss Austen's last novel *Persuasion*, published a year after her death, is famous for its portraiture of the heroine Anne Elliot. It has become an accepted tradition to infer from Anne's experience the love-story of the author's own life. The character of Anne is delicately drawn, from within so to speak, in a graver tone and with deep feeling. It is easy to see the gradual softening of the novelist's satirical mood by her own more tender passion. Late in the story Captain Wentworth, in love with

Anne, has come to Bath. They have been engaged, separated by the intruding Lady Russell, and are now again come together. There are other persons present: Lady Dalrymple is there; and, with her, the Elliots, and their hangers-on; and they are warming themselves and testing their wits before the fire in the Octagon Room. Wentworth enters, and Anne and he meet for a few moments' conversation that is broken off by the invading Lady Dalrymple and her coterie. But by the glances of those moments the lovers seal their united destiny:

Anne saw nothing, thought nothing, of the brilliancy of the room. Her happiness was from within. Her eyes were bright, and her cheeks glowed;—but she knew nothing about it. She was thinking only of the last half-hour, and as they passed to their seats her mind took a hasty range over it. His choice of subjects, his expressions, and still more his manner and look . . . his half-averted eyes and more than half-expressive glance all declared that he had a heart returning to her at last; that anger, resentment, avoidance were no more; and that they were succeeded, not merely by friendship and regard, but by the tenderness of the past. Yes, some share of the tenderness of the past! She could not contemplate the change as implying less. He must love her.

**OBSERVATION AND ANALYSIS**

Two things especially hold our attention as we read one of Jane Austen's novels. The first is her power to observe closely every detail of life around about her: domestic life in rural England, the minute consequences of happenings in Chawton, in Winchester, in Bath; the seasons, their foliage, their temperate influence on the people of whom she writes; the people themselves, seldom rich, yet never poor; the men with good incomes, gentlemen, looking for wives; ladies of leisure and match-making mothers; aspiring daughters, socially schooled, alert to pick up good husbands; clergymen and doctors; lawyers and men of business; dinners, theaters, fine horses and carriages; evenings at tea, with good music, riding for exercise; the play and interplay of human emotions, fallings out and reconciliations; the struggle for position, for social recognition, for the satisfaction of life's desires. These are her themes and on them she dwells, lightly, objectively, and without the philosophical misgivings or disturbing inner conflicts that waylay and haunt the idealist. Her photographic art is unexcelled. She is, like the medieval Chaucer, a benevolent realist. But her sense of humor and her keen, delicate relish for the playful save her from personal disillusionment and any show of contempt for men and women.

## SELECTION AND SYNTHESIS

But we are even more impressed by her artistic powers of selection, organization, and literary composition. She does not merely list the items of her story but composes them into a work of a singularly well proportioned and attractive pattern. Looking beyond the observable facts, she achieves the meaningful synthesis that is the true and creative intent of her art. Her place in our literature is not great. But it is secure. By adding thought to fact, giving some touch of grace to a human fault, or seeing some sign of order in the outward display of chance—by letting some handshake or bow, for instance, be the gesture and symbol of a hidden truth—she is able to create for her readers a miniature world of reality and enduring value. For these gifts a grateful posterity will not let her name be forgotten.

# CHARLES LAMB

## CHARACTER AND ANCESTRY

Passing from the novel to the essay, we turn to three writers who invite our especial study. They are Charles Lamb, William

Hazlitt, and Thomas De Quincey. Of the three, Lamb is personally the most interesting. He attracts us by the manner in which his writing so closely reflects what he himself was: an eminently good-natured man, of a gentle but frolicsome manner; sympathetic, wistful, sensible, yet daringly bold, admiring Nature but liking more his fellow-men; a gourmet with a relish for the simple little things of daily life; a tearful humorist; an epicure of words; a man tenderly gallant toward women, but a man's man. Wordsworth summed it all up when he said of him:

O, he was *good,* if e'er a good man lived.

Lamb was born in 1775, in London, in the Temple fronting on the Thames. His father was a lawyer's clerk in the Temple; his mother was Elizabeth Field. There were, altogether, seven children of whom three survived childhood, and of them Charles was the youngest, and Mary twelve years his senior. His father, though a plain man, possessed in a fair measure the gifts of humor, clear judgment and good taste. Charles, writing of his father, said: "He was a man of incorrigible . . . honesty. A good fellow withal, and "would strike" . . . He never forgot rank, where something better was not concerned."

## FORMATIVE INFLUENCES

Lamb's early education was fragmentary. He was sent first to William Bird's school, a dingy place where the birch rod ruled the teaching of the languages and arithmetic. At eight Charles was entered at Christ's Hospital where he remained until he was fifteen. He was an amiable but sensitive child, suffering much from an excited fancy and from cruel treatment. Throughout his life, and afterwards in studies of him, he came to be known by the attribute "gentle." From the beginning of his accountable years to his death he was the indisputable pilgrim of the imagination. The world was actual to him, and cruelly at odds with what a man of his temperament had the right to expect; but fancy was his queen in it, and a quizzically tender humor was his way of yielding her obedience. At Christ's Hospital he learned Latin and became enamored of the poetry of Bowles, a popular writer of pathetic and graceful verse; and, most important of all, he met and became attached to Coleridge. This boyhood attachment proved to be the most signal experience of his life. It was once strained in 1797, when Lamb was twenty-two, and Coleridge, though only twenty-five, was already too mature and metaphysical for Lamb to follow him. But the bond between the two men was unbreakable; for when, in 1834, Lamb received word of his friend's death he fell into repeating aloud "Coleridge is dead!" as if nothing else thereafter could matter to the world and to him. He lived indeed only five weeks longer, as if, to quote the familiar lines, finding his dearest friend gone and trying to get on alone for a little while, "he liked it not—and died."

### FAMILY AFFECTION

For an intimate knowledge of the private life of Charles Lamb and of his sister Mary it is best to begin by reading *My Relations* and *Mackery End*, two of the *Essays of Elia*. In them Charles—it was with much pleasure that he heard persons call him by his Christian name—writing of Mary, who was ten years his senior, said that she "was tumbled early, by accident or design, into a spacious closet of good old English reading, without much selection or prohibition, and browsed at will upon that fair and wholesome pasturage." It is of interest to note here also his life-long remembrance of the formative influence of his grandmother, Mrs. Field, who died at a good old age and to whom he once dedicated these lines as one of his first literary attempts:

> On a green hill top
> Hard by the house of prayer, a modest roof,
> And not distinguished from its neighbor barn
> Save by a slender tapering length of spire,
> The Grandame sleeps. A plain stone barely tells
> The name and date to the chance passenger.

## THE YOUNG AUTHOR

It was about the year 1791, when Coleridge was writing creditable poems for the *Morning Chronicle,* that Lamb also began his venture into literature. He was just then entering on his almost life-long employment with the East India House. His work at the desk, involving a simple daily routine, gave him supportable occupation, assurance against poverty, and time to put his thought to writing, to a closer association with Coleridge, to a study of the sonnets of Bowles, and to his love affair with Ann Simmons, afterward in the essays called Alice, and of whom, in an amateur sonnet, he wrote:

> And does the lonely glade
> Still court the footsteps of the fair-haired maid?
> Still in her locks the gales of summer sigh?
> While I forlorn do wander, reckless where,
> And 'mid my wanderings meet no Anna there.

## SORROW AND SONG

The years 1795-6 were trying for Lamb. Not yet twenty-one, he suffered an attack of mental disorder which forced him to spend six weeks, as he said "very agreeably," in a madhouse. It was at this time that Mary, overburdened with worry, fell victim to a fit of madness and fatally stabbed her mother. The next four years were filled with sorrow, with literary beginnings and failures, and with the first hopes of success. In 1800 he fell in love with Hester Savory; and her death, in 1803, inspired the deeply moving lines of the ballad *Hester*. Hester was a Quaker girl but full of the life that was to Lamb's liking. So much the more poignant was the pain he felt when he wrote of her:

> A month or more hath she been dead,
> Yet cannot I by force be led
> To think upon the wormy bed,
>     And her together.

> A springy motion in her gait,
> A rising step, did indicate
> Of pride and joy no common rate,
>     That flushed her spirit.

> A waking eye, a prying mind,
> A heart that stirs, is hard to bind,
> A hawk's keen sight ye cannot blind,
>     Ye could not Hester.

In 1798 he had written *Rosamund Gray,* a prose tale on which he had lavished that delicacy of fancy and feeling for which he was to become famous. The poet Shelley, reading it in 1819, wrote to Leigh Hunt: "What a lovely thing is his—Lamb's— *Rosamund Gray*! How much knowledge of the sweetest and deepest part of our nature is in it!" In 1798, also, Lamb had published a volume of verses, in association with Charles Lloyd. That winter and during a part of the year 1799, there had occured his sad falling out with Coleridge who, in company with William and Dorothy Wordsworth, had gone to Germany— Wordsworth, to write the Lucy Poems; Coleridge, to study philosophy. Coleridge bore no grudge and Lamb could not endure one. Before the year ended the friendship was resumed, fully and for always. We may imply from lines written months before—now preferably held to refer to a petty quarrel with Charles Lloyd—that Lamb condemned only himself:

> I have a friend, a kinder friend has no man.
> Like an ingrate, I left my friend abruptly;
> Left him, to muse on the old familiar faces.

Besides these trials there was that of finding a place to live. Mary's mental illness so persistently tended to arouse suspicion in their landlords that in a moment of deep discouragement, Charles wrote to Coleridge: "We are in a manner *marked*. I am completely shipwrecked . . . I almost wish that Mary was dead." Yet he did not mean this, actually. Mary, it proved, was to outlive him. And there were better days ahead.

## GRADUAL LITERARY SUCCESS

The year 1800 marked a turning point. For in that year Charles, with Mary in better health, took up residence with her in the Temple, in London, where he was to live for seventeen years. Here he began to write in earnest. Yet all that he was at first invited to contribute to the *Chronicle* or the *Post* was a joke or two a day. It was like writing for bread. Actually, his heart was set on writing a play, which he did. It turned out to be an Elizabethan tragedy, in five acts, called *John Woodvil.* It failed. Jeffrey, in the *Edinburgh Review,* barely noticed it; Southey, loyal and friendly, remarked on the "exquisite silliness of the story." In 1805 Lamb met Hazlitt. In 1806 he wrote to his friend Manning that Mary and he had begun the writing of the *Tales from Shakespeare.* The work was an immediate success and the *Tales,* published in 1807, not only established Lamb as a writer but brought Shakespeare and the Elizabethan drama generally to the attention of the reading public.

**ESSAY AND DRAMA**

But it was in the *Essays of Elia,* published in a collected edition in 1823, that the Lamb we know made his appearance. The *Last Essays of Elia* were published ten years later. The first volume, in its final form, contained twenty-eight essays; the second, twenty-three. The *Essays,* the *Tales,* his letters, and the immortal little poem *The Old Familiar Faces* are now his enduring monument. Besides these, the novelette *Rosamund Gray,* the already mentioned tragedy *John Woodvil,* the farcial comedy *Mr. H.,* and the *Specimens of English Dramatic Poets,* are valuable writings to the special student. They show that Lamb was intensely interested in the drama and a good esthetic critic of it. But they also indicate that he could not himself produce a good play; the reason, perhaps, being that he was a homely and practical philosopher rather than a profound and disciplined thinker; and that he did not have the dramatist's interest in major events, in the history of ideas and in social institutions, nor his special gift of organization, of inventing a plot and of writing with detached objectivity. Referring to the comedy *Mr. H.,* he himself said: "A smokey man must write smokey farces." It is reported that when *Mr. H.* was hissed for its lamentable stage failure, Lamb gleefully joined in the hisses.

**INTERPRETATIVE CRITIC**

No man in his time "felt" Shakespeare better, perceptively and appreciatively, than Charles Lamb. He read the great dramatist, so to speak, from within; for his own life, fully understood, was itself tragicomical. Compared to his two close friends who lectured on Shakespeare, Lamb was not as brilliantly impressionistic as Hazlitt, and far less critical, scholarly and eloquent than Coleridge of whom he himself said: "I cannot think a thought, I cannot make a criticism on men or books, without an ineffectual turning and reference to him. He was the proof and touchstone of all my cogitations." Lamb's opinions on Shakespeare were those of a gifted amateur. His view that the plays *Hamlet* and *King Lear* were written for the mind and are therefore better read—by those who can understand them— than listened to, contains a notable half-truth. In the *Tragedies of Shakespeare* he says:

The Lear of Shakespeare cannot be acted. . . . The actors might more easily propose to personate the Satan of Milton upon a stage, or one of Michael Angelo's terrible figures. The greatness of Lear is not in corporal dimension, but in intellectual: the explosions of his passion are terrible as a volcano: They are storms turning up and disclosing to the bottom that sea, his mind, with all its vast riches. It is his mind which is laid bare.

But this view, held by itself, does not sufficiently recognize that life is lived in a setting of history, and that history itself is enacted drama; nor does it take into account the living power of the spoken word. Lamb, a shy and diffident stammerer, possessed no such gift of its public use.

## STRANGERS AND FRIENDS

Charles Lamb, like every informal essayist, was to the last degree himself. He was modest and sensitive, affectionate toward his friends, jolly and unselfconscious in sympathetic company, but nervous among strangers, ready and sure in his resort to wit, fond of whip-cracking puns above the heads of his hearers, of playing Harlequin or Puck in a motley crowd, and of putting a thorn into the flesh of fools. In all this now obvious pathetic hunger for innocent fun he was misunderstood by Thomas Carlyle who once remarked that Charles Lamb's talk was "contemptibly small." William Macready the actor, too, misunderstood him if we may judge from Macready's remark after an appointed meeting with Lamb: "I noted an odd saying of Lamb's that 'the last breath he drew in he wished might be through a pipe, and exhaled in a pun'." A classic example of this quizzical attitude toward Lamb is presented to us in the occasion of the famous Haydon Christmas dinner, of 1817, at which Wordsworth and Lamb and Keats were honored guests. There was also present, Haydon writes, a comptroller of stamps who felt himself elevated to equality in the presence of Lamb, a fellow-comptroller. To quote Haydon:

When we retired to tea we found the Comptroller. In introducing him to Wordsworth I forgot to say who he was. After a little time the Comptroller looked down, looked up, and said to Wordsworth: "Don't you think, sir, Milton was a great genius?" Keats looked at me, Wordsworth looked at the Comptroller. Lamb, who was dozing by the fire, turned around and said, "Pray, sir, did you say Milton was a great genius?" "No, sir; I asked Mr. Wordsworth if he were not." "Oh," said Lamb, "then you are a silly fellow." "Charles! my dear Charles!" said Wordsworth. But Lamb, perfectly innocent of the confusion he had created, was off again by the fire.

## ESSENTIAL CHARACTER

In reality Lamb was a patient, considerate and affectionate man. England's best known contemporary writers were his close friends: Wordsworth, Coleridge, Keats, Hunt, Hazlitt, Southey, De Quincey and Shelley—these, and many plain people he knew, openly admired him. He was small of stature, odd in manner and appearance and, as we have said, he stammered. Because of this last handicap he was, as he himself reports,

More apt to discharge his occasional conversation in a quaint aphorism, or a poor quibble, than in set or edifying speeches; and has consequently been libelled as a person always aiming at wit;

which, as he told a dull fellow who charged him with it, is at least as good as aiming at dullness.

But he rose above these disadvantages, now psychologically explainable; and those who knew him well talked of him with endearing respect, using, as he liked so well, his Christian name.

## FEAST FOR READERS

Lamb's title to fame rests on the *Essays of Elia*. To the seasoned reader the mere list of them has a pleasing suggestiveness: *Mrs. Battle's Opinion on Whist,* that touches delightfully on human nature and play; *A Chapter on Ears,* which, with intentional humor, begins, "I have no ears," and continues the initial leisurely sentence for nearly 150 words before closing with the words "for music;" *The Old Benchers of the Inner Temple,* containing, in the character of Lovell, Lamb's descriptive tribute to his father; *Christ's Hospital Five and Thirty Years Ago,* which may be said to be dedicated to Coleridge; *The Two Races of Men*—meaning those who borrow and those who lend—in which he calls the men who borrow the *great race* and lists the greatest of them: Alcibiades, Falstaff, Richard Steele, and the contemporary playwright Sheridan. Above these pieces, one cannot forbear to mention the better known *Dream Children,* with its reticent yet self-revealing pathos; and *The Praise of Chimney-Sweepers,* in which the author's pity and wit join to express reverence, as he says, for

these young Africans of our own growth—these almost clergy imps, who . . . from their little pulpits (the tops of chimneys), in the nipping air of a December morning, preach a lesson of patience to mankind. . . . Reader, if thou meetest one of these small gentry in thy early rambles, it is good to give him a penny. It is better to give him twopence. . . . Him shouldst thou haply encounter . . . , regale him with a sumptuous basin (of sweet sassafras tea) and a slice of delicate bread and butter—so may thy culinary fires . . . curl up a lighter volume to the welkin—so may the descending soot never taint thy costly well-ingredienced soups!

The list of selected essays must include *A Dissertation Upon Roast Pig*, which is a kind of feast to the gustatory sense and the literary taste; *Poor Relations*, that is replete with Lamb's deft touches in character study; the autobiographic *The Super-annuated Man;* and *Old China*, which in its own way sums up what men and women hold worthiest in the after-years of life when its joys and sorrows can be seen in the tranquil perspective of an afternoon at tea.

## THE LETTERS

To the essays and poems of Lamb we must add his letters. In them his likes and dislikes break eruptively through the general calm of his thoughts, adding a photographic touch of the man and his surroundings to the literary portraiture of his thoughts in the *Essays*. None is more familiar, or representative of this sharp edge of Lamb's expression of his choice of things, than the letter to Wordsworth in which he allows the poet his preference for the natural wonders of the Lake Country, while he himself prefers the city. Thrusting his blade into the battle, he says:

Separate from the pleasure of your company, I don't much care if I never see a mountain in my life. . . . The lighted shops of the Strand and Fleet Street; the innumerable trades, tradesmen and customers, coaches, wagons, playhouses; all the bustle and wickedness round about Covent Garden; . . . the crowds, the very dirt and mud, the sun shining upon houses and pavements, the print shops, the old book stalls, coffee houses, streams of soups from kitchens;—all these things work themselves into my mind, and feed me, without a power of satiating me. The wonder of these sights impels me into night walks about her (London's) crowded streets, and I often shed tears in the motley Strand from fulness of joy at so much life.

## LAST DAYS

Lamb ended his active duties at the East India House in 1825. Thereafter he lived on a pension of about four hundred pounds a year, making frequent visits to Herefordshire, taking moderately long walks into the country, writing leisurely, and going often to the British Museum. Later, in 1827, Charles and Mary moved to Enfield and, after several years, to Edmonton. There, in 1834, Lamb died and was buried in the Edmonton churchyard. Mary Lamb outlived him to 1847.

## FINAL ESTIMATE

As a writer Lamb owed much to the seventeenth century. He was drawn, by the choice of his own good reading, to the well of pure English found in Burton's *Anatomy* and Browne's *Hydriotaphia*, and it was in them that he found the prose of antique flavor and deep feeling that suited his taste. He was, we have noted, an Epicurean in his taste of words, and one who habitually steeped his mind in the poetry of Shakespeare and Marlowe. In one of his letters he said: "I prefer the affections to the sciences." He had, Thomas De Quincey wrote, an "angelically benign" temper. To De Quincey he was "the exquisite Elia." It is become a respected practice to record after Lamb's name these traits as belonging especially to him: a talented author's sharp wit and genial humor, a poet's fancy, a woman's devoted tenderness, and a suffering man's understanding of life. Almost everything close to our daily human experience lies buried beneath his sentences. Reading him is a continual unearthing of allusions: to books, to people, to remote times, to intimate places. It is as if something we had long since believed to be past, or dead, were rising up and coming back to life again and, in our waiting moments, were associating itself with our half-forgotten thoughts.

## SUMMARY

In Lamb's writings we find a style of prose that at times comes close to the poetry of Wordsworth. The emotions breaking through it are deep and genuine. The mood is one of intimacy. Its accents are those of humor and pathos. Tears, tempered with laughter, are its Romantic substance. Reading one of Lamb's essays, we feel and think with him. We go with him down the London street on which he liked to walk, to the "motley Strand" where, as he says, he "often shed tears for fulness of joy at so much life". His voice, as he talks to us, is friendly; his talk is touched with humor; he indulges "in a quaint aphorism, or a poor quibble"; he enjoys making private "edifying speeches"; he seems, to outsiders, to be "always aiming at wit" which, he remarks, "is at least as good as aiming at dullness". He stammers. Writing is his avocation, his irresistible hobby; he is not a professional author; his occupation is that of a clerk in the East India House, checking imports and exports —a position he holds for thirty-three years. When, in 1825, he retires, he writes of the mood in which he finds himself in an essay, *The Superannuated Man.* In a letter to Wordsworth he describes his feeling as "like passing from life into eternity". In the essay he is more whimsical, and adds, in the kind of dissertative style that Lamb can manage so well:

It was like passing from Time into Eternity—for it is a sort of Eternity for a man to have Time all to himself. It seemed to me I had more time on my hands than I could manage.

Finally, there is a quality in Lamb, related to the odd and whimsical in him. It is the deeper one of joy, immersed in sorrow. It makes him, in a special sense, the most Romantic of our prose writers. None of them, in any age, so interfuses tears and laughter to get so sublimated and pure a product as is found, for example, in the essay *Dream-Children: A Reverie,* written shortly after the death of his brother John, in 1821. In it he thinks of his bachelorhood, his loneliness; of "Alice," that is, Ann Simmons, the girl he once loved; of his sister Mary's periodic insanity; and of the family life that might have been his, had he married; and, so dreaming, sees little Alice,

The soul of the first Alice. . . . And while I stood gazing, both the children gradually grew fainter to my view, receding, and still receding till nothing at last but two mournful features were seen in the uttermost distance, which without speech, strangely impressed upon me the effects of speech: "We are not of Alice, nor of thee, nor are we children at all. . . . We are nothing; less than nothing, and dreams."

# HAZLITT AND DE QUINCEY

**A COMPARISON**

There is good reason for studying the work of these two writers together. Their writings are not alike, and certainly not of one piece; but the men were close contemporaries and looked together on the same world and lived in the same England. Both men were expressly Romantic, and both were literary critics. In both the "literature of knowledge" was aptly and forcibly interfused with, the "literature of power." Hazlitt was intent on communicating literary knowledge, and he did so with imagination and gusto. De Quincey revelled in the world of imagination with a technician's definitive and itemizing logic and a necromancer's skill. Hazlitt wrote with a fiery intellect, De Quincey with a subtilized one. Hazlitt's words, when he is stirred, leap up like flames; De Quincey's sentences, mysteriously composed, rise like a vapor and distil themselves like ether in the mind. Hazlitt is essentially the scholar; De Quincey's temper is philosophical. The fame of Hazlitt rests on his contribution to literary criticism, that of De Quincey on his impassioned, strangely powerful poetical prose.

## CONCERNING COLERIDGE

A comparison of the two writers is best brought out by what each saw in the character and genius of Coleridge. Hazlitt, remembering how the younger Coleridge preached, likens him admiringly to a voice crying in the wilderness, an "eagle dallying with the wind." De Quincey, in melancholy reminscences, pictures the older Coleridge as a man haunted by a past happiness and "blank mementoes of power extinct," and driven as by some dark spirit from the Lake Region to the city and the world of men. Hazlitt, in 1825, writes of Coleridge whose progress through philosophy he has traced by stages from Hartley to Berkeley, from Berkeley to Huss, and from Huss to Spinoza:

"But poetry redeemed him from this spectral philosophy, and he bathed his heart in beauty, and gazed at the golden light of heaven, and drank of the spirit of the universe."

De Quincey, in his *Reminiscences of the English Lake Poets,* says Coleridge, tormented and exiled from nature,

"fled from poetry and all commerce with his own soul; burying himself in the profoundest abstractions from life and human sensibilities."

Both friends and critics were right; only they saw Coleridge from opposite directions. It was a choice between poetry and philosophy; and it became, in the course of time, an issue between them. Hazlitt began with philosophy, with ideas and their application to life, and moved toward a consummation of these ideas in the vision and intuition of poetry. De Quincey's mind was by its composition and nature steeped in poetry, and continually engaged in and working outward toward an expres-

sion of tangible reality. He sought an anchorage of truth for
the imagination, a sound and final resting place for reason.
Perhaps the difference between the two writers is best expressed by saying that Hazlitt's thoughts came to him as if
unexpectedly assembled, or by rapid accretion; whereas De
Quincey's foliated slowly, branch by branch, as if from some
mysterious and dark root within him.

## LIVING WITH BOOKS

William Hazlitt was born in 1778 at Maidstone where his
father was a Unitarian minister. Hazlitt himself said: "I started
in life with the French Revolution"—a statement that both
dated and characterized him. When William was two years
old his father moved to Ireland, and three years later the family
emigrated to America; but after several unhappy years there,
returned to England and settled at Wem, in Shropshire. William
was now ten, and Wem remained his home until he was twenty-
two. Here he read the Bible, began to study Latin and Greek,
and spent many happy hours among his father's theological
books. A little after that he began to read French, and to
develop the preference for solitude and egocentric brooding
that later revealed his individual strength and weakness. At
eighteen he was reading Burke; at nineteen, Rousseau whose
*Confessions* and novel *Eloise* were feeding his romantic nature;
and Fielding's *Tom Jones* and Smollett's *Peregrine Pickle* were
becoming more actual and real to him than life in Wem.

## MEETING TWO POETS

In 1798, when Hazlitt was twenty, he met Coleridge. Hearing
him preach, he was moved, he says, as by a voice ascending
"like a stream of rich distilled perfumes;" and, after a few weeks
of eager expectation, he went to visit him. Hazlitt, after twenty-

five years, records the still undimmed recollection in *My Frst Acquaintance with Poets;* and, a little later, sums it up by saying that while listening to Coleridge he felt as if he were listening to the music of the spheres, and that it seemed to him then that

"Poetry and Philosophy had met together, Truth and Genius had embraced, under the eye and sanction of Religion."

At this time he also met Wordsworth with whom, because of Hazlitt's volatile and opposite nature, he soon started an argument. The net result of the visit with these two poets was that it irretrievably claimed him for literature. It had earlier been planned that he should prepare to become a clergyman; but he had by now come to prefer Rousseau and Shakespeare to Unitarian theology.

## THREE CONCURRENT PURSUITS

Yet the call to literature did not come immediately. Instead Hazlitt turned to painting. He went to Paris and spent much time in the Louvre studying and copying the masters, especially Titian of whom he was enamored, revelling in the experience, and so altogether using up, at home and abroad, the ten years between 1798 and 1808 in following Madam Art, his elusive mistress. Nor was he more successful in marriage than in art. In 1808 he married Sarah Stoddart, but was divorced in 1822. Two years later he was married to Mrs. Bridgewater from whom he almost immediately separated. The ground of the difficulty was that Hazlitt was too easily irritated and too fond of his own thoughts to live under domestic restraint. But fortunately, by 1808, he had begun to write; and it was Leigh Hunt who offered to give space in *The Examiner* to his compositions. Essays from Hazlitt's pen now quickly began to attract the attention of the reviewers. At about this time, also, he began to lecture, first on philosophy, then on poetry. The two fields of interest were in some mysterious way united in his mind as he undertook to address his audiences, quite at random, on Hobbes, on Jonathan Edwards and on Shakespeare. Besides much trenchant dramatic criticism, he wrote lively essays on men and manners. His *Lectures on the Elizabethan Poets* were published in 1818; *Table Talk*, a collection of familiar essays, appeared in 1822; *The Spirit of the Age*, a masterly and daring volume of critical essays on his contemporaries, followed in 1825. These, all told, were his best works. He wrote, in addition, a *Life of Napoleon Buonaparte* which ran into four volumes, and into which he put rather more praise than history. Among his informal essays these are most typical of Hazlitt's brilliant self-exhibitive style: *On Going on a Journey; On Gusto; On Disagreeable People; On the Pleasure of Hating; On Taste; On Reading Old Books; On Living to One's Self;* and *On the Fear of Death.*

## PASSION AND INTUITION

Hazlitt was no mild writer. *The Spirit of the Age,* he said, was written in "mellowed animosity." In it he dealt with his friends and the men around him, "never meanly," but as one fearing to be afraid and intent on being just. In this attitude of mind he over-prized his own liberty and his sense of justice, too often forgetting what Charles Lamb whom he admired so well knew, that charity is a surer key to the hidden treasure of a poet's soul than the critic's arbitrary taste. His intuitive sense in purely literary matters almost never failed Hazlitt. He knew good books and poems and paintings when he saw them; and he knew and openly admired goodness in people; but his vigorous and sometimes violent nature was extremely restive against opposition. He had, we may say, the Old Testament spirit of a Calvinist: his zealous courage; his passion for individual freedom; and his sense of being guided by a divine moral law. He could not, like Lamb, be subtly critical, or quaintly nostalgic, or sadly humorous, or tenderly affectionate; or, like De Quincey placate the evil demon and soothe the human spirit with labyrinthine tours of logic and stately cadent rhythms. He talked, as he was moved, of Plato, of Spinoza, of Jacob Boehme; and he whipped out, because he could not help it, some adroit comment on Coleridge's understanding of them. But he knew little of these great men's abysmal insight into truth; and he had none of the deeper tranquil wisdom of such a man as Wordsworth. Hazlitt's mind was keyed to action, to intellectual activity, to the stirring of the will and the imagination, to the explorative urge and the sudden joy of discovery. When he wrote of books he marched through them like a soldier through an open field. There was nothing "literary" or pedantically bookish about him. And he was the same journeying and robust critic toward men. It was easy for him to be colloquial, idiomatic, and unaffectedly himself. His zest for life and for literature was phenomenal; and it is probably a just criticism of him to say that he was the master of the art of a great style, a style that was at once a dance and a triumph, a triumph of life.

### BRILLIANT STYLE

An excellent example of Hazlitt's success with the character sketch is the familiar passage on the magnitude and progress of Coleridge's mind. A single paragraph will illustrate, beyond any further analysis, Hazlitt's particular literary talent.

Let us draw the curtain, and unlock the shrine. Learning rocked him in his cradle. . . . At sixteen he wrote his *Ode on Chatterton*. . . .

At Christ's Hospital, where he was brought up, he was the idol of those among his schoolfellows who mingled with their bookish studies the music of thought and of humanity; and he was usually attended round the cloisters by a group of those whose hearts, even then, burnt within them as he talked, and where the sounds yet linger to mock *Elia* on his way, still turning pensive to the past! One of the finest and rarest parts of Mr. Coleridge's conversation, is when he expatiates on the Greek tragedians—on the subtle reasonings and melting pathos of Euripides, on the harmonious gracefulness of Sophocles, ... on the high-wrought trumpet-tongued eloquence of Aeschylus. ... As the impassioned critic speaks and rises in his theme, you would think you heard the voice of the Man (Prometheus) hated by the Gods, contending with the wild winds as they roar, and his eye glitters with the spirit of Antiquity!

## SUBLIME RHETORIC

In the next moment Hazlitt sees Coleridge engaged, in preoccupied study, with "Hartley's tribes of mind," and their doctrine of Necessity. Then, as an escape from Dr. Priestley's materialism, "where he felt himself imprisoned by the logician's spell, like Ariel in the cloven pine-tree," Coleridge is depicted as "enamored of Bishop Berkeley's fairyworld," and, in his inspired conversation, as essaying to "build the universe, like a brave poetical fiction, of fine words." After that, it seems out of sheer pleasure, Hazlitt follows Coleridge through "a huge pile of learning, unwieldy, enormous," to Leibnitz; and from him, as from a rainbow, he traces Coleridge's descent "ten thousand fathoms down" to the simpler faith of a Christian. At last, so chastened and rising again, and, by the help of Spinoza, taking "the vast chain of being in his hand," Coleridge is all but transfigured before Hazlitt's eyes in the next portion of the essay, as he continues:

But poetry redeemed him from this spectral philosophy, and he bathed his heart in beauty, and gazed at the golden light of heaven, and drank of the spirit of the universe . . . and, wedded with truth in Plato's shade, and in the writings of Proclus and Plotinus saw the ideas of things in the eternal mind, and unfolded all of Duns Scotus and Thomas Behmen, and walked hand in hand with Swedenborg through the pavilions of the New Jerusalem.

## LAST DAYS

Hazlitt worked hard and long to complete the *Life of Napoleon;* and it was finally printed in 1830. Critics, if they looked for history, found instead an impassioned praise of Buonaparte—a strange thing in a life-long rebel like Hazlitt— and the work had a small sale. By then, too, Hazlitt was ill, irrecoverably so. Yet even in the struggle with death his mind was strong and clear, and during his last days Charles Lamb was continually at his bedside. He died in September of the year 1830.

## DE QUINCEY'S BOYHOOD DAYS

Thomas De Quincey was born in 1785; and he lived to 1859, almost thirty years after Hazlitt's death. His literary life extended into the Victorian age; but he belonged by both tradition and temperament to the school of the Romantics. He was a Manchester merchant's son, educated successively in Bath, at Winkfield, and in the Manchester Grammar School from which, when he was seventeen, he ran away. He had been a child prodigy, and had by then mastered Latin, learned to write in Greek, been invited to Eton as the guest of Lord Westport, seen the King at Windsor Castle, visited London and traveled, in company with Lord Westport, to Ireland. He knew the Bible, could discuss theology, and had read Euripides—all this when at seventeen he chose to quit the grammar school.

**SCHOLAR AND GENIUS**

The remaining months of 1802 young De Quincey spent wandering leisurely into Wales, and then finding his way to London where for a year, except for the charity of the street, he lived homeless and destitute. In 1803, he entered Oxford and was there intermittently until 1809, reading prodigiously, especially in English and German literature and studying Hebrew. He read all that Wordsworth wrote and delved into the work of Coleridge. It was during this time that he began to take opium. In 1807 he met Coleridge; and he was presently introduced to Southey. Coleridge was then lecturing on poetry and the fine arts in London, but was, as De Quincey later said, personally in a state of profound dejection. Between the years 1809 and 1816 De Quincey lived in the Lake Region, occupying the Grasmere cottage lately vacated by the Wordsworths. By then the Lake District had become famous. Wordsworth, having given it fame, was now forty and living with his family at Rydal Mount; and there his sister Dorothy was the talented hostess to their visitors. Southey lived there; so also did Coleridge, until 1810, sharing at intermittent periods the Wordsworth home. Now De Quincey too settled there; taking long walks; finding himself generously adopted by the Wordsworth family; habitually in need of money; yet making new friends, and going on periodic visits to Edinburgh; but chiefly reading and taking notes on his reading, until, as one of his admirers later said, by his lively conversation, set to measures in a most pleasing musical cadence, he could range at will, in good company, from strict logic to extreme fancy,

from beeves to butterflies, and thence to the soul's immortality, to Plato, and Kant, and Schelling, and Fichte, to Milton's early years and Shakespeare's Sonnets, to Wordsworth and Coleridge, to Homer and Aeschylus, to St. Thomas of Aquin, St. Basil, and St. Chrysostom.

## FIRST LITERARY SUCCESS

But with all this expanding range of knowledge, by now, in 1816, De Quincey had published nothing significant, and he was thirty-one. When in due time he came to public attention, it was as the editor of a little country journal, the *Westmoreland Gazette*. Now married and still living at Grasmere, and struggling against inadequate financial income and his acquired habit of opium, he accepted the editorship simply as a last resort. As we should expect, he overwhelmed the journal's readers with his learning, and the promise of more learning, until it all but failed. Driven by necessity, he visited Edinburgh, hoping there to find work as a contributor to *Blackwood's Magazine* of which Lockhart and his friend Wilson were the editorial critics. So five years passed. Then, in 1821, the opportunity came to write for the *London Magazine*. Keats, who died that year, had published poems in it; Lamb was sending new *Essays of Elia* to it; and De Quincey's *Confessions of an Opium-Eater* were alloted the major space of 47 pages in two succeeding issues, after which the way to a literary career was fully open to him. The *Confessions* appeared in book form in 1822, and were thereafter gradually expanded until the complete edition of them was published in 1856. Their success was immediate and lasting. No English autobiography till then, had been so intimately self-revealing and at the same time so nobly classical. Its lofty poetical prose had the encompassing effect of organ music; it bordered on the eloquence and dignity of ancient Hebrew poetry, as for example such a single sentence as this amply illustrates:

O just, subtle, and mighty opium! that to the hearts of poor and rich alike, for the wounds that will never heal and for "the pangs that tempt the spirit to rebel," bringest an assuaging balm; eloquent opium! that with thy potent rhetoric stealest away the purposes of wrath, and, to the guilty man, for one night givest back the hopes of youth and hands washed pure from blood.

## IN LONDON

The years with the *London Magazine*, between 1821 and 1824 were productive ones. Articles like those on the Germans Richter and Herder, and on the English political economist Malthus, blazed the "The Opium-Eater"—the name by which De Quincey was first known to his readers—into fame. During this time, and until 1825, he lived chiefly in London. There, near his publishers and, as Thomas Hood said, "in the midst of a German Ocean of Literature," in a room in Covent Garden, he worked, famous, but preferring to be alone, eccentric and silent and shy. Though he still struggled with opium, actually it was poverty that haunted him, now as before; and it was his continual fear of the creditor's bailiff that, to his sorrow, kept De Quincey away from his family in Grasmere till late in 1825.

## WORD FROM CARLYLE

During the next five years De Quincey lived alternately at Grasmere and at Edinburgh, and continued writing for *Blackwood's Magazine*. At this important time in his career he came to know Thomas Carlyle, and to find in him the understanding fellow writer who, in 1828, in a letter to De Quincey, gave him encouragement to pursue the profession of an author by saying:

"Believe it, you are well loved here, and none feels better than I what a spirit is for the present eclipsed in clouds. For the present it can only be; time and chance are for all men; that troublous season will end."

## FULL YEARS

In 1830 the De Quincey family moved to Edinburgh. There, in a picturesque yet modern city, for the next ten years he worked, writing articles now for *Blackwood's,* and then for *Tait's Magazine;* and there were many of them: additional essays on Kant; essays on English politics; an article on Charlemagne, another on *The Revolution of Greece,* a longer one on the *Revolt of the Tartars;* criticisms of the work of Wordsworth and Coleridge; a series of articles on *Style and Rhetoric;* and, perhaps most significant of all, more essays or sketches on the biography of an opium-eater, which ran into an extended series between the years 1834 and 1853 and came finally to be published as the autobiography of De Quincey. Besides these there were four other important pieces of writing. Outstanding among them was the *Suspiria De Profundis,* which was begun in 1845, and consisted altogether of six parts. It is a dream poem of organ-throated sounds and stately cadences, woven into a subterranean theme of sighs and strange hauntings of the soul; occult, rhythmical, and liturgical; suggesting the author's own experience of profound sorrow; and well illustrated for us in the inimitable section called *Levana and Our Sisters of Sorrow,* in which, after naming the three Ladies of *Tears, Sighs,* and *Darkness,* the author says of the last of these:

"But the third sister, who is also the youngest—Hush! whisper, whilst we talk of *her!* Her kingdom is not large, or else no flesh would live. . . . She is the defier of God. She also is the mother of lunacies, and the suggestress of suicides. Deep lie the roots of her power; but narrow is the nation that she rules. . . . Madonna (Our Lady of Tears) moves with uncertain steps, fast or slow, but still with tragic grace. Our Lady of Sighs creeps timidly and stealthily. But this youngest sister moves with incalculable motions, bounding, and with a tiger's leaps."

## CRITICISM OF LITERATURE

In 1847 De Quincey wrote the romantic-lyric biography *Joan of Arc;* and in 1848 he followed it—in an essay on the Poetry of Pope—with the well-known dissertation on *The Literature of Knowledge and the Literature of Power,* in which, making a distinction that has now become classical, De Quincey said:

There is, first, the literature of *knowledge;* and secondly, the literature of *power.* The function of the first is to—*teach;* the function of the second is to—*move:* the first is a rudder; the second, an oar or a sail. The first speaks to the *mere* discursive understanding; the second speaks ultimately, it may happen, to the higher understanding or reason, but always *through* affections of pleasure and sympathy.

## EXTRAORDINARY STYLE

In 1849 there issued from his pen, in strange galloping sensations of speed, the graphic account of *The English Mail-Coach.* In contains the *Dream Fugue: The Vision of Sudden Death* in which fantasy and rhythm unite to produce an effect of terror. De Quincey himself described it as a "duel between life and death." The story is a masterpiece of suspense and retarded motion; anticipated horror impinges on the idyllic scene of the two lovers riding in a gig through Gothic aisles of umbrageous trees. The *Dream Fugue* transports the scene, giving it the symbolism of a lament of some sweet lost hope personified in "a girl adorned with a garland with white roses about her head for some great festival." De Quincey's description follows her in cadences of trembling fear as she runs toward the perilous quicksands; and what Professor Oliver Elton calls De Quincey's master-faculty, "his union of logic, imagination, and narrative skill," is well illustrated in the ensuing vision:

"Faster and faster she ran; round a promontory of rocks she wheeled out of sight; in an instant I also wheeled round it, but only to see the treacherous sands gather over her head. Already her person was buried; only the fair young head and the diadem of white roses around it were still visible to the pitying heavens; and, last of all, was visible one white marble arm. I saw by the early twilight this fair young head, as it was sinking down to darkness—saw this marble arm, as it rose above her head and her treacherous grave, tossing, faltering, rising, clutching, as at some false deceiving hand stretched out from the clouds. . . . The head, the diadem, the arm—these all had sunk; at last over these also the cruel quicksand had closed; and no memorial of the fair young girl remained on earth, except my own solitary tears, and the funeral bells from the desert seas, that, rising again more softly, sang a requiem over the grave of the buried child, and over her blighted dawn."

## FAME AND SOLITUDE

De Quincey's life, after 1830, was lonely and sorrowful. From the obtainable records it seems clear enough that he found his purest individual pleasure in the company of his family. Yet poverty and sorrow, and some strange trait in his frail nature, mostly denied him this joy. His youngest son, a child of five years, died in 1833; his eldest son, eighteen years of age, died in 1835; the death of his wife, not yet forty, followed in 1837. De Quincey was now fifty-two. The remaining six children kept house together at Lasswade, just outside Edinburgh, while the father, though often at home with them, spent long periods of time in Glasgow and in separate lodgings in Edinburgh. There, among his books and sheets of neatly written manuscript, he kept vigil with his thoughts, a frail little man of a bad digestion, struggling with the evil of opium—twice, after that time critically, once in 1844, and again in 1848—and writing, with amazing productivity, article after article for *Tait's* and *Blackwood's;* the chief stimulus to this productivity being his daily need of money. One biographer, writing of this period in his life, refers to him as "The brainworn veteran." Yet he wrote with astonishing freshness and power, and literary Edinburgh quickly took notice of this fact. Everyone talked of him; but he himself was nowhere to be found except by the few who knew the cloistered rooms in which the gentle shy man lived.

## CLOSING YEARS

In 1849 De Quincey met and began to write for Mr. James Hogg and his *Weekly Instructor*. Out of this meeting grew the plan to gather together the vast assortment of De Quincey's essays and articles into what was to become the edited collection of his works. The first volume appeared in 1853; the fourteenth, in 1860. At the same time an American edition of his collected writings began to appear, and was completed in 1855. The Edinburgh edition preoccupied De Quincey's attention during these literary years spent in solitude in the now famous Lathian Street rooms. He died in 1859, and was buried in Edinburgh.

## SUMMARY

Besides De Quincey's gentleness of spirit and manner, his instinctive love of solitude, his intellectual curiosity and wide learning, his subtle logical faculty, his fantastic display of the imagination, his brooding melancholy temperament—or, rather, because of these dominant traits in his nature—he is noted for his extraordinary prose style. Yielding easily enough to analysis, it defies imitation. It is most simply defined as impassioned and poetical: a prose that should be spoken, since it gathers effect by the order and sound of the words, calling on the emotions, directing and focusing them; holding them in check, like waves of the slowly incoming sea, by the cadence of the periodic clause; until, as they break, they spend themselves in some exquisite vision and display of tears. It is the prose of life's pulse: the pulse's "magnificent come and go." The primary source of it is a sense of life's essential sorrowful passion, perceived as a creative force of man's existence; and, so passing through the channel of expression into rhythm, is directed to culminate, through the subtle infusion of lofty thought, in the pure essence of a dream vision. By this psychological process De Quincey attains heights of literary achievement which resemble—though they are otherwise different from—those of religious inspiration.

# THE LESSER ROMANTICS

## ROBERT SOUTHEY

He was born in 1774, in Bristol. At eighteen he was sufficiently gifted and radical to write an essay against flogging for which he was expelled from the Westminister School. A little later he entered Oxford. When he was twenty he met Coleridge who was then twenty-two, and together they dreamed the dream of a Pantisocracy, that state of society in which a perfect environment would make virtue natural and inevitable. In 1795 Southey married Edith Fricker, Coleridge's wife's sister. The next year he spent in Portugal. In 1800 he went to Spain. By now, besides the cause of political freedom, literature claimed his attention. He did not, like Wordsworth, know the "god-like hour" of his dedication to literature; instead, writing was a vocation to him, a literary day's labor and a moral duty. In the course of the years he had come, rather sensibly, to believe that neither the primitivism taught by Rousseau nor the rationalism proposed by Godwin could be made the basis of a civilized society. Instead he was convinced that it was the moral man as hero, disciplined in self-control and freed from childish superstition and from evil passion, who alone could free a nation and set it on its way to virtue; and to this sound, if over-simplified, belief he set himself to make a positive contribution by his writing. In this undertaking he was measurably successful.

## THE EPIC MOTIVE

Southey wrote, besides numerous other pieces, four long narrative poems and four noteworthy biographies. The poems, in their broad intent, are noble; but they do not have the hidden power to haunt and waylay the reader. The biographies are models of a clear and solid prose, of character study, and of epic structure. Of the four longer poems, *Thalaba the Destroyer,* in which Arabian legend is intertwined with Mohammedan mythology, is the most supernaturalistic; *Madoc,* combining Welsh and Mexican legend, is the most discriminating history; *The Curse of Kehama,* in which the mighty Raja's curse turns into a blessing, and which is essentially a treatment of Hindu mythology, is the most clearly moral and religious; and *Roderick, the Last of the Goths,* a tragic poem in which the hero grapples fiercely with life's problems, with evil in himself and in his environment, is the most realistic and true to life. The four important *Lives* Southey wrote were those of John Bunyan, John Wesley, William Cowper, and Lord Nelson. Of them the *Life of Nelson,* a model in character study, is deservedly famous. A typical example of his lucid, manly and graphic prose, and of his gift of good narrative, is Southey's account of the Battle of Trafalgar. The battle has reached its climax and Lord Nelson is mortally wounded. He is on board the flag ship *Victory* when Hardy, his captain, after three hours of fighting, announces that the enemy is routed.

"Once, amid his sufferings Nelson had expressed a wish that he were dead; but immediately the spirit subdued the pains of death, and he wished to live a little longer; doubtless that he might hear the completion of the victory which he had seen so gloriously begun. That consolation—that joy—that triumph, was afforded him. He lived to know that the victory was decisive; and the last guns which were fired at the flying enemy were heard a minute or two before he expired."

Southey concludes with this paragraph resembling an Athenian peroration, touched with the fire of biblical prophecy:

"The most triumphant death is that of the martyr; the most awful that of the martyred patriot; the most splendid that of the hero in the hour of victory; and if the chariot and the horses of fire had been vouchsafed for Nelson's translation, he could scarcely have departed in a brighter blaze of glory. He has left us, not indeed his mantle of inspiration, but a name and an example which are at this hour inspiring thousands of the youth of England—a name which is our pride, and an example which will continue to be our shield and our strength."

Other creditable works of which Southey was either the author or the editor included abbreviated versions of medieval Spanish romances; moral and political essays; ecclesiastical writings; a *History of Brazil;* annotated texts of Malory's *Morte D'Arthur* and Bunyan's *Pilgrim's Progress;* and, perhaps more important than all these, a body of letters which show us the loyal and gentle-spirited man behind his vast works.

## ENGLISH CONSERVATISM

He wrote voluminously, diligently, honestly, conservatively. He was respected for his integrity, honored by being made poet laureate of England, and trusted as a friend of other and younger writers. He was a political Tory, but an unselfish one; and when he opposed the Reform Bill of 1832, he did so—we must say—sincerely. His attitude on social questions was conservative, equally against despotism and democracy. It was his belief that a state should be governed by men who were self-disciplined and morally courageous; but apparently, once at least, as poet laureate, he forgot his convictions and wrote an elegy on the death of George III, for which he was taken to task by Lord Byron in a parodied *Vision of Judgment,* one of the severest satires of the language. The precipitate candor and brilliance of Byron were the exact opposite of Southey's wide and too weighty learning. Byron's pointed thrust at Southey, that

> He meant no harm in scribbling; 'twas his way
> Upon all topics; 'twas besides his bread,
> Of which he butter'd both sides,

was not without justification. Yet, if in the contest between them, the trophy of wit went to Byron, that of good conduct belonged undeniably to Southey.

## SATISFIED LIFE

Southey lived a full life, making industry a virtue, and writing rather too incessantly to be kept from being dull. But there is no record that his was a dull existence. For, surrounded by the more than ten thousand books that made up his private library, and fond of his family, and of good food—he confessed his keen taste for gooseberry tarts and old Rhenish wine—he spent his days in advancing the cause of literature, altogether nearly fifty active years of them, leaving to us—who now mostly pass by his major works—a little treasury of poetry in the form of a few ballads like *The Battle of Blenheim,* with its satirical refrain, "But 'twas a famous victory," a handful of lyrics like *The Holly-Tree,* and the epitaphic *My Days Among the Dead are Passed,* in which he wrote:

> My hopes are with the dead, anon
> My place with them will be,

> And I with them shall travel on
> Through all futurity;
> Yet leaving here a name, I trust,
> That will not perish in the dust.

It may perhaps be well for those of us accustomed to thinking of Southey as didactic only, and so dull, to remember that he proved his Romantic understanding of childhood by composing the ever-popular nursery story of *The Three Bears,* in the subtitle of which he gives the hint that he understands also the ways of adults, adding that it is

> A tale which may content the minds,
> Of learned men and grave philosophers,

and further punctuating the implied truth of the tale with these bold headlines:

> Somebody Has Been at My Porridge!
> Somebody Has Been Sitting in My Chair!
> Somebody Has Been Lying in My Bed!

## WALTER SAVAGE LANDOR

Walter Savage Landor belonged to two periods in English literature: the Romantic and the Victorian. He was born in 1775, when Wordsworth was five years old, and Coleridge, three; he wrote his well known lyric *Rose Aylmer* when Keats was ten years of age, and Shelley was thirteen; and, fifty-seven years later, in 1863, after publishing his *Last Fruits from an Old Tree,* he wrote in the same pure lyrical vein:

> To my ninth decade I have totter'd on,
>   And no soft arm bends now my steps to steady;
> She, who once led me where she would, is gone,
>   So when he calls me, Death shall find me ready.

Landor died in 1864, outliving Elizabeth Barrett Browning by three years. It was Robert Browning who helped support him to the end. Thus, in Landor's long life, was the entire Romantic movement spanned, as by a bridge resting ultimately on classical foundations. For in its attention to form, and its accent on self-control, Landor's poetry was classical; though by temperament—in his alternate expressions of tender affection and violent passion—he was certainly a revolutionary and a Romantic.

Landor was a picturesque character and a man of genius. He was born in Warwickshire. He excelled in Latin at Rugby; and it is reported that he was jeered at Oxford as a "mad Jacobin." His pugnacious, yet generous nature remained a dominant and puzzling trait in him throughout his long life. He quarreled with his father, but admired him. Leaving home, he settled in South Wales to study classical and English literature, unabashedly accepting the financial support of his father who, ten years later, at his death, left his son, who was then thirty, a small fortune; but most of which, before very long, he lost through his tactless generosity. At thirty-six he married Julia Thuillier who was twenty, dear to him, and with whom he quarreled. His life was spent almost equally between Italy and England: during the years between 1815 and 1835 he lived in Como and Pisa and Florence; between 1838 and 1858 at Bath; and from 1858 to 1864, the year of his death, again in Florence.

## LITERARY BEGINNINGS

Landor's literary career began in 1798 with the appearance of his epic poem *Gebir*. Its atmosphere is Oriental. Its theme is war and love: the conquering soldier is slain by the treacherous woman, and the worldly city he has built is destroyed by supernatural magic. Landor himself wrote a Latin version of the poem. That the Ancients and Milton were his models is evident in these chaste and august lines on the sea shell:

> Apply
> Its polisht lips to your attentive ear;
> And it remembers its august abode,
> And murmers as the ocean murmers here.

## MAN AND POET

Landor's important works appeared at intervals of ten years. After *Gebir, in* 1798, he published the first of the *Imaginary Conversations* in 1824; *Pericles and Aspasia* in 1836; the earliest of the *Hellenics* in 1847. On these, and on a group of short personal poems and epigrams, his fame as a minor poet and literary figure rests secure. Landor the man and his art are often at wide variance. He was temperamentally violent, yet worshipped still beauty and artistic restraint. He could offend the living; but of the dead he wrote as if he stood in some cathedral or Greek temple:

> Rose Aylmer, whom these wakeful eyes
> May weep, but never see,
> A night of memories and of sighs
> I consecrate to thee.

Perhaps the only persons who fully understood him were Robert and Elizabeth Barrett Browning in whose home in Florence he felt completely at ease and secure. In their presence the strange antithesis of what was classical and romantic in his nature was resolved and, as by some rebirth, given living form in those statuesque creations of still beauty that survive as examples of his pure art. Even when, as it happened, he had dashed to the floor a plate of food he did not like, Elizabeth could write in a letter: "Robert succeeded in soothing him, and the poor old lion is very quiet on the whole, roaring softly to beguile the time in Latin alcaics against his wife and Louis Napoleon."

## HIS ENDURING ART

Landor was majestical without the suggestion of the mystical. Nothing that he writes is adumbrated; everything is vividly and outwardly cold and solid. Its warmth, the pent up passion unmistakably present in it, is carefully concealed as in some marble Grecian urn. A familiar example of this calm, controlled and polished style, heavily charged with emotion, is the Imaginary Conversation *Iphigenia and Agamemnon* in which the daughter is about to die at the priest's hands in order to persuade the angry goddess Artemis to let the ships sail on the siege against Troy. The father is broken-hearted. Tears course down his cheek. He is silent. The daughter speaks:

> "O father! if the ships are now detained,
> And all your vows move not the Gods above,
> When the knife strikes me, there will be one prayer
> The less to them: and purer can there be
> Any, or more fervent than the daughter's prayer
> For her dear father's safety and success?"
> A groan that shook him shook not his resolve.
> An aged man now entered, and without
> One word, stepped slowly on, and took the wrist
> Of the pale maiden. She looked up and saw
> The fillet of the priest and calm cold eyes.
> Then turned she where her parent stood, and cried,
> "O father! grieve no more: the ships can sail."

Yet, for all this, the paradox of his character remains. He liked children, as he liked flowers, for what they actually were. But against this, in somber contrast, though the bare facts appeared otherwise, late in his life he could write, and not absurdly:

> I strove with none, for none was worth my strife,
> Nature I loved, and next to Nature, Art;
> I warmed both hands before the fire of life,
> It sinks, and I am ready to depart.

### THOMAS CAMPBELL

Campbell was the Scottish Highland son of a Glasgow merchant. He was born in the year 1777. By his native Scottish sense of freedom he was destined to interest himself in the cause of France in the years following the Revolution; in the liberation of the negro slave; in the national struggle of Poland; and in England's naval strength and command of the seas. But his patriotic absorption was in song, not in soldiery. Love of his country was a romantic feeling in him, gallant and moving, fed by the humanitarian ideal of the improvement of conditions for the natural development and happiness of man. At the same time his plain Scottish sagacity made him realistic enough to see in the British navy the power that could restore order and reason to a world upset by Napoleon.

### MELODY AND EMOTION

The best poetry of Campbell was written during the ten years between 1799 and 1809. None of it is profound or searching. Its commendable trait is its fluency of popular feeling. His one long poem of merit is his *Pleasures of Hope;* and its title is a commentary on what it contains. The occasional felicity of expression in it, and the poet's point of view, are both apparent in such random lines as these:

> 'Tis distance lends enchantment to the view,
> And robes the mountains in its azure hue.

### SONGS OF ENGLAND

Besides this poem, there are three war songs inseparable from Campbell's name. They are, *Hohenlinden, The Battle of the Baltic,* and *Ye Mariners of England;* the first and last of which are little masterpieces. The poet had himself been in Bavaria, in 1800, when the French fought the Austrians there and, from an elevated point, had seen an actual battle at Ratisbon, north-east of Munich on the Danube. The suddenness, the pictur-esqueness, the glory and the tragedy of Hohenlinden are vividly depicted; and, in the last lines, the benumbing stillness:

> Few, few, shall part where many meet!
> The snow shall be their winding-sheet,
> And every turf beneath their feet
> Shall be a soldier's sepulchre.

*The Battle of The Baltic* ends in the same quiescent mood; only now the melody is that of a wind-harp heard above the rolling, incoming sea:

> Soft sigh the winds of Heaven o'er their grave!
> While the billow mournful rolls
> And the mermaid's song condoles,
> Singing Glory to the souls
> Of the brave!

The critic George Saintsbury well sums up the still popular estimate of the poet: "Campbell holds the place of the best singer of war in a race and language which are those of the best singers and not the worst fighters in the history of the world,—in the race of Nelson and the language of Shakespeare. Not easily shall a man win higher praise than this."

## THOMAS MOORE

Moore was Irish to the core of his being. He was born in Dublin, in 1779. His mother gave him, as he later said, his "boudoir education." He learned very early to sing, to play the piano, to write verse, and to dislike Ireland's subjugation to British rule. While at the University of Dublin he made a trans-lation of the Odes of Anacreon which he took with him to Lon-don. He was then twenty-one, handsome, sociable, sincere, and gifted with a melodious voice, and he became immediately popular in London. His *Odes of Anacreon,* convivial, exotic, flirtatious, were published in 1800. A second volume of poems followed in 1801; and in 1807 appeared the first small collection of his *Irish Melodies.* The collection was to grow year by year until 1835 and to become the work by which he is now remembered. Meanwhile, in 1803, he was appointed admiralty registrar at Bermuda; but, assigning the work to a deputy, he spent a year visiting the United States. In 1811 he was married, and very happily, to Elizabeth Dyke, then sixteen and half his age, whom in frank devotion he everywhere called his "darling Bessy," and who bore him five children.

## HIS MAJOR POEM

In 1817 Moore published *Lalla Rookh,* a work in verse held together by passages of prose. The poem's setting is Oriental. One, the second, of its four stories suggests the nature of their theme. In it the beautiful air-spirit Peri must present a gift in order to enter Paradise. She brings, first, a drop of a young patriot's blood; then a once loved and now forsaken maiden's sigh of grief. But the gate of Paradise remains closed until she brings a criminal's tear shed in answer to a little child's prayer. Longman's, the publishers, paid three thousand pounds for the manuscript, but *Lalla Rookh* never became as famous as its author. There is a now very familiar story that Lady Holland, entertaining Moore at dinner, surprised him by saying: "I have not read your Larry O'Rourke; I don't like Irish stories."

## HIS PROSE WORK

Besides poems, Moore wrote several works of prose. One of them was his novel *The Epicurean,* the story of a young third century Greek who went to Egypt in quest of the secret of eternal life, found Alethe who was a Christian, was converted to Christianity through her influence, and, after her martyrdom, received the death sentence of hard labor in the mines. Moore also wrote three biographies: one of Sheridan; another of Lord Fitzgerald; and a third and official one of Byron, his intimate friend, who left his personal memoirs to Moore who, after writing the *Life of Lord Byron*, destroyed them.

## THE LYRIC GIFT

It is a little difficult to estimate the place of Thomas Moore in English literature. He was a melodist who knew, in season, how to be grave and gay, how to make the instrument of his verse give forth the plaintive or the stirring note, to make it breathe a sultry and exotic air, or sigh in a sweet and sentimental tone,—as in the poem beginning:

> Oft, in a stilly night,
>  Ere Slumber's chain has bound me,
> Fond Memory brings the light
>  Of other days around me.

His poems cannot be fully appreciated apart from the tunes which accompany them. Their intellectual content is scant. The poet, for instance, takes the simple idea that time brings change; touches it with the memory of some historic age; calls in emotions on the waves of pleasing sound; gives the composition the stillness and temper of his Celtic genius—and the pleasing result is verse like this:

> The harp that once through Tara's halls
>  The soul of music shed,
> Now hangs as mute on Tara's walls,
>  As if that soul were fled.
> So sleeps the pride of former days,
>  So glory's thrill is o'er,
> And hearts that once beat high for praise
>  Now feel that pulse no more!

**293**

The best of Moore's poetry revolves about this theme: life is good; but it cannot last; the moment of its rich fullness must go. Summer is a short season of fruition; every living thing moves toward its ripening. That moment is life's joy. Then comes the turning of leaves in the autumn sun; the grass withers and the flower fades. It was so with Moore's own life. Near the end of it he said in his journal: "The last of my five children is gone, and we are left desolate and alone; not a single relation have I in this world." That is the theme, and the inescapable art, of the song beginning:

> 'Tis the last rose of summer
> Left blooming alone;
> All her lovely companions
> Are faded and gone.

## ROMANTICISM IN TWILIGHT

We can think of no more fitting and final commentary on Moore than these just quoted lines: the immediacy of their sensory appeal; the lively intelligence behind them; their subdued plaintive tone; the absence in them of philosophic depth, of strong passion or transcendent vision; their mellow odor of Indian summer and nostalgia. Moore's poetry represents romanticism in sweet and genial decay. In a summary estimate of him, we may recall Arthur Symons' remark that

"Moore as a poet is the Irishman as the Englishman imagines him to be. . . . All the Irish quicksilver is in him; he registers change with every shift in the weather. . . . But the voice of the peasant is not in him; there is in him nothing of that uneasy, listening conscience which watches the earth for signs, and is never alone in solitude. . . . He gave pleasure, but the quality of that pleasure must be considered, and it will be seen that it was not the quality of poetic pleasure. . . . Herrick wrote drinking songs, and he left in them some of the mournful ecstasy of the vine. But, in the drinking songs of Tom Moore, only the lees are left."

("Romantic Movement in English Poetry," p. 200-2, E. P. Dutton & Co., Publishers, N. Y., 1909.)

## LEIGH HUNT

In Hunt the romantic movement found a man without genius but of abundant talent. His varied interests, versatility, and his vital energy gave a timely impetus to the movement in its later career. The *Examiner,* the *Autobiography,* and a few choice lyrics like *The Glove and the Lions, Abou Ben Adhem* and *Jenny Kissed Me,* are his modest literary monument. The last of these, the graceful *Rondeau,* still pleases us as it must have pleased Thomas and Jane Carlyle for whom it was written:

> Jenny kissed me when we met,
>   Jumping from the chair she sat in;
> Time, you thief, who love to get
>   Sweets into your list, put that in;
> Say I'm weary, say I'm sad,
>   Say that health and wealth have missed me,
> Say I'm growing old, but add,
>   Jenny kissed me.

But Hunt's fame rests chiefly on what he did for others in the literary world who were greater than himself, notably Byron, Shelley and Keats who owed him much and to whose names his own is now closely attached. His judgment of contemporary writers was unsurpassed. He edited the *Examiner* which had a career of fourteen years, and the *Liberal* which lasted but three years, being cut off by Shelley's death. He wrote a long poem, *The Story of Rimini,* based on Dante's tragic love-story of Paolo and Francesca; he translated Tasso's pastoral *Aminta* with graceful skill; he wrote a tract on Christianity; and, most important to his age and to us, he became the author of works of literary criticism, among the best of which were his *Imagination and Fancy, Wit and Humour,* and *Men, Women, and Books.*

## LITERARY PATRON AND CRITIC

In the first of these three critical volumes there appeared, in 1844, an essay entitled *What is Poetry?* In it Hunt did two things: he commended poetry by quoting it, aptly, tactfully, and with a feeling of its worth; and he offered an elementary definition of poetry as art, giving particular attention to Romantic poetry as the expression of imaginative passion. Such powers of critical analysis and intellectual subtlety, important for historical study and indispensable to original and philosophical insight, as for example Coleridge possessed, were not his. It was Hunt's special talent to appreciate a good poem and to hail and defend the good—and especially the young—poet. In estimating his work it should be remembered that his entry into literature was made through journalism, that his interests were wide, representing the age, and included political and social questions, such as Parliamentary reform, education, child labor, the London prison laws, and a larger freedom for Roman Catholics; and that the *Examiner* was made the instrument of his activities as a reformer, a patron of young writers, and a critic of English manners and letters. Readers of literature are well reminded that for daring to say what most Englishmen thought of the Prince Regent—referring to him as "a violator of his word . . . a despiser of domestic ties," in short, a "fat Adonis of fifty"—Hunt spent two years in prison where he was visited by Lamb, Hazlitt and Byron, and became a deservedly popular hero. The editors of *Blackwood's,* as they thought proper, slandered him indecently, and with him Keats, his then devoted friend, provoking, by their contemptuous references

to the "Cockney School" of poets, these explanatory lines of
Keats:

> What though, for showing truth to flatter'd state,
> Kind Hunt was shut in prison, yet has he,
> In his immortal spirit, been as free
> As the sky-searching lark, and as elate . . .
> In Spenser's halls he stray'd, and bowers fair,
> Culling enchanted flowers; and he flew
> With daring Milton through the fields of air;
> To regions of his own genius true
> Took happy flights.

## CRITICAL VERDICT

It is tempting to dwell on Hunt's short-comings. He had, we
may say, no eye for business, no talent in politics, though his
writing carried him continually into public affairs. He imposed
too easily on his best friends, of whom nevertheless he had and
kept a considerable number; among them were Hazlitt, Moore,
Byron, Shelley and Keats, and later also Dickens, Thackeray,
Browning and Carlyle. His insight into abstract and philosophical matters was superficial; he could not dwell with high
seriousness on questions of moral duty, deity and the immortal
life. He contented himself, in writing verse, with what was
close at hand, intimate, in good taste, tending toward the delicacy of the feminine, the luxurious and languid pleasures, without sharpening his fancy to a keen edge of rapture, letting the
lines "trot and amble", and avoiding—except unsuccessfully in
the *Story of Rimini*—attempts at writing in a noble tragic strain.
Keats, himself later aware of Hunt's shortcomings, recognized
in the lesser poet the especial gift by which he was to influence
the age, and wrote in a sonnet to *Leigh Hunt, Esq.*,

> And I shall ever bless my destiny,
> That in a time, when under pleasant trees

> Pan is no longer sought, I feel a free,
> A leafy luxury, seeing I could please
> With these poor offerings, a man like thee.

That, we conclude, is praise enough for one content, without feasting with the Olympian gods, to wait on the tables of the great.

## THOMAS HOOD

Something now remains to be said of Thomas Hood who was born in 1799 and died in 1845. His verse was of two kinds: serious and light, reflecting his chief traits of humor and humanitarianism. He worked against the sad odds of poverty and ill health. But friends, among them Browning and Dickens, helped by their contributions to *Hood's Magazine* to support the editor-poet and so to save him for literature. A great day for him came when, in 1843, in the Christmas issue of *Punch,* he saw published his poem *The Song of the Shirt.* In 1826 there had come from the press, in London, a volume by him entitled *Whims and Oddities* containing both verse and prose. His punning ballads in it had given him a reputation for droll and stark humor; and he must have well deserved it for writing lines like these about Sally Brown's forlorn lover:

> "O Sally Brown, O Sally Brown,
> How could you serve me so?
> I've met with many a breeze before
> But never such a blow!"

> Then reading on his 'bacco box
> He heaved a bitter sigh,
> And then began to eye his pipe,
> And then to pipe his eye . . .

His death, which happen'd in his berth,
  At forty-odd befell:
They went and told the sexton, and
  The sexton toll'd the bell.

## HUMANITARIANISM

But in *The Song of the Shirt* Hood now exhibited an emotional and a social quality unguessed at in the earlier verses. Here was a realism with a thrust at human conscience, suited to the temper of the early Victorians to whom the poem by time and right belonged, and to whose humanitarian outlook it owed its prolonged popularity. For by the year 1843 far-sighted men, looking on an industrialized England, had begun to press hard for the social reforms that were to be the Parliament's answer to the poet's cry of anguish:

Oh, God! that bread should be so dear,
And flesh and blood so cheap!

Equally humanitarian in its pathos and appeal to Christian charity was the poem *The Bridge of Sighs*. Cutting through conventional sentiment, its clear short lines register the heart-beat of pity felt by the poet as he tells the story of the unfortunate girl drowned in the river, and then tranquilizes the sharp note of tragedy with the tenderly muted touch of the sleep of death, when he says:

Make no deep scrutiny
Into her mutiny
  Rash and undutiful:
Past all dishonour,
Death has left on her
  Only the beautiful.

Looking again at the small select body of Hood's poetry, we are impressed by its variety and the poet's versatility. In it we find an amazing verbal dexterity, a sharp wit, a sturdy humorous treatment of a grim theme, as for example in the poem *The Last Man.* Then, in a moment, we trace the poet's return to the lighter delicate touch of the verses,

> I remember, I remember,
> The house where I was born,
> The little window where the sun
> Came peeping in at morn.

After that there is the intended silly sophistication of the poem *French and English,* which advises us never to go to France, where

> *Chaises* stand for chairs,
> They christen letters *Billies,*
> They call their mothers *mares,*
> And all their daughters *fillies.*

Finally, these impressions seem all to be swept away by the strident note of social reform in *The Song of the Shirt,* and the tender pathos of *The Bridge of Sighs.* One wonders, musing and reflecting on how much talent lay underground with Thomas Hood when he died at forty-six.

# THE LITERARY REVIEWS

## ENGLISH LIFE AND LETTERS

Something, in conclusion, should be said about the literary editors and reviewers of the Romantic period. They were, to look at them generally, watchful judicious observers of English life and manners rather than literary critics. England was their chief concern, and the course of literature was therefore a responsibility they could not shun or ignore. Behind them, lodged firmly in their consciousness, lay the 18th century with its aloof and formal intellectualism; before them, still unexplored, lay the Victorian era of objective scientific criticism. Between the two trends was a deep-rooted dual conflict: the first was between reason and imagination; the second, more radical and divisive, was between an inherited classical and Christian tradition and a rising materialistic and secular conception of life and society. The poets themselves sensed the conflict and took issues in the struggle. The reviewers, as the bold nationalistic critics of the time, looked with a cold eye on the struggle, adjudicated current disputes, and condemned or approved what they examined, according to their Whig or Tory positions.

## THE EDINBURGH REVIEW

Between 1800 and 1825 five such important reviews, or journals, were established. The first of them was the *Edinburgh Review*, founded in 1802 by Francis Jeffrey, assisted by Henry Brougham and Sidney Smith. Its position was at first mildly Tory; but in the course of the decade it became gradually, and at last completely, Whig. Its career extended through 127 years—to 1929; and its attitude toward the Romantic writers was in the main rather fair. Hazlitt contributed to it, as later also did Macaulay, Carlyle and Arnold. The Lake poets were the most severely criticized in it. Even Hazlitt — who sometimes waves before us the red flag of his own defiance when he cannot at once find his way into another and perhaps superior mind — writing in the September, 1816 issue of the *Edinburgh,* could say of Coleridge whom he professed to respect, and of the *Kubla Khan:*

Upon the whole, we look upon this publication as one of the most notable pieces of impertinence of which the press has lately been guilty; and one of the boldest experiments that has yet been made on the patience or understanding of the public.

Against such criticism uttered in the *Edinburgh* strain we need now only to apply to Coleridge the unanswerable plea of Shakespeare:

> I am that I am; and they that level
> At my abuses reckon up their own.

Jeffrey, himself a quick-witted lawyer, writing in the fact-listing, judicatory Eighteenth century style, later so much praised and imitated by Macaulay, tended to treat every poet whose work he reviewed as a prisoner at the bar; and he attempted, with the utmost honesty of a Scottish judge, to conduct trials of all men who produced literature, with his own grey eye set on the precept implied in the remark he once made to Sir Walter Scott, that "the *Review* . . . has but two legs to stand on. Literature, no doubt, is one of them: but its *Right leg* is Politics."

## THE QUARTERLY REVIEW

In 1809 Sir Walter Scott, by then unwilling any longer to read the *Edinburgh Review*, though he had earlier contributed to it, went to London and there founded the *Quarterly Review*. William Gifford became its first editor; John Lockhart and John Croker were appointed his near associates. The *Quarterly* was unmitigatedly Tory; it denounced the then popular criticism of church and state; it condemned the romanticism of the younger poets; it upheld the established principles of literary style. In it, in 1818, appeared the well-known attack on Keats' *Endymion*, of which Lord Byron wrote:

> Who killed John Keats?
> "I" says the *Quarterly*,

So cruel and Tartarly,
"Twas one of my feats."

After 1824, with Lockhart as editor, its attitude toward the older poets was one of relative tolerance; so much so that by 1834, the year of Coleridge's death, Hartley Coleridge, his son, writing for the *Quarterly,* could say:

It is this remarkable power of making his verse musical that gives a peculiar character to Mr. Coleridge's lyric poems. In some of the smaller pieces, as in the conclusion of the "Kubla Khan," for example, not only the lines by themselves are musical, but the whole passage sounds all at once as an outburst or crash of harps in the still air of autumn. The verses seem as if *played* to the ear upon some unseen instrument.

Yet the *Quarterly,* like its rival the *Edinburgh,* was a law unto itself. It resembled a closed corporation trading on its own views of literature, scholarship, politics and science, praising what was Tory, condemning what was Whig. The reviewer in it wrote without signing his name; the editor trimmed or added to the articles he published; the contributing poet was often shot at from the dark; and all was done in the supposed interest of the general public of which the *Review* was the self appointed spokesman. Such generally, was the order and estate of literary journalism in the sparse years between 1825 and 1830.

## BLACKWOOD'S MAGAZINE

The third magazine of importance was *Blackwood's.* It was begun in 1817, in Edinburgh, and was published monthly. John Lockhart who was Scott's son-in-law and John Wilson, a close friend of De Quincey, were the men whose special talents assured its success. "The first of these men," says a modern writer, "could deliver a swashing blow; the second was the master of the *coup de grace.*" De Quincey we have earlier said, contributed regularly to it, giving it, through his *Confessions,* the status of literature. Its reviews were merciless toward the younger English poets, particularly toward Hunt and Keats for whom Lockhart invented the derisive nickname "The Cockney School." *Blackwood's* over-praised Scott; accepted Byron; did justice to Wordsworth; but was rather uneasily critical toward Coleridge, ignorantly suspicious of Shelley, cruel toward Keats, and openly slanderous (in the issue of October, 1817) toward Hunt. Nevertheless the magazine was kept from being merely vituperative and addicted to scolding by the sturdy and forthright honesty of Mr. Wilson. "Christopher North," by which name Wilson is known in *Noctes Ambrosianae,* a series of articles published in *Blackwood's,* was in fact an extraordinary man. His robust imagination astonished Edinburgh where he lectured on moral philosophy; and his oratory often quite eclipsed his coveted reputation for logic. He admired Wordsworth, and wanted, like him, to be *sublime.* But there was a non-Wordsworthian strain of the convivial in him that De Quincey called "a large expansiveness of heart" and that hints at the nights of exuberant and witty talk of the literary coterie at the Ambrose.

## THE LONDON MAGAZINE

A blot on the escutcheon of *Blackwood's* was its tragic quarrel with the *London Magazine.* In a called-for opposition to *Blackwood's,* a group of writers among them Hazlitt, Lamb, De Quincey and Hood, had started *London's* in 1820 and had nursed it along toward a distinguished career when, in 1829, the editor of *Blackwood's* challenged and killed the editor of *London's* in a duel. The shock of the event subdued further offensive criticism, and opened the way for the new *West-*

*minster Review,* founded in 1824 by Jeremy Bentham and James Mill, leaders of the new and radical Utilitarian movement, with the rise of which the Romantic period may be said to have come to an end.

# BIBLIOGRAPHY

**GENERAL**

Abercrombie, L. *Romanticism,* The Viking Press, Inc., 1927.

Babbitt, Irving. *Rousseau and Romanticism,* Houghton Mifflin Co., 1919.

Bate, W. J. *From Classic to Romantic,* Harvard University Press, 1946.

Beach, J. W. *The Concept of Nature in Nineteenth-Century English Poetry,* The Macmillan Co., 1936.

Beers, H. A. *A History of English Romanticism in the Nineteenth Century,* Henry Holt & Co., Inc., 1901.

Bernbaum, Ernest. *Guide Through the Romantic Movement,* The Ronald Press Company, 1949.

Brinton, C. *The Political Ideas of the English Romanticists,* Oxford University Press, Inc., 1926.

Brooks, Cleanth. *Modern Poetry and the Tradition,* University of North Carolina Press, 1939.

Bush, Douglas. *Mythology and the Romantic Tradition in English Poetry,* Harvard University Press, 1937.

Dowden, E. *The French Revolution and English Literature,* Charles Scribner's Sons, 1897.

Eliot, T. S. *The Sacred Wood,* Barnes & Noble, Inc., 1920.

Elton, Oliver. *A Survey of English Literature: 1780-1830,* 2 Vols., The Macmillan Co., 1920.

Evans, B. I. *Tradition and Romanticism,* Longmans, Green & Co., 1940.

Fairchild, H. N. *The Romantic Quest,* Columbia University Press, 1931.

Herford, C. H. *The Age of Wordsworth,* E. P. Dutton & Co., Inc., 1930.

Pater, Walter. *Appreciations,* The Macmillan Co., 1889.

Phelps, Wm. L. *The Beginnings of the English Romantic Movement,* Ginn & Company, 1893.

Railo, Eino. *The Haunted Castle: Elements of English Romanticism,* E. P. Dutton & Co., Inc., 1927.

Symons, A. *Collected Works,* v. 13, *The Romantic Movement in English Poetry,* Gabriel Wells, 1924.

Tinker, C. B. *Nature's Simple Plan,* Princeton University Press, 1922.

Trevelyan, G. M. *British History in the Nineteenth Century,* Longmans, Green & Co., 1930.

## JAMES THOMSON: 1700-1748

Macaulay, Geo. C. *James Thomson,* The Macmillan Co., 1907.

McKillop, Alan D. *The Background of Thomson's Seasons,* University of Minnesota Press, 1942.

Robertson, J. Logie, edit. *Complete Poetical Works,* Oxford University Press, Inc., 1908.

## THOMAS GRAY: 1716-1771

Arnold, Matthew. *Essays in Criticism, Second Series,* St. Martin's Press, Inc., 1888.

Crofts, J., edit. *Gray: Poetry and Prose,* Oxford University Press, Inc., 1926.

Hudson, W. H. *Gray and His Poetry,* F. W. Dodge Corporation, 1918.

Jones, W. P. *Thomas Gray, Scholar,* Harvard University Press, 1937.

Reed, Amy L. *The Background of Gray's Elegy: Melancholy Poetry, 1700-1751,* Columbia University Press, 1924.

Tovey, D. C. *Gray and His Friends,* Putnam, 1890.

Toynbee and Whibley, edits. *The Correspondence of Thomas Gray,* Oxford University Press, Inc., 1935.

## WILLIAM COLLINS: 1721-1759

Ainsworth, E. G. *Poor Collins: His Life, his Art, and his Influence,* Cornell University Press, 1937.

Blunden, E., edit. *The Poems of William Collins,* Oxford University Press, Inc., 1929.

Bronson, W. C., edit. *Poetical Works,* Ginn & Company, 1898.

Garrod, H. W. *The Poetry of Collins,* Oxford University Press, Inc., 1928.

Johnson, Samuel. *Lives of the Poets,* edit., E. P. Dutton & Co., Inc., 1905.

Kennedy, Wilma L. *English Heritage of Coleridge;* Ch. on Collins, Yale University Press,, 1947.

# BIBLIOGRAPHY

### JAMES MACPHERSON: 1736-1796

Nutt, A. *Ossian and Ossianic Literature*, Charles Scribner's Sons, 1899.

Saunders, T. B. *The Life and Letters of James Macpherson*, S. Sonnenschein & Co., 1894.

Sharp, W., edit. *The Works of Ossian*, Edinburgh Press, 1896.

Smart, J. S. *James Macpherson: An Episode in Literature*, David Nutt, 1905.

Snyder, E. D. *The Celtic Revival in English Literature: 1760-1800*, Harvard University Press, 1923.

### THOMAS CHATTERTON: 1752-1770

Hare, M. E., edit. *The Rowley Poems*, Oxford University Press, Inc., 1911.

Ingram, J. H. *The True Chatterton*, Charles Scribner's Sons, 1910.

Meyerstein, E. H. W. *The Life of Thomas Chatterton*, Charles Scribner's Sons, 1930.

Penzoldt, E. *The Marvelous Boy*, Harcourt, Brace & Co., 1931.

### WILLIAM COWPER: 1731-1800

Cecil, David, edit. *Selections of Cowper's Poetry*, Methuen & Co., 1933.

Cecil, David. *The Stricken Deer*, Constable & Co., 1929.

Fausset, H. l'A. *William Cowper*, P. Smith, 1928.

Hartley, L. C. *William Cowper, Humanitarian*, University of North Carolina Press, 1938.

Wright, Thomas. *The Life of William Cowper*, Author, 1921.

Wright, Thomas, edit. *Cowper's Correspondence*, 4 Vols., Dodd, Mead & Co., 1904.

### GEORGE CRABBE: 1754-1832

Ainger, A. *Crabbe*, The Macmillan Co., 1903.

Carlyle, A. J. and R. W., edits. *Works of George Crabbe*, Oxford University Press, Inc., 1915.

Evans, J. H. *The Poems of George Crabbe*, The Macmillan Co., 1933.

Huchon, R. *George Crabbe and His Times*, transl. by Clarke, E. P. Dutton & Co., Inc., 1907.

### ROBERT BURNS: 1759-1796

Dick, J. C. *Songs of Robert Burns: With Melodies*, Oxford University Press, Inc., 1907.

Ferguson, J. deL., edit. *Robert Burns' Letters,* Oxford University Press, Inc., 1931.

Ferguson, J. deL. *Pride and Passion: Robert Burns,* Oxford University Press, Inc., 1939.

Hecht, Hans. *Robert Burns: The Man and His Work,* transl. by Lymburn, W. B. Saunders Co., 1936.

Henley, W. E. and Henderson, edits. *The Centenary Burns,* T. C. & E. C. Jack, 1896.

Snyder, F. B. *Robert Burns,* University of Chicago Press, 1936.

## WILLIAM BLAKE: 1757-1827

Binyon, Lawrence, edit. *Poems of Blake,* The Macmillan Co., 1931.

Binyon, Lawrence. *The Engraved Designs of William Blake,* Charles Scribner's Sons, 1926.

Chesterton, G. K. *William Blake,* E. P. Dutton & Co., Inc., 1910.

Damon, S. Foster. *William Blake: His Philosophy and Symbols,* P. Smith, 1947.

Figgis, Darrell. *The Paintings of William Blake,* Charles Scribner's Sons, 1925.

Frye, Northrup. *Fearful Symmetry,* Princeton University Press, 1947.

Kazin, Alfred, edit. *The Portable Blake,* The Viking Press, Inc., 1946.

Keynes, Geoffrey, edit. *Poetry and Prose of William Blake,* Random House, 1927.

Murry, J. Middleton. *William Blake,* Jonathan Cape, 1933.

Percival, Milton O. *William Blake's Circle of Destiny,* Columbia University Press, 1938.

Plowman, Max. *Introduction to the Study of Blake,* E. P. Dutton & Co., Inc., 1927.

Schorer, Mark. *William Blake,* Henry Holt & Co., Inc., 1946.

Swinburne, A. C. *William Blake,* Charles Scribner's Sons, 1925.

White, Helen. *The Mysticism of William Blake,* University of Wisconsin Press, 1927.

Wilson, Mona. *The Life of William Blake,* Random House, 1927.

## WILLIAM WORDSWORTH: 1770-1850

Arnold, Matthew. *Essays in Criticism, Second Series,* St. Martin's Press, Inc., 1888.

Batho, Edith C. *The Later Wordsworth,* The Macmillan Co., 1933.

Beatty, Arthur. *William Wordsworth: His Doctrine and Art,* University of Wisconsin Press, 1927.

George, A. J., edit. *The Prelude,* abridged ed., D. C. Heath, 1935.

# BIBLIOGRAPHY

Grierson, H. J. *Milton and Wordsworth,* The Macmillan Co., 1937.

Griggs, E. L. edit. *Wordsworth and Coleridge,* Princeton University Press, 1939.

Harper, Geo. McL. *William Wordsworth,* Charles Scribner's Sons, 1929.

Herford, C. H. *Wordsworth,* E. P. Dutton & Co., Inc., 1930.

Hutchinson, Thomas, edit. *William Wordsworth, Poetical Works,* Oxford University Press, Inc., 1928.

Legouis, Emile. *The Early Life of Wordsworth,* E. P. Dutton & Co., Inc., 1921.

Martin, A. D., *The Religion of Wordsworth,* G. Allen, 1936.

Meyer, Geo., W. *Wordsworth's Formative Years,* University of Michigan Press, 1943.

Patton, C. H., *The Rediscovery of Wordsworth,* Stratford Co., 1935.

Peek, Katherine M. *Wordsworth in England,* Author, Rosemont College, Rosemont, Pennsylvania, 1943.

Raleigh, Walter. *Wordsworth,* Longmans, Green & Co., Inc., 1913.

Read, Herbert. *Wordsworth,* Jonathan Cape, 1930.

Selincourt, E. de, edit. *The Prelude,* abridged ed., Oxford University Press, Inc., 1935.

Smith, J. C. *Wordsworth,* Oliver, 1944.

Stallknecht, N. P. *Strange Seas of Thought,* Duke University Press, 1945.

Winwar, Frances. *Farewell the Banner: Coleridge, Wordsworth and Dorothy,* Doubleday & Company, Inc., 1938.

Wordsworth, Dorothy. *The Journals,* edit., E. de Selincourt, St. Martin's Press, Inc., 1924.

Wordsworth, Dorothy. *Letters,* edit., E. de Selincourt, Oxford University Press, Inc., 1944.

## SAMUEL TAYLOR COLERIDGE: 1772-1834

Chambers, E. K. *Samuel T. Coleridge,* Oxford University Press, Inc., 1938.

Charpentier, John. *Coleridge, the Sublime Somnambulist,* Dodd, Mead & Co., 1929.

Coleridge, E. H., edit. *Complete Poetical Works,* 2 Vols., Oxford University Press, Inc., 1912.

Fausset, H. l'A. *Samuel Taylor Coleridge,* Jonathan Cape, 1934.

Griggs, E. L., edit. *The Best of Coleridge,* The Ronald Press Company, 1932.

Griggs, E. L. edit. *Wordsworth and Coleridge,* Princeton University Press, 1939.

Hanson, Lawrence. *The Life of Coleridge: The Early Years,* Oxford University Press, Inc., 1939.

Howard, Claud. *Coleridge's Idealism: Kant and the Cambridge Platonists,* Richard G. Badger, 1924.

Kennedy, W. L. *The English Heritage of Coleridge of Bristol,* Yale University Press, 1947.

Lowes, John Livingston. *The Road to Xanadu,* Houghton Mifflin Co., 1927.

Muirhead, J. H., *Coleridge as Philosopher,* Humanities Press, Inc., 1930.

Potter, Stephen. *Coleridge and S. T. C.,* Jonathan Cape, 1935.

Richards, I. A. *Coleridge on Imagination,* Harcourt, Brace & Co., 1935.

Sanders, C. R. *Coleridge and the Broad Church Movement,* Duke University Press, 1942.

Shawcross, John, edit. *Biographia Literaria,* 2 Vols., Oxford University Press, Inc., 1907.

Traill, H. D. *Samuel Taylor Coleridge,* The Macmillan Co., 1884.

Winwar, Frances. *Farewell the Banner: Coleridge, Wordsworth and Dorothy,* Doubleday & Company, Inc., 1938.

## SIR WALTER SCOTT: 1771-1832

Baker, Ernest A. *The History of the English Novel,* Vol. VI, Witherby, 1935.

Ball, Margaret. *Sir Walter Scott as a Critic of Literature,* Columbia University Press, 1907.

Buchan, John. *Sir Walter Scott,* Cassell & Co., 1933.

Grierson, H. J. C. *Sir Walter Scott, Bart.,* Columbia University Press, 1938.

Hillhouse, J. T. *The Waverley Novels and Their Critics,* Oxford University Press, Inc., 1936.

Hudson, W. H. *Sir Walter Scott,* Sands: London, 1901.

Lang, Andrew, edit. *Waverley Novels,* 25 Vols., L. C. Page & Company, 1902-1904.

Lockhart, J. G. *Life of Sir Walter Scott,* The Macmillan Co., 1839. Mod. editions available.

Saintsbury, George. *Life of Sir Walter Scott,* Charles Scribner's Sons, 1897.

Scudder, H. E., edit. *Scott's Complete Poetical Works,* Appleton-Century-Crofts, Inc., 1900.

Walpole, Hugh, edit. *The Waverley Pageant,* Harper & Brothers, 1932.

# BIBLIOGRAPHY

### CHARLES LAMB: 1775-1834

Blunden, Edmund. *Charles Lamb and His Contemporaries,* The Macmillan Co., 1937.

Howe, W. D. *Charles Lamb and His Friends,* The Bobbs-Merrill Company, 1944.

Hutchinson, Thomas, edit. *Prose and Verse of Charles and Mary Lamb,* Oxford University Press, Inc., 1924.

Johnson, Edith. *Lamb Always Elia,* Methuen & Co., 1935.

Lucas, E. V. *Life of Charles Lamb,* 2 Vols., 5th ed., Methuen & Co., 1921.

Morley, F. V. *Lamb Before Elia,* Jonathan Cape, 1932.

Ward, A. C. *The Frolic and the Gentle,* Methuen & Co., 1934.

Williams, Orlo. *Charles Lamb,* Duckworth, 1934.

### WILLIAM HAZLITT: 1778-1830

Birrell, A. *William Hazlitt,* The Macmillan Co., 1902.

Howe, P. P. *Life of William Hazlitt,* rev. ed., Penguin Books, Inc., 1947.

Howe, P. P. *The Complete Works of William Hazlitt,* 21 Vols., Dent, 1930-1934.

Maclean, Catherine. *Born Under Saturn,* The Macmillan Co., 1944.

Schneider, Elisabeth. *The Aesthetics of William Hazlitt,* University of Pennsylvania Press, 1933.

Zeitlin, Jacob. *Hazlitt on English Literature,* Oxford University Press, Inc., 1913.

### THOMAS DE QUINCEY: 1785-1859

Abrams, M. H. *The Milk of Paradise,* Harvard University Press, 1934.

Bonner, W. H., edit. *De Quincey at Work: His Letters,* University of Buffalo Press, 1936.

Eaton, H. A. *Thomas De Quincey: A Biography,* Oxford University Press, Inc., 1936.

Eaton, H. A., edit. *A Diary of Thomas De Quincey: 1803,* Harcourt Brace & Co., Inc., 1928.

Fowler, J. H. *De Quincey as Literary Critic,* Oxford University Press, Inc., 1922.

Hogg, J. *De Quincey and His Friends,* London, 1895.

Masson, David, edit. *Collected Writings of De Quincey,* 14 Vols., The Macmillan Co., 1890.

Metcalf, J. C. *De Quincey: A Portrait,* Harvard University Press, 1940.

Proctor, Sigmund K. *Thomas De Quincey's Theory of Literature,* University of Michigan Press, 1943.

Sackville-West, E. *Thomas De Quincey, His Life and Work,* Yale University Press, 1936.

Salt, Henry. *De Quincey,* Macmillan, 1904.

## ROBERT SOUTHEY: 1774-1843

Dowden, Edward. *Southey,* The Macmillan Co., 1906.

Fitzgerald, M. H., edit. *Poetical Works of Robert Southey,* Oxford University Press, Inc., 1909.

Fitzgerald, M. H., edit. *Southey's Life of Wesley,* 2 Vols., Oxford University Press, Inc., 1925.

Gollancz, Emma, edit. *Southey's Life of Nelson,* The Macmillan Co., 1896.

Haller, William. *The Early Life of Robert Southey,* Columbia University Press, 1917.

Simmons, Jack. *Southey,* Yale University Press, 1948.

## JANE AUSTEN: 1775-1817

Austen-Leigh, W. and R. *Jane Austen: Her Life and Letters,* E. P. Dutton & Co., Inc., 1913.

Bailey, John. *Introduction to Jane Austen,* Oxford University Press, Inc., 1931.

Chapman, R. W., edit. *Jane Austen: Novels,* Oxford University Press, Inc., 1934.

Lascelles, M. *Jane Austen and Her Art,* Oxford University Press, Inc., 1939.

Rawlence, Guy. *Jane Austen,* Duckworth, 1934.

Rhydderch, D. *Jane Austen: Her Life and Art,* P. Smith, 1936.

Seymour, B. K. *Jane Austen,* M. Joseph, 1937.

## THOMAS CAMPBELL: 1777-1844

Beattie, William. *Life and Letters of Thomas Campbell,* 2 Vols., Harper & Brothers, 1850.

Campbell, Lewis., edit. *Selected Poems of Thomas Campbell,* The Macmillan Co., 1904.

Dixon, W. M. *An Apology for the Arts,* St. Martin's Press, Inc., 1944.

Elton, Oliver. *Survey of English Literature: 1780-1830,* The Macmillan Co., 1912.

Hadden, J. C. *Thomas Campbell,* Charles Scribner's Sons, 1900.

Robertson, John L., edit. *Thomas Campbell: Complete Poetical Works,* Oxford University Press, Inc., 1907.

## WALTER SAVAGE LANDOR: 1775-1864

Colvin, Sidney. *Landor;* English Men of Letters Series, The Macmillan Co., 1888.

Colvin, Sidney, edit. *Landor: Selections,* Prose and Poetry, The Macmillan Co., 1895.

Elkin, Felice. *Landor's Studies of Italian Life and Literature,* University of Pennsylvania Press, 1934.

Ellis, Havelock, edit. *Imaginary Conversations and Poems,* E. P. Dutton & Co., Inc., 1933.

Elwin, Malcom. *Savage Landor,* The Macmillan Co., 1941.

Goldmark, Ruth. *Studies in Influence of the Classics on English Literature,* Columbia University Press, 1918.

Minchin, H. C. *Last Days, Letters, and Conversations,* Methuen & Co., 1934.

Selincourt, E. de, edit. *Imaginary Conversations,* Oxford University Press, Inc., 1914.

Welby, T. Earle and Stephen Wheeler, edits. *Complete Works of Landor,* 16 Vols., Chapman & Hall, 1927-1936.

## THOMAS MOORE: 1779-1852

Falkiner, C. L., edit. *Selected Poems,* The Macmillan Co., 1903.

Godley, A. D., edit. *Poetical Works of Thomas Moore,* Oxford University Press, Inc., 1910.

Gunning, J. P. *Moore, Poet and Patriot,* Gill: Dublin, 1900.

Gwynn, S. L. *Thomas Moore;* English Men of Letters Series, The Macmillan Co., 1924.

Jones, Howard M. *The Harp That Once: The Life Of Thomas Moore,* Henry Holt & Co., Inc., 1937.

Priestley, J. B., edit. *Tom Moore's Diary,* Cambridge University Press, 1925.

Strong, L. A. G. *The Minstrel Boy,* Alfred A. Knopf, Inc., 1937.

## LEIGH HUNT: 1784-1859

Blunden, Edmund Charles, edit. *Autobiography;* World Classics, Oxford University Press, Inc., 1928.

Blunden, Edmund Charles. *Leigh Hunt and His Circle,* Harper & Brothers, 1930.

Brewer, Luther, A. *My Leigh Hunt Library.* Bibliography. Torch Press, 1932.

Johnson, R. B., edit. *Essays and Poems: Leigh Hunt,* 2 Vols., The Macmillan Co., 1891.

Johnson, R. B., edit. *Prefaces by Leigh Hunt,* W. M. Hill, Chicago, 1927.

Johnson, R. B., *Leigh Hunt: His Life,* Macmillan, 1896.

Milford, H. S., edit. Hunt's *Poetical Works,* Oxford University Press, Inc., 1923.

Miller, Barnette. *Leigh Hunt's Relations with Byron, Shelley, and Keats,* Columbia University Press, 1910.

Monkhouse, William Cosmo. *Life of Leigh Hunt,* Charles Scribner's Sons, 1893.

## THOMAS HOOD: 1799-1845

Ainger, Alfred, edit. *Hood's Poems,* 2 Vols., The Macmillan Co., 1897. Good *Introduction.*

Henley, W. E. *Views and Reviews;* essay on Hood, The Macmillan Co., 1921.

Hudson, W. H. *A Quiet Corner in a Library;* essay on Hood, Rand McNally & Co., 1915.

Jerrold, W. C., edit. *Hood's Complete Poetical Works,* Oxford University Press, 1911.

Jerrold, W. C., edit. *Hood's Poems,* 2 Vols., Oxford University Press, Inc., 1897. Good *Introduction.*

Jerrold, W. C. *Thomas Hood: His Life and Times,* John Lane Co., 1909.

Marchand, L. A. *Letters of Thomas Hood,* Rutgers University Press, 1945.

More, Paul E. *Shelburne Essays;* essay on Hood, Houghton Mifflin Co., 1910.

Saintsbury, George E. B. *Collected Essays and Papers;* essay on Hood, E. P. Dutton & Co., Inc., 1923.

## LORD BYRON: 1788-1824

Briscoe, W. A., edit. *Byron the Poet,* Routledge: London, 1924.

Chew, S. C. *Byron in England,* Charles Scribner's Sons, 1924.

Coleridge, E. H., edit. *Works of Lord Byron: Poetry,* 7 Vols., new ed., Murray: London, 1922.

# BIBLIOGRAPHY

Coleridge, E. H., edit. Byron's *Poetical Works:* one-vol. rev. ed., Murray: London, 1930.

Drinkwater, John. *The Pilgrim of Eternity,* George H. Doran Company, 1925.

Fox, Sir John. *The Byron Mystery,* Richards: London, 1924.

Goode, C. T. *Byron as a Critic,* Stechert, 1923.

Howarth, R. G., edit. *Letters of Lord Byron;* selected, E. P. Dutton & Co., Inc., 1933.

Lovelace, Ralph. *Astarte,* Charles Scribner's Sons, 1921.

Maurois, André. *Byron,* Jonathan Cape, 1936.

Mayne, Ethel C. *Byron,* 2 vols., rev. ed., Charles Scribner's Sons, 1924.

Moore, Thomas. *Life of Lord Byron; His Letters and Journals,* Bigelow, Brown & Co., 1830.

More, Paul E., edit. Byron's *Complete Poetical Works;* one-vol. ed., Houghton Mifflin Co., 1906.

Nichol, John. *Byron,* The Macmillan Co., 1908.

Nicolson, H. G. *Byron: The Last Journey,* Constable & Co., 1934.

Prothero, R. E., edit. *Works of Lord Byron: Letters and Journals,* Charles Scribner's Sons, 1922.

Quennell, Peter. *Byron,* Duckworth, 1934.

Quennell, Peter. *Byron: The Years of Fame,* The Viking Press, Inc., 1935.

Quennell, Peter. *Byron in Italy,* The Viking Press, Inc., 1941.

Rice, R. A., edit. *The Best of Byron:* selections, Thomas Nelson & Sons, 1933.

Rice, R. A. *Lord Byron's British Reputation,* Smith College Press, 1924.

Spender, H. *Byron and Greece,* Charles Scribner's Sons, 1924.

Trueblood, P. G. *The Flowering of Byron's Genius,* Stanford University Press, 1945.

Winwar, Frances. *The Romantic Rebels,* Little, Brown & Co., 1935.

## PERCY BYSSHE SHELLEY: 1792-1822

Barnard, Ellsworth. *Shelley's Religion,* University of Minnesota Press, 1937.

Barrell, Joseph. *Shelley and the Thought of His Time,* Yale University Press, 1947.

Campbell, Mrs. O. W. *Shelley and the Unromantics,* Scribners, 1924.

Clarke, Isabel. *Shelley and Byron,* Hutchinson & Co., 1934.

Dowden, Edward. *The Life of Percy Bysshe Shelley,* 2 vols., Charles Scribner's Sons, 1896.

Edmunds, E. W. *Shelley and His Poetry,* F. W. Dodge Corporation, 1918.

Grabo, C. H. *The Magic Plant: The Growth of Shelley's Mind,* University of North Carolina Press, 1936.

Grabo, C. H. *A Newton Among Poets,* University of North Carolina Press, 1930.

Hughes, A. M. D. *The Nascent Mind of Shelley,* Oxford University Press, Inc., 1947.

Hutchinson, Thomas, edit. *Complete Poetical Works of Shelley,* Oxford University Press, Inc., 1933.

Ingpen, Roger and Peck, Walter E., edits. *Complete Works of Shelley,* 10 vols., Charles Scribner's Sons, 1926-1930.

Ingpen, Roger. *Shelley in England,* Houghton Mifflin Co., 1917.

Knight, G. Wilson. *The Starlit Dome;* essay on Shelley, Oxford University Press, Inc., 1941.

Maurois, André. *Ariel: A Shelley Romance,* Appleton-Century-Crofts, Inc., 1924.

Power, Julia A. *Shelley in America,* University of Nebraska Extension Division, 1940.

Read, Herbert. *In Defense of Shelley,* Heinemann, 1936.

Salt, H. S. *Percy Bysshe Shelley,* Charles Scribner's Sons, 1896.

Stovall, Floyd. *Desire and Restraint in Shelley,* Duke University Press, 1931.

Strong, A. T. *Three Studies in Shelley,* Oxford University Press, Inc., 1922.

Symonds, J. A. *Shelley;* English Men of Letters Series, The Macmillan Co., 1902.

Thompson, Francis. *Collected Works, III;* essay on Shelley, Newman, 1913.

Weaver, Bennett. *Toward the Understanding of Shelley,* University of Michigan Press, 1932.

White, Newman I., edit. *The Best of Shelley,* The Ronald Press Company, 1932.

White, Newman I. *The Unextinguished Hearth,* Duke University Press, 1938.

White, Newman I. *Shelley,* Alfred A. Knopf, Inc., 1940.

Woodberry, G. E., edit. *Shelley's Complete Poetical Works,* Houghto Mifflin Co., 1908.

# BIBLIOGRAPHY

## JOHN KEATS: 1795-1821

Bate, W. J. *The Stylistic Development of Keats,* Modern Language Association, 1945.

Beyer, W. W. *Keats and the Daemon King,* Oxford University Press, Inc., 1947.

Bridges, Robert. *A Critical Introduction to Keats,* Privately printed, 1895.

Brown, C. A. *The Life of John Keats,* Oxford University Press, Inc., 1937.

Caldwell, J. R. *John Keats' Fancy,* Cornell University Press, 1945.

Colvin, Sidney. *John Keats: His Life and Poetry,* Charles Scribner's Sons, 1925.

Evans, B. I. *Keats,* Duckworth, 1934.

Fairchild, H. N. *The Romantic Quest,* Columbia University Press, 1931.

Fausset, H. l'A. *Keats: A Study in Development,* Martin Secker: London, 1922.

Finney, C. L. *The Evolution of Keats' Poetry,* 2 vols., Harvard University Press, 1936.

Ford, G. H. *Keats and the Victorians,* Yale University Press, 1944.

Forman, H. B., edit. *Keats: Letters,* Oxford University Press, Inc., 1935.

Garrod, H. W. *Keats,* Oxford University Press, Inc., 1939.

Hewlett, D. *Adonais: A Life of John Keats,* Hurst, 1939.

Lowell, Amy. *John Keats,* 2 vols., Houghton Mifflin Co., 1925.

Murry, John M. *Keats and Shakespeare,* Oxford University Press, Inc., 1925.

Murry, John M. *Studies in Keats: New and Old,* Oxford University Press, Inc., 1939.

Ridley, M. R. *Keats' Craftmanship,* Oxford University Press, Inc., 1933.

Selincourt, Ernest de, edit. *Poems of Keats,* 5th ed., British Book Centre, 1926.

Spurgeon, Caroline. *Keats' Shakespeare,* Oxford University Press, Inc., 1929.

Thorpe, Clarence D. *The Mind of John Keats,* Oxford University Press, Inc., 1926.

Thorpe, C. D., edit. *John Keats: Complete Poems and Selected Letters,* Odyssey, 1935.

Weller, E. V., edit. *Autobiography;* based on Keats' letters, Stanford University Press, 1934.

Winwar, Frances. *The Romantic Rebels,* Little, Brown & Co., 1935.

# *Index*

*Address to the Irish People* 174
*Adonais* 177, 193-197
*Aids to Reflection* 120-1
Akenside, Mark 23
*Alastor* 179-80
*Ancient Mariner, The* 102-4
*Antiquary, The* 239
Austen, Jane 247-54
*Autumn, Ode To* 226

*Battle of the Baltic, The* 290
*Battle of Blenheim, The* 285
Beattie, James 39-40
*Beppo* 152, 220
Berkeley, Bishop 12
*Biographia Literaria* 113-18
*Blackwoods Magazine* 303-4
Blair, Robert 16
Blake, William 50-4
Bowles, William Lisle 96-7
Brawne, Fanny, 228
*Bride of Abydos, The* 138-9
*Bride of Lammermoor* 240
*Bridge of Sighs, The* 299
*Bright Star, Would I Were* 228
Burns, Robert 45-50
Byron, Lord 125-164
    Byron: His Ancestry 128
    Byron: Boyhood Days 129
    Byron: His Character 134
    Byron: Defenders and Critics
        136
    Byron: Exile from England
        142-50
    Byron and Goethe 126
    Byron: Harrow and Cambridge
        129-30
    Byron: Literary Productivity
        150-163
    Byron: Man and Poet 161

*Cain* 155
Cambridge Platonists 97
Campbell, Thomas 290-1
*Cap and Bells* 230
Carlyle, Thomas 45-6
*Castle of Indolence* 22
*Cenci, The* 187
*Chapman's Homer, Sonnet on* 207
Chatterton, Thomas 37-8
*Childe Harold* 143-4
*Christabel* 106-109
*Clarissa* 248
Clarke, Charles Cowden 202-3
Classical tradition 15
*Cloud, The* 191
Coleridge, Samuel Taylor 91-124
    Coleridge and Carlyle 123
    Coleridge: His Critical
        Method 112-118
    Coleridge: Estimates of him
        118-24
    Coleridge: His Early Youth
        94-105
    Coleridge: German Philosophy
        106-7
    Coleridge and Hazlitt 100
    Coleridge: Imagination and
        Intuition 117-8
    Coleridge: Intellectual Poet
        91-4
    Coleridge and Lamb 118
    Coleridge: His Later Years 118
    Coleridge: Maturing Years 99
    Coleridge Lectures on
        Shakespeare 112
    Coleridge and Shelley 123
Collins, William 25-27
*Confessions of an Opium-Eater* 276
*Coronach* 236
*Corsair, The* 138

Cowper, William 41-5
Crabbe, George 40
*Cupid and Psyche* 224

De Quincey, Thomas 267-281
*Defense of Poetry* 192
Deism 19
*Dejection, Ode to* 110
*Dejection, Stanzas Written in* 175
*Departing Year, Ode to the* 100
*Dirge, A* 176
*Divine Comedy, The* 170
*Don Juan* 158-9
*Dream Children* 263
*Dream Fugue, The* 279
Dryden, John 17
*Duty, Ode to* 77

*Edinburgh Review, The* 301
*Endymion* 208-9
*English Bards and Scottish
    Reviewers* 131
*Eolian Harp, The* 99
*Epipsychidion* 193-4
*Essays of Elia* 256-60
*Euganean Hills, Among The* 187
*Euphues* 247
*Eve of St. Agnes, The* 215-6
*Examiner, The* 295-6
*Excursion, The* 82

*Faerie Queene, The* 248
*Fame, Sonnets On* 228
*Fatal Sisters* 29-31
*Fear, Ode to* 28
*Foscari, The Two* 154
*France, Ode to* 111
French Revolution, The 100

*Giaour, The* 138
Godwin, William 97
*Going On a Journey* 271
Goldsmith, Oliver 40
Gothic Literature 38
Gray, Thomas 28-32
Gray's *Elegy* 29-30
Grecian Art 27-8
*Grecian Urn, Ode on a* 226-7
*Guy Mannering* 238

Hartley, David 83
Hazlitt, William 267-74
Hazlitt and Coleridge 268-70
Hazlitt and De Quincey 267-81
*Heart of Midlothian* 239
*Hebrew Melodies* 141
*Hellas* 193
*Hester* 258
*Highland Mary* 45
*Hohenlinden* 290
*Holy Living and Dying* 230
Hood, Thomas 298-9
Hunt, Leigh 295
*Hymn Before Sunrise* 183
*Hymn to Intellectual Beauty* 167
*Hyperion* 213

*Iliad, The* 243
*Imaginary Conversations* 288
*Immortality, Ode on* 80
*Indian Serenade, The* 178
*Irish Melodies* 292
*Isabella* 219-20
*Ivanhoe* 240

Johnson, Samuel 29

Keats, John 201-32
    Keats: His Career in Outline 203
    Keats: His Critics 210
    Keats: His Early Education 202
    Keats: His Letters 230
    Keats: His Miraculous Year
        214-28
    Keats: His Self-criticism 210
    Keats: His Reading of
        Shakespeare 206
    Keats: His Study of Spenser 203
    Keats: Influence of Virgil 204
*Kubla Khan* 105-6

*Lady of the Lake, The* 237-8
*Lake Region, The* 275
Lamb, Charles 254-266
    Lamb and Coleridge 256
    Lamb: His Friends 261
    Lamb: Literary Critics 260
Lamb, Mary 255
*Lament of Tasso, The* 145

Lamia 217-19
Landor, Walter Savage 286-8
Laodamia 89
Lara 138
Lay of the Last Minstrel 236
Lockhart, John 236
London Magazine 304
Lucy Gray 88
Lucy Poems 63-4
Lyrical Ballads 72, 101

Macpherson, James 36
Manfred 148-50
Mansfield Park 250
Marmion 237
Mask of Anarchy 189
Mazeppa 157
Melancholy, Ode to 225
Mermaid Tavern, Lines on the 213
Michael 74-5
Minstrelsy of the Scottish
    Border 236-7
Mont Blanc 182
Moore, Thomas 291-4
Napoleon, Life of 242
Nelson, Life of 283-4
Nightingale, Ode on a 213
Night Thoughts 23-4

Odes of Keats 224-7
Old China 263-4
Old Familiar Faces 259
Old Mortality 239
Ossianic Poems 36-7
Otho: A Drama 218, 229

Pains of Sleep 110
Pamela 248
Pantisocracy, The 95
Peregrine Pickle 249
Personal Talk 76
Persuasion 252
Phantom of Delight 80
Pilgrim's Progress 248
Platonism 19
Pleasures of Hope 290
Pleasures of the Imagination 23
Pleasures of Melancholy 33
Political Justice: Godwin 179

Poor Relations 264
Pope, Alexander 21
Prelude, The 83-4

Pride and Prejudice 251-2
Prisoner of Chillon 147
Prometheus Unbound 184-5
Prophecy of Dante 153
Psyche, Ode to 224

Quarterly Review, the 302
Queen Mab 177-8

Religious Musings 97-8
Retirement 43
Revolt of Islam 183-4
Reynolds, John 203
Rob Roy 239
Rokeby 234
Romantic Spirit 15
Rosamond Gray 258
Rousseau 169
Rowley Poems 38

Sardanapalus 153-4
Schoolmistress 34
Scott, Sir Walter 233-247
Seasons, The 21
Sense and Sensibility 251
Sensibility, School of 96
Sensitive Plant, The 190-1
Shelley, Percy Bysshe 165-199
    Shelley and Byron 165
    Shelley: Eton and Oxford
        170-1
    Shelley and Godwin 166-7
    Shelley: His Golden Years
        184-199
    Shelley: His Critics 195
    Shelley: Man and Poet 165-6
    Shelley's Platonism 167, 193
    Shelley's Radicalism 173-4
Shelley, Mary 179, 183
Shenstone, William 34
She Walks in Beauty 126
Siege of Corinth 138
Skylark, To A 191
Sleep and Poetry 207
Smart, Christopher 35

Solitary Reaper, The 79
Song of the Shirt 298-300
Songs of Experience 53
Songs of Innocence 52
Song to the Men of England 190
Southey, Robert 282-6
Spinoza 182
Spirit of the Age, The 271
Suspiria De Profundis 278
Symposim, The 194

Table Talk 122
Tales From Shakespeare 260-1
Talisman, The 241
Task, The 43
Thomson, James 20-22
Tintern Abbey 74
Tom Jones 248
Tristram Shandy 249
Turkish Tales 138

Vision of Judgment 150

Utopia 248

Warton, Thomas 33
Waverly 238
West Wind, Ode to the 188
Wordsworth, William 57-83
  Wordsworth: His Boyhood 61
  Wordsworth: At Cambridge 64
  Wordsworth: In France 65
  Wordsworth: His Healing
    Power 87
  Wordsworth: His Literary
    Style 87-8
  Wordsworth: Lyrical Poet 72
  Wordsworth and Nature 57-8
  Wordsworth: His Personality 78
  Wordsworth: Philosophical
    Poet 80-1
  Wordsworth's Preface 73
  Wordsworth: Songs and
    Sonnets 75
Work Without Hope 119

Young, Edward 23-4
Youth and Age 118-9

# Barron's College Reviews

## WORLD LITERATURE SERIES

An inexpensive paperbound series of expertly written books designed to clarify the great literary works for study or general reading. Each volume contains detailed summaries, interpretations and criticisms of all major and many minor works, historical backgrounds, and biographical data.

**CHAUCER'S CANTERBURY TALES**
By *Hopper*. Set as interlinear translation to preserve vitality of the original poetry, each Middle English line coupled with a line of modern English. Introduction, and notes. (selected) $1.50

**CONTEMPORARY LITERATURE**
By *Heiney*. An absorbing survey of more than 125 important 20th Century American, Russian and European writers. Summaries in detail, interpretations, bibliographies. 554 pp. $1.95

**CLASSICAL DRAMA**
By *Reinhold*. A brilliant insight into the classic era, basis of all subsequent drama. Summaries, interpretations: 85 extant Greek and Roman plays. Glossary, bibliography. 342 pp. $1.95

**CLASSICS, GREEK AND ROMAN**
By *Reinhold*. Crisp, readable guide to each author: details of his life, list of works, thought and style analyzed, main work summarized. Mythology, glossary, bibliography. 390 pp. $1.95

**ENGLISH LITERATURE, Volume I**
By *Grebanier*. Reliable complete, guide to major and minor writers, and development of literary trends. Summaries, critiques from Old English Period through 18th Century. $1.95

**ENGLISH LITERATURE, Volume II**
By *Grebanier*. 18th Century Pre-Romanticism through 20th Century; analyses of the authors; vivid summaries; interpretations of works and their relation to historical trends. $1.95

**ENGLISH ROMANTIC WRITERS**
By *Battenhouse*. A stimulus to independent study and understanding of the lyrical age of Keats, Shelley, Byron and others. Historical influences; interpretation of works. 322 pp. $1.95

**EUROPEAN LITERATURE, Volume I**
By *Hopper* and *Grebanier* Early Middle Ages to Romantic Movement. Guide to movements, authors, works: French, Italian, Spanish, German, Russian and others. Summaries, critiques. $1.50

**EUROPEAN LITERATURE, Volume II**
By *Hopper* and *Grebanier*. Literary tour, without language barriers, mid-1700's on. French, German, Italian, Scandinavian, Russian authors and their works. Resumes, criticisms. $1.75

**RECENT AMERICAN LITERATURE**
By *Heiney*. Companion to *Contemporary Literature*, surveying top American writers from 1880 on. Trends in poetry, fiction, criticism, drama. Interpretations, summaries of works. $1.95

## Other Reviews

COLLEGE ALGEBRA by *Peters*.  500 pp. $1.95

PRINCIPLES OF GEOGRAPHY, Physical and Cultural, by *Doerr, Guernsey* and *Van Cleef*. 320 pp. $1.95

HISTORY OF EDUCATION by *Frost*. 205 pp. $1.25

SPELLING YOUR WAY TO SUCCESS by *Mersand*. 173 pp. 98¢

ESSENTIALS OF EFFECTIVE WRITING by *Hopper* and *Gale*.  224 pp. $1.50

PRACTICE FOR EFFECTIVE WRITING by *Hopper* and *Gale*.  176 pp. $1.50

**BARRON'S EDUCATIONAL SERIES, INC.**
343 Great Neck Road, Great Neck, N.Y.